SCOTLAND AND THE BORDERS OF ROMANTICISM

Scotland and the Borders of Romanticism is the first published collection of critical essays devoted to Scottish writing between 1745 and 1830 – a key period marking the contested divide between the Scottish Enlightenment and Romanticism in British literary history. Essays in the volume, by leading scholars from Scotland, England, Canada, and the USA, address a range of major figures and topics, among them Hume and the Romantic imagination, Burns's poetry, the Scottish song and ballad revivals, gender and national tradition, the prose fiction of Walter Scott and James Hogg, the national theatre of Joanna Baillie, the Romantic varieties of historicism and antiquarianism, Romantic Orientalism, and Scotland as a site of English cultural fantasies. The essays undertake a collective rethinking of the national and period categories that have structured British literary history, by examining the relations between the concepts of Enlightenment and Romanticism as well as between Scottish and English writing.

Leith Davis is Associate Professor of English at Simon Fraser University. She is the author of *Acts of Union: Scotland and the Literary Negotiation of the British Nation, 1707–1830* (1998) and numerous articles on Scottish and Irish literature of the eighteenth century and Romantic era.

Ian Duncan is Professor of English at the University of California, Berkeley. He is the author of *Modern Romance and Transformations of the Novel: The Gothic, Scott, Dickens* (Cambridge, 1992) and numerous articles on eighteenth- and nineteenth-century Scottish literature. He has edited Walter Scott's *Rob Roy* and *Ivanhoe* and James Hogg's *Winter Evening Tales*.

Janet Sorensen is Associate Professor of English at Indiana University at Bloomington. She is the author of *The Grammar of Empire in Eighteenth-Century British Writing* (Cambridge, 2000) and she has written many articles on eighteenth-century topics.

SCOTLAND AND THE BORDERS OF ROMANTICISM

EDITED BY

LEITH DAVIS
Simon Fraser University

IAN DUNCAN
University of California, Berkeley

JANET SORENSEN
Indiana University

CAMBRIDGE
UNIVERSITY PRESS

PUBLISHED BY THE PRESS SYNDICATE OF THE UNIVERSITY OF CAMBRIDGE
The Pitt Building, Trumpington Street, Cambridge, United Kingdom

CAMBRIDGE UNIVERSITY PRESS
The Edinburgh Building, Cambridge, CB2 2RU, UK
40 West 20th Street, New York, NY 10011-4211, USA
477 Williamstown Road, Port Melbourne, VIC 3207, Australia
Ruiz de Alarcón 13, 28014 Madrid, Spain
Dock House, The Waterfront, Cape Town 8001, South Africa

http://www.cambridge.org

First published 2004

Printed in the United Kingdom at the University Press, Cambridge

Typeface Adobe Garamond 11/12.5 pt   *System* LATEX 2ε   [TB]

A catalogue record for this book is available from the British Library

Library of Congress Cataloguing in Publication data

Scotland and the borders of romanticism / edited by Leith Davis, Ian Duncan, Janet Sorensen.
p. cm.
Includes bibliographical references and index.
ISBN 0 521 83283 7
1. Scottish literature – 18th century – History and criticism.   2. Romanticism – Scotland.
3. Scottish literature – 19th century – History and criticism.   4. Scottish Borders (England and
Scotland) – Intellectual life.   5. Scottish Borders (England and Scotland) – In literature.
6. Romanticism – Scottish Borders (England and Scotland)   7. Borders Region (Scotland) –
Intellectual life.   8. Scotland – Intellectual life – 18th century.   9. Scotland – Intellectual life –
19th century.   10. Borders Region (Scotland) – In literature.   11. Scotland – In literature.
I. Davis, Leith, 1960–   II. Duncan, Ian.   III. Sorensen, Janet.
PR8549.S35   2004
820.9′145′0941–dc22   2003065283

ISBN 0 521 83283 7 hardback

Contents

Contributors

ALYSON BARDSLEY (Assistant Professor, Department of English, Speech, and World Literature, College of Staten Island, City University of New York)

JOHN BARRELL (Professor of English, Centre for Eighteenth-Century Studies, University of York)

ADRIANA CRACIUN (Lecturer, Department of English, Birkbeck College, University of London)

CAIRNS CRAIG (Professor of Scottish and Modern Literature, and Director of the Centre for the History of Ideas in Scotland, University of Edinburgh)

LEITH DAVIS (Associate Professor, Department of English, Simon Fraser University)

IAN DUNCAN (Professor of English, University of California, Berkeley)

INA FERRIS (Professor of English, University of Ottawa)

PENNY FIELDING (Senior Lecturer, Department of English, University of Edinburgh)

PETER J. MANNING (Professor and Chair, Department of English, Stony Brook University)

SUSAN MANNING (Grierson Professor of English Literature, University of Edinburgh)

JEROME MCGANN (John Stewart Bryan Professor, Department of English, University of Virginia)

ANN WIERDA ROWLAND (Assistant Professor, Department of English, Harvard University)

JANET SORENSEN (Associate Professor, Department of English, Indiana University at Bloomington)

JAMES WATT (Lecturer, Department of English and Related Literature, University of York)

Acknowledgments

The editors would like to thank research assistants Nick Nace at the University of California at Berkeley and Chris Lendrum, Leeanne Romane, and Karina Vernon at Simon Fraser University for their help with *Scotland and the Borders of Romanticism*. Material assistance was provided by the Committee on Research of the Academic Senate and the Townsend Humanities Center at the University of California, Berkeley, the Social Sciences and Humanities Research Council of Canada, and the Office of the Dean of Arts at Simon Fraser University. We also thank Linda Bree at Cambridge University Press for her support and the team that oversaw production: Katie Bright, Audrey Cotterell, Rachel de Wachter, Lucille Murby, and Jackie Warren.

John Barrell's chapter first appeared in *The London Review of Books* 18: 4 (1996): 14–15. Earlier versions of Leith Davis's and Peter Manning's chapters were published in *The Wordsworth Circle*, 31 (2000): 99–7 and 80–3. Thanks to the editor of *The Wordsworth Circle*, Marilyn Gaull, for her support.

Introduction

Ian Duncan, with Leith Davis and Janet Sorensen

SCOTLAND IN ROMANTICISM

"What a hobbling pace the Scottish Pegasus seems to have adopted in these days," grumbled William Wordsworth in a letter to R. P. Gillies (February 14, 1815). Wordsworth condemns the "insupportable slovenliness and neglect of syntax and grammar, by which James Hogg's writings are disfigured"; such solecisms may be "excusable in [Hogg] from his education, but Walter Scott knows, and ought to do, better." Both poets can be summarily dismissed: "They neither of them write a language which has any pretension to be called English."[1] Wordsworth's complaint cuts across distinct if overlapping conceptions of the institutional framework of British Romantic literature: as a *market*, in which Scottish writing enjoys a notable success, and as a *canon*, from which it must be purged – on the grounds of a national deficiency, a linguistic unfitness "to be called English."[2]

Wordsworth's verdict has proven remarkably durable. Modern literary criticism in Great Britain and North America adopted the view of Romanticism as a unitary phenomenon, the *agon* of a mighty handful of lyric poets with a Kantian (later Heideggerian) problematic of the transcendental imagination.[3] Some Romanticisms are more Romantic than others: some are the real thing, while others are premature or belated, or simply false – anachronistic or fraudulent simulacra. British Romanticism is English, from Blake and *Lyrical Ballads* in the 1790s to Keats, Shelley, and Byron (cut off from his own Scottish roots), prematurely dead in the early 1820s. Scotland, neither English nor foreign, stands for an *inauthentic* Romanticism, defined by a mystified – purely ideological – commitment to history and folklore. Rather than being a site of Romantic production, Scotland's fate is to have become a Romantic object or commodity: glamorous scenery visited by the Wordsworths, Turner, Queen Victoria, steam-train parties of tourists; a series of kitsch, fake, more or less reactionary "inventions of tradition," from Ossian and Scott to Fiona MacLeod and

Brigadoon.[4] Nor is this simply an English story, since Scottish nationalist critics have devised a compelling variant, denouncing their modern tradition as inorganic, self-divided, alienated from its vital sources – the proof of that alienation (as we shall see) being Scotland's lack of a genuine Romantic movement.

The term "Romanticism" has come under intense scrutiny and debate in literary studies in Great Britain and North America in the last couple of decades.[5] Only very recently has that debate begun to address the term's anglocentric underpinnings. While post-structuralist, feminist, and New Historicist critiques have opened some of the aesthetic boundaries that defined Romantic-era writing, the likeliest instruments for rethinking its geopolitical borders would seem to be provided by post-colonial theory. As critical projects within Scottish studies itself have made clear, though, Scotland occupies an anomalous position in the topology of post-colonialism – shifting between the coordinates of colonized and colonizer, the producer as much as recipient of a "global English."[6] Although England was unquestionably the dominant partner, politically and economically, at the Treaty of Union (1707), Scotland enjoyed far more opportunity to capitalize on the new arrangement than the other ancient nations (Ireland, Wales) absorbed into the British state. The articles of Union allowed Scots to participate in the new imperial economy, and preserved the key national institutions – the Presbyterian church, banking and legal systems, schools and universities – that supported a dynamic entrepreneurial and professional middle class. The Lowland burghs – especially the four university cities, above all Edinburgh – accommodated one of the most advanced civil societies in Europe. At the same time, Scotland held within its borders a culturally alien, increasingly "backward" "Celtic fringe," the Highlands, in which something like colonial conditions prevailed: military and legal repression, economic underdevelopment. Scotland itself reproduced the split condition both of an imperial Great Britain and of the nascent world-system of which Britain was the political-economic core.

Far from being peripheral, then, Lowland Scotland became one of the generative centers of European and North Atlantic literary culture in the century between David Hume's *Treatise of Human Nature* (1739–40) and Thomas Carlyle's *The French Revolution* (1837). In the balance of an emerging imperial world order, Scottish innovations in moral philosophy, the social sciences, history, rhetoric, poetry, periodical journalism, and the novel matched or outweighed their English counterparts. The intellectuals of the so-called Scottish Enlightenment – David Hume, Adam Smith, Adam Ferguson, John Millar, William Robertson, Thomas Reid, Dugald Stewart,

Lord Kames, and others – developed a new, synthetic account of human nature, historical process, and the dynamics of social formation, in a cosmopolitan or universal order of modernity. At the same time, poets and scholars began to invoke the national past, ancestral origins, and regional popular traditions in a series of attempts to reimagine Scottish identity in the conditions of imperial Union. In the early 1760s James Macpherson's collections of "Poems of Ossian" founded European Romanticism on a scandalous invention of lost cultural origins. In the 1780s Robert Burns crafted the first modern vernacular style in British poetry. In the first quarter of the nineteenth century, Scott's historical novels combined those distinctively Scottish inventions, a universal modernity and a national past, to define the governing form of Western narrative for the next hundred years. At the same time, a succession of Edinburgh periodicals – *The Edinburgh Review* (1802), *Blackwood's Edinburgh Magazine* (1817), *Chambers's Edinburgh Journal* (1832) – established the main medium of nineteenth-century public discussion. And to list these epoch-making achievements is to overlook such strikingly original experiments as Joanna Baillie's theatre of the passions and the anti-novelistic fictions of James Hogg and John Galt.

This Scottish literary history describes rhythms of continuity, change, and disjunction quite different from the English model to which it has been subordinated. Against that English model, Scotland could only loom as an intermittent, shadowy anachronism, a temporal as well as spatial border of Romanticism. In Scotland, "Classical" and "Romantic" cultural forms occupy the same historical moment and institutional base, rather than defining successive stages or periods. Macpherson's *Fingal*, founding document of a global Romanticism, is not just contemporary with the scientific projects of the Scottish Enlightenment but one of its typical inventions, in a contemporaneity that defies the English schema of a teleological development of Romanticism proper from Augustan Neoclassicism through a liminal "Pre-romanticism."[7] The French Revolution provides the epochal fulcrum, or rather fracture, in the English story: a metaphysical rather than historical event, an apocalyptic or traumatic break in the flow of history, through which other states of being gleam into visibility, however fugitive. In the time of disillusion that succeeds it, with the stifling resumption of history as usual, the revolutionary rift generates the compensatory Romantic investment in a poetic language which is the trace of a force alien to the normative ordering of social life – some of its names are desire, the imagination, difference.[8]

Scottish cultural history, according to this model, does not just fail to produce an authentic Romanticism: it manufactures false substitutes, it oppresses the real thing. On the one hand, the theme-park Highland heritage of Macpherson and Scott, simulations of past lost worlds; on the other, the punitive campaigns waged against the Lake and Cockney schools by *The Edinburgh Review* and *Blackwood's*. The Scottish Enlightenment legacy of political economy, propagated in *The Edinburgh Review* and its utilitarian offshoots, becomes the formidable disciplinary antagonist of a post-Romantic discourse of "culture," throughout the nineteenth century and well into the twentieth. This opposition was itself an artefact of Scottish Romanticism, an ideological projection of the political conflict between *The Edinburgh Review* and *Blackwood's*.[9] In other words, it is as though the differential structure of Scottish cultural history cast a repressive shadow over the English Romantic movement: its signature of developmental blockage, the split between an aridly rational political economy and a lachrymose Ossianism, could only reiterate itself, with an ever heavier ideological and normalizing emphasis. Scotland, in short, produced the Victorians.

As Romanticism acquired its conceptual coherence as a "system of norms," in the retrospect of Victorian cultural criticism, the Scots were closed out of it. Samuel Johnson's denunciation of Ossian became the standard modern verdict. The success of Macpherson's translations in translation, from Berlin to Bogota, furnished further proof of their ontological "vacuity," since poetry is what escapes translation.[10] Burns might have anticipated Wordsworth's commitment to a "language really spoken by men," but the prematurity (and naïveté) of his attempt was marked by its realization in a provincial and rustic dialect, as well as its fixation on the social surfaces of life. Matthew Arnold reinforced the ban with the judgment that Burns lacked "high seriousness," the epic or rather tragic tone of the metropolis.[11] If Scott fared better in the nineteenth century it was because he was a novelist, and the novel, with its mimetic investment in manners and history, was a Victorian rather than a Romantic genre. Victorian forefathers did not wear well in the era of Modernism. F. R. Leavis expelled Scott from the Great Tradition on the grounds of his being "an inspired folklorist." Georg Lukács, programmatic anti-Modernist, reclaimed Scott as the founder of the historical novel – but by divorcing him from Romanticism.[12] Other figures who had enjoyed degrees of success or controversy in their time, such as Baillie and Hogg, sank out of sight altogether by the early twentieth century. Hogg led the half-life of a local curiosity, "the Ettrick Shepherd" or clown-sage of *Blackwood's*, until André Gide promoted *The Private Memoirs and Confessions of a Justified Sinner* into a Modernist canon of accursed books. Scholarly interest has returned in very recent years to

Baillie, whose neglect was dictated by gender rather than nationality: it was a fellow Scot, Francis Jeffrey, who argued that women's exclusion from public life disqualified them from the genre of tragedy.[13]

Romanticism was instituted as a critical object, the site of a critical practice, in the university after World War II, especially in the United States, which generated an ideologically potent account of lyric poetry as the authentic utterance or (later) trace of an ontological difference which escaped or resisted the collective pressures of society and history.[14] The visionary company of five English poets constituted the bright origins of a Romanticism that (paradoxically) became world-historical by becoming American. Wordsworth remained a touchstone, both for the post-structuralist turn of the 1970s[15] and for the New Historicism of the 1980s.[16] Meanwhile English criticism, historically and socially attuned much earlier, and anyway less interested in an ideologically substantive category of "Romanticism," observed nationalist boundaries: its chief subaltern counter-example to mainstream Romanticism is John Clare.[17] The most productive rethinking of the Romantic canon over the last decade or so has taken place through feminist projects of reclamation and critique;[18] if these too have so far tended to reproduce rather than unsettle a normative anglocentricism, as a glance at recent classroom anthologies will show, they also encourage further attention to what has been left out. Still, "Scotland" as often as not continues to play the role of an oppressive anti-Romanticism in some of these new accounts: a force of mere worldliness, or of imperial ideology, for example, in the person of Scott.[19]

The strength of the tradition is shown by its persistence even in so scrupulously reflective a study as Jerome Christensen's recent *Romanticism at the End of History*. Christensen, the author of notable books on Hume and Byron, reclaims a coherent, indeed authentic "Romantic movement," if as a continually deferred project rather than a "system of norms," in the teeth of New Historicist and ideological critiques. Wordsworth and Coleridge remain standard-bearers, thanks to the capable imagination with which both poets continued to reflect upon their predicament, through and after their revolutionary disappointment and accommodation to Pittite reaction. *The Edinburgh Review* and Scott feature prominently in Christensen's story, but as figureheads of an official, hegemonic apparatus – even if Scott, technically more resourceful and self-conscious, plays the part of a literary Metternich, chancellor of the new legitimacy, while *The Edinburgh Review* is more like the police, a relatively unwitting, corporate agency. As representatives of "the novel" and "the Scottish Enlightenment," respectively, they form the dark wall of "normal history," or of ideology itself, against which an ethical and anti-ideological "Romantic hope" may be flickeringly visible.[20]

Scotland as the lack, or simulation, or repression of Romanticism: the theme pervades the cultural histories produced by Scottish critics. Indeed, it provides the historiographic crux of the modern nationalist analysis of Scottish literature, the "Caledonian Antisyzygy" or diagnostic figure of a self-divided, internally contradictory national character.[21] The schizoid figure of Romanticism's negation is itself, of course, quintessentially "Romantic" – and typical of "semi-peripheral" national representations, from Hoffmann and Hogg to Poe and Dostoevksy. What differentiates the Scottish from the English analysis is the insistent Scots identification of the *nation* as the excluded category that bears Romantic value – that numinous condition exiled from "normal history," authentic because of exile.

Thus Edwin Muir, writing at the height of the modern nationalist "Renaissance" in the 1930s, identifies a fatal "dissociation of sensibility" in Scottish culture, its primary symptom a linguistic split between thought (English, the language of Enlightenment philosophy) and feeling (Scots, the language of the folk and Burns's lyrics).[22] A generation later David Craig deplores Scotland's lack of a "Great Tradition," the representation of an organic national society, so that its literature can only chart the widening gulf between literati and populace.[23] As Cairns Craig has argued, such narratives create their image of a divided Scottish culture by projecting it against an idealized English model: Muir adapts T. S. Eliot's account of English poetry, with Scott in the place of Milton, while David Craig draws on Leavis.[24] These models of a split tradition may yield different appraisals of particular figures. David Craig, for example, joins in the mission to salvage an attractively bawdy, rough, insurgent Burns from the Victorian cult of sentimentality that had so exasperated Hugh MacDiarmid.[25] This new-modelled Burns (drawn by a woman novelist and critic, Catherine Carswell, in her 1930 biography of the poet) personified the masculine values of muscular assertiveness, virile heterosexuality, and "horizontal brotherhood" that typify emergent nationalisms.[26] More recently, in work that is beginning to transform our understanding of the period, scholars have recovered the contexts of a "Radical Burns" in eighteenth-century popular democratic politics.[27]

With remarkable unanimity, nationalist cultural histories identify the nineteenth century as the era when the Scottish tradition became extinct – or at the very least, went into hibernation. They converge, in particular, on Scott, anathematized for replacing a living heritage with a reactionary effigy. Muir's evocation of Scott in post-Enlightenment Edinburgh – elaborate invention screening "a very curious emptiness" – recalls the Johnsonian verdict on Macpherson ("let us not fill the vacuity with Ossian").[28] Scott combines both tendencies already described, Enlightenment anti-Romanticism and a sentimental pseudo-Romanticism, in a lethal synthesis. Even Tom Nairn, who mounts a scathing critique of "Antisyzygy" historiography in order to rescue the Scottish Enlightenment from nationalist proscription, reiterates its discovery of a disappearance of national tradition, "a very curious emptiness," at the opening of the nineteenth century. Adapting Lukács's thesis, Nairn finds Scott to be a "valedictory realist" whose works invoke the national past not to revive it, as a source of alternative possibility for the present, but to pronounce it dead. Here, though, the historiographic principle is made explicit: Scott personifies a larger emptiness, the lack of a Scottish Romantic movement, which in Nairn's analysis must be defined by an oppositional nationalist politics.[29]

Not only Scott, then, but the resplendent literary production of Scott's Edinburgh – Constable, Blackwood and their reviews, the fictions of Hogg, Galt, Mary Brunton, Susan Ferrier, Christian Johnstone, John Lockhart – all this fails to constitute a "Romanticism," or rather, it amplifies an anti-Romanticism born of the socioeconomic prematurity of post-Union civil society and its cultural expression, the Scottish Enlightenment. In other words, the very vitality of Enlightenment mortified the successive developmental stage, by rendering it superfluous – a mortification already evident in the contemporaneous excrescence of "Ossian." Dissident voices, even Burns's, were censored, ignored, or patronized by an increasingly conservative Edinburgh establishment. After 1794, and a more bitter repression of Jacobin sympathizers even than occurred in England, the Scots intelligentsia could only choose from among different counter-revolutionary postures: the post-Enlightenment liberal positivism of *The Edinburgh Review* or the reactionary pseudo-Romanticism of *Blackwood's*.

Nairn has been perhaps the most influential figure in a notable "return to Scotland" in British cultural studies of the last decade or so. *The Break-Up of Britain*, provoked by the 1970s devolution controversy, framed Scotland's status in the Union as exemplary of modern nationalist development through its very contradictions. Nairn's analysis helped instigate a rethinking of the categories of nation, nationality, and nationalism, at first by historians and political scientists and then by literary critics, given massive impetus by the end of the Cold War. Nairn's more recent work revisits the question in the wake of the 1999 referendum and its defiance of long-standing assumptions about Scotland's destiny in the United Kingdom.[30] The political and historiographic debates around devolution have nourished accounts of a Scottish cultural history in which the Union need no longer represent a "metaphysical disaster" (Nairn's term) or even an "end of history." Some of these accounts, while making better sense of "subaltern" figures such as Burns and Hogg, have continued to produce Macpherson and Scott as touchstones for an inauthentic nationalism, a negative Romanticism. In a series of powerful, often revelatory recastings of a variegatedly British rather than monolithically English cultural history, Murray Pittock finds Scott completing Macpherson's task by ringing down the "tartan curtain" upon a populist and revolutionary Jacobitism – an authentic national tradition – and replacing it with a nostalgic facsimile. Colin Kidd stresses the Enlightenment rather than Romantic genealogy of a Whig historiographic repudiation of Scotland's pre-modern past, to which Scott gives popular legitimacy.[31]

Other commentators construct their versions of Scottish literary history on principles of heterogeneous inclusiveness and continuity. Cairns Craig's probing critique of an Anglo-British, centrist, and organicist model of culture studies the Scottish contribution to a mixed, hybrid, imperial nineteenth-century "English literature."[32] In an analogous project, Robert Crawford reconstitutes a long-durational modern Scottish literary history in which gaps and contradictions, far from being fatal, are generative; its continuities flow across territorial borders to other sites of the imperial anglophone periphery, as "devolution" becomes a global principle.[33] The approach was anticipated by Susan Manning's study (following the pioneering work of Andrew Hook) of the ideological and formal relations between Scottish and North American writing (and between Calvinism and Enlightenment) in the eighteenth and nineteenth centuries. Manning's more recent work specifies the cultural condition she analyzes – an open-ended dialectic between principles of organic wholeness and centrifugal fragmentation – as a "Romantic" one (with philosophical roots in Hume).[34] Penny Fielding has excavated the ideological foundation of a Romantic national culture in the binary opposition between orality and literacy.[35] Meanwhile, recent Burns scholarship is bringing to light a larger tradition of Scottish dissenting literature, with (as Liam McIlvanney shows) indigenous cultural roots as well as links to contemporary English and Irish radicalism.[36] Together with Pittock's work on Jacobitism, this sets Scottish writing in the context of an alternative pan-British Romanticism that has been effectively submerged by literary history's preoccupation with metropolitan models of tradition.

North American scholars, meanwhile, have not hesitated to mobilize the insights of post-colonial studies in their more recent (late-1990s) turn to Scotland, with special reliance on the analysis of "internal colonialism."[37] At their most fruitful, such studies have attended to the reciprocal if uneven dynamics of Scotland's relation to England in the Union. Leith Davis traces the ineluctable, vexed dialectic between English and Scottish constructions of literature and tradition in the century after 1707. Janet Sorensen reads the primary role played by Scottish intellectuals, and by English intellectuals addressing the Scottish case, in the eighteenth-century standardization of English as a national (i.e., imperial) language. In an analogous move, Clifford Siskin discusses the role of Scottish philosophy and the figure of Jacobitism in the modern (i.e., Romantic) formation of a national, literature-based culture.[38] These North American projects have tended to absorb the traditional period category of Romanticism into the "long eighteenth century," a chronological artefact of the New Historicism. The phenomena of periodization already remarked – the contemporaneity of Smith and Ossian, the continuities between the Enlightenment and *The Edinburgh Review* – suit Scotland especially well to the new diachrony: witness the recent boom in Macpherson studies, or the salience of Scottish cases in recent projects on historicism and the emotions.[39] Does this development – the return to intelligibility of Scottish cultural history in the framework of the "long eighteenth century" – signal, then, a definitive abandonment of "Romanticism" as a historical category? – one which, bound to the ideology of cultural nationalism, could only distort the Scottish case, and has outlived its usefulness elsewhere?

Recent studies of the novel as national form show that a wholesale abandonment would be premature. Katie Trumpener's *Bardic Nationalism* re-situates the novel at the center of Romanticism by turning a pervasive assumption – the identification between Romanticism and nationalism – into the object of analysis. Trumpener attends to the geographically dispersed production of "the nation" across the modern British imperium, and the primacy of semi-peripheral sites, notably Ireland and Scotland, in generating the new cultural nationalisms.[40] And as nationalism, so historicism: both are Romantic inventions as much as they may be limiting conditions. James Chandler's *England in 1819* reads Scott and the Scottish Enlightenment philosophers as productive rather than blocking forces in the cultural field of British Romanticism. By explicitly framing chronology and periodization as its critical questions, Chandler's analysis is able to specify anachronism as one of the constitutive tropes of a distinctive practice of Romantic historicism, theorized by Scottish Enlightenment philosophical historians and amplified by Scott – whose writings highlight the "anachronistic" relation between England and Scotland as the discourse's own historical condition.[41]

Such projects help us to view Scotland as a critical site for the invention or production of "Romanticism": not in itself but always as part of a larger political, economic, and cultural geography, encompassing not only "Britain" – London, Northern England, Ireland – but Europe, North America, and an expanding world-horizon of colonized and dominated territories, constituting, in Trumpener's phrase, "the transcolonial consciousness and transperipheral circuits of influence to which empire gives rise."[42] The case of Scotland may thus provoke a salutary defamiliarization of some of the fundamental categories that structure literary history, including the temporal borders of periodization and the topological borders of nationality. This critical rethinking – rather than an objective survey – is the project of the present volume of essays.

SCOTLAND AND THE BORDERS OF ROMANTICISM

In the opening chapter of *Scotland and the Borders of Romanticism* Cairns Craig reopens a famous crux in the early formation of Romanticism as a theoretical project: Coleridge's dismissal of associationist psychology for a Kantian poetics of the transcendental imagination. Craig shows how Coleridge secured his idealist turn by substituting David Hartley for the more formidable philosophical authority of David Hume. While Coleridge could easily refute Hartley's reductive, mechanistic account of associationism, Hume's shadow – in a classic pattern of repression – continued to vex Coleridge's thought. The Humean model of the imagination as a cognitive and socializing faculty, meanwhile, would pose a "novelistic" alternative, exemplified in Scott's historical fiction, to the "lyric" model of English Romantic poetry.

The double repudiation of Scotland and Enlightenment, condensed in the spectre of Hume, marks a periodic as well as a national border of English Romanticism. Romanticism's spatial and temporal limits have been drawn, of course, in a set of antinomies familiar to literary scholars: between epistemological categories of theoretical abstraction and material particularity, and their geopolitical and historiographic equivalents – global versus local knowledges, universal versus culturally specific histories; between social exchange and alienated individualism as the matrix of experience and feeling; between orality and literacy, writing and speech or song. If we have grown used to the deconstruction of binary oppositions as a procedure within Romantic writing (until, as Marc Redfield puts it, "any entity marked as romantic will turn out to resist its own romanticism"),[43] the larger national-period boundary remains in place: Scottish Enlightenment, English Romanticism. The essays in this volume explore an Enlightenment that was always, in these terms, Romantic, and a Romanticism that did not need to cast off Enlightenment to come into its own – at least, not until quite late in the game.

The Scottish universities nourished both those archetypal projects of Romanticism and Enlightenment, the *Poems of Ossian* and the treatises of Adam Smith, the philosophical links between which are traced in Ian Duncan's chapter. Macpherson matriculated at King's College, Aberdeen, which (close to the Highlands) pioneered a curricular attention to "primitive" cultural conditions; his quest for an ancient Gaelic epic was promoted by urban intellectuals like Hugh Blair, the first Regius Professor of Rhetoric and Belles Lettres at Edinburgh.[44] Smith himself had founded this new branch of the "science of man" at mid-century, extending the conjectural and comparative methods of philosophical history to the discipline of national language formation. The institutional framework of eighteenth-century Scottish civil society – religious, financial, legal, and academic – sustained a broadly dispersed "Republic of Letters," from working-men's reading and debating clubs in the Lowland parishes and market towns to the universities and polite literary societies in the cities. In contrast, as John Brewer has emphasized, English literature in the "Age of Johnson" was overwhelmingly commercial and entrepreneurial, with its main institutional base in booksellers' shops.[45] The adjacency of the English market, with new colonial markets looming beyond it, provided a dynamic opening for Scottish literary production; philosophical blockbusters such as *The Wealth of Nations* and Hume's *History of England* were incubated in the Scottish universities (and accessory institutions, such as the Speculative Society and Faculty of Advocates' Library) and sold to the English book trade.[46]

The French Revolution provoked a crisis of ideological legitimation in this Scottish republic of letters. The Anti-Jacobin crackdown, strengthened by the monopolistic control of institutions under William Pitt's "Scotch manager," Secretary of State Henry Dundas, issued in a general repression: the transportation of "Friends of the People," official warnings to philo-revolutionary professors like Dugald Stewart and John Millar, and a Tory stranglehold on appointments and promotions. Accordingly, the projects of Enlightenment shifted their institutional base, from the university curriculum to an industrializing literary marketplace. After 1800 Edinburgh became the British centre for innovative publishing in periodicals and fiction, the ascendant – booksellers' – genres of the post-Enlightenment. *The Edinburgh Review* was founded by a set of young Whig lawyers blocked from preferment under the Dundas regime and financed by an enterprising Whig bookseller, Archibald Constable, who would also go on to publish the Waverley novels.

Post-Enlightenment cultural production was increasingly typified, in addition, by those private, amateur, quasi-illegitimate discourses that had grown up on the fringes of the university curricula: overlapping with them, disavowed by the professors, but by now infiltrating the approaches of philosophical history and conjectural anthropology. Antiquarian research, ballad and song collection, and vernacular poetry revival made up a broad continuum, the matrix of the nationalist genres of the post-Enlightenment. Susan Manning's chapter in the present volume shows how antiquarianism came to exert a contaminating if not disintegrating pressure on the field of philosophical history that had officially rejected it; while Ina Ferris gives a complementary view of the ironical and melancholy inflexions of historicism carried by the "private" genre of the novel.

After all, the discourse of rhetoric and belles lettres had strained in contrary directions. On the one hand, recognizing the historical integrity of primitive cultural conditions, it opened philosophical space for "Romantic" projects of revival. On the other, its ideological commitment to politeness tended to condemn regional vernacular forms, those contemporaneous "relics" of traditional ways of life, as "rude and barbarous," obsolescent and moribund. Language marked the fault-line of class difference disguised as historical destiny: Blair defended the dead Gaelic of Ossian, preserved in English prose, and exhorted Burns to abandon live Scots for English. The consolidation and diversification of the vernacular revival brought no release – quite the contrary – of the structural tension between its (vulgar, heterogeneous, dissident) materials and the official frames (nationalist, historicist, canonical, philological) set up to contain them. Leith Davis's chapter finds Burns speculating on the double valency written into eighteenth-century collections of Scottish song: between the affirmation of a universal Britishness (downplaying social and political differences) and the counter-claim of an irreducible, potentially unruly Scottishness. Ann Rowland studies the formalism of the ballad revival in Scott's generation as a technique with which collectors sought to neutralize a scandalous content – in this case, maternal infanticide – that troubled their legitimating myth of national memory and cultural transmission. In Adriana Craciun's discussion it is the poet herself – Anne Bannerman – who bears the stigma of illegitimacy in the sign of her gender, as a masculine critical establishment relegates her work to a decadent, "Gothic" branch of the ballad tradition, obliterating a general milieu of female cultural production.

The cultural breach with Enlightenment, defined by the antagonistic formation of a "Romantic ideology," came late in Scotland, with the founding of *Blackwood's Edinburgh Magazine* in 1817: the post-war battle over Reform precipitated rival, Whig and Tory ideological constellations, Romanticism as (at last) Counter-Enlightenment. In programmatic contrast to *The Edinburgh Review*, *Blackwood's* formally embraced the nationalist discourses of the post-Enlightenment – antiquarianism, vernacular poetry, prose fiction. Along with its spin-offs, notably Lockhart's polemical anatomy of Scottish culture *Peter's Letters to his Kinsfolk* (1819), *Blackwood's* founded a modern (Romantic) discourse of cultural nationalism, which included the "Antisyzygy" critique of a divided tradition, as well as the apotheosis of Scott as national man-of-letters hero – an operation that required, however, the excision of Scott's own philosophical roots in Humean empiricism.

The centrality of Scott to the post-Enlightenment phase of Scottish Romanticism, appropriated as it was by *Blackwood's*, needs to be understood rather than retroactively debunked. Scott played a "Johnsonian" role in the cultural politics of early nineteenth-century Edinburgh, exploiting Tory patronage networks and weaving networks of his own. The cultural position he occupied, mediating between (traditional) Whig–Enlightenment and (new) Tory–Romantic formations, has often been misconstrued as a psychological complex of "Hanoverian head and Jacobite heart," a commitment to progress tempered (or subverted) by baronial nostalgia. The situation was at once more objective and more productive than such formulations tend to allow. Scott's late experiments with representing national difference along an imperial axis, as James Watt argues in these pages, draw on Enlightenment stadial history while dismantling both its "pre-ordained, homogenizing trajectory of societal development" and an emergent, racializing discourse of Romantic Orientalism. Scott's centrality installs the "Border" chronotope of a dynamic liminality rather than an imperial dead centre, the space-time of an historical modernity that (in Ina Ferris's account) looks backwards in order to move forwards; figured in the relentlessly reflexive, ironical strategies of an aesthetic that Jerome McGann, in his contribution to this volume, calls "Romantic postmodernity."

Scholarly editors as well as critics are doing invaluable work recovering marginalized and dissenting figures from the nineteenth-century shadow

of Scott's reputation, and bringing to light the alternative aesthetic and political possibilities opened in their writings.[47] Of the cases addressed in the
present collection, Baillie and Hogg figured prominently among Scott's
network of friends and protégés. Scott was the dominant figure in both
their literary careers, although Baillie's reputation anteceded Scott's (and
her friendship with him), while some of Hogg's most distinctive works articulate a fierce, intimate struggle with his patron, involving – as John Barrell
suggests in these pages – a repudiation of the Enlightenment consensus
Scott represented. If gentlewoman and ex-shepherd produced their work,
in Hogg's case vexatiously, within the aegis of polite literary circles, Anne
Bannerman wrote decisively from outside. The location of these figures
poses, in another register, the question with which Penny Fielding opens
her chapter: "Where was Scottish Romanticism?" Their literary production
occupies a topology not just of formal institutions but (as Craciun insists) of
informal networks of patronage, friendship, influence – "residual" but especially potent in the tightly-knit society of post-Enlightenment Edinburgh,
coexisting with its "advanced" cultural formations (entrepreneurial publishers, a proto-professional public sphere).

Modern and archaic at once, yet again: Scotland's temporal unevenness
found its spatial equivalence in the dialectic between discourses of locality
and abstraction, the former representing ancient, traditionally embedded
ways of life, the latter a scientific, universalizing framework of taxonomies
and systems. If (as Duncan's chapter suggests) Enlightenment writing invested powerfully in an abstraction of time and space, a Romantic attention
to locality (as Fielding shows) continued to invoke that abstract horizon,
whether or not it was specified, historically and geographically, as the glob-
alizing political economy of empire. Blackwoodian cultural nationalism
sought to fix an affirmative, synecdochic relation between an intensively
local chronotope and what Saree Makdisi (describing the dialectic) has
called "universal empire."[48] Fielding finds a productive unsettling of that
relation in Burns's poems, which dissolve the binary opposition between
a particular geography of enunciation and an unspecified human universality to apprehend, instead, the here and now through "global structures
which are themselves the product of writing and naming." Alyson Bardsley
explores the formal tension between place and space in Baillie's writing: the
imaginary, abstract, mobile potentiality claimed for both theatre and nation runs aground as soon as dramatic action is historically and materially
specified. And Peter Manning discusses two visits to Scotland by eminent
English authors at the time of the great Reform bill. North of the border, Cobbett glimpses signs of a British political future, while Wordsworth

escapes – not just from a troubling historical present, but from his own former poetic practice – into the reverie of a pure pastness, the form of memory
without content: Romantic Scotland as the blank of a poet's mind.

NOTES

1. *The Letters of William and Dorothy Wordsworth*, ed. Ernest de Selincourt, 8 vols.,
   III, *The Middle Years, Part 2: 1812–1820*, 2nd edn, rev. Mary Moorman and Alan
   G. Hill (Oxford: Clarendon Press, 1970), 196–7.
2. On the linguistic politics of "English" in the period see Janet Sorensen,
   The Grammar of Empire in Eighteenth-Century British Writing (Cambridge:
   Cambridge University Press, 2000). On the relations between canon and mar-
   ket see, e.g., Michael Gamer, *Romanticism and the Gothic: Genre, Reception, and
   Canon Formation* (Cambridge: Cambridge University Press, 2000).
3. In a formative exchange, René Wellek affirmed the authority of a Kantian–
   Coleridgean "system of norms" against Arthur O. Lovejoy's proposal for a di-
   versity of local practices: Lovejoy, "On the Discrimination of Romanticisms,"
   PMLA 39 (1924): 229–53; Wellek, "The Concept of 'Romanticism' in Literary
   History," *Comparative Literature* 1 (1949): 1–23; 147–72.
4. See Andrew Hook's account of Scotland's emergence "as a kind of romantic
   archetype, its very existence offering confirmation of what were becoming key
   aspects of the ideology of romanticism": "Scotland and Romanticism: The
   International Scene," in Hook (ed.), *The History of Scottish Literature: Volume
   2, 1660–1800*, 4 vols. (Aberdeen: Aberdeen University Press, 1987), 307–21 (316).
5. See Marc Redfield's recent summary and critique: "Both as a term and a field,
   romanticism has suffered instabilities to the degree that it has functioned as a
   trope for aesthetics – as, that is, the figurative locus of 'aesthetic ideology' and
   'theory'": *The Politics of Aesthetics: Nationalism, Gender, Romanticism* (Stanford:
   Stanford University Press, 2003), 9–34 (9). Highlights of the (broadly) historicist
   critique of "Romanticism" include: Jerome McGann, *The Romantic Ideology:
   A Critical Investigation* (Chicago: University of Chicago Press, 1983); Clifford
   Siskin, *The Historicity of Romantic Discourse* (New York: Oxford University
   Press, 1988); David Simpson, *Romanticism, Nationalism, and the Revolt Against
   Theory* (Chicago: University of Chicago Press, 1993); and the essays in Mary
   A. Favret and Nicola J. Watson (eds.), *At the Limits of Romanticism: Essays in
   Cultural, Feminist, and Materialist Criticism* (Bloomington: Indiana University
   Press, 1994). See also the works listed in endnotes to follow. More recent work in
   Romantic historicism has followed John Guillory's redirection of the canonicity
   debate from issues of representation to relations of literary production: see
   Cultural Capital: The Problem of Literary Canon Formation (Chicago: University
   of Chicago Press, 1993).
6. Exemplary here is Leith Davis, *Acts of Union: Scotland and the Literary Negotia-
   tion of the British Nation, 1707–1830* (Stanford: Stanford University Press, 1998).
   On Scotland as matrix of "global English" see Robert Crawford, *Devolving
   English Literature* (Oxford: Clarendon Press, 1992).

7. For a forthright defence of the model see Marshall Brown, *Preromanticism* (Stanford: Stanford University Press, 1991).

8. The standard critique is McGann, *Romantic Ideology*. Among later studies that restore historical and critical complexity to this Romantic project see, e.g., Frances Ferguson, *Solitude and the Sublime: Romanticism and the Aesthetics of Individuation* (New York: Routledge, 1992); Steven Goldsmith, *Unbuilding Jerusalem: Apocalypse and Romantic Representation* (Ithaca: Cornell University Press, 1993); Forest Pyle, *The Ideology of Imagination: Subject and Society in the Discourse of Romanticism* (Stanford: Stanford University Press, 1995); Paul H. Fry, *A Defense of Poetry: Reflections on the Occasion of Writing* (Stanford: Stanford University Press, 1995).

9. See Ian Duncan, "Edinburgh, Capital of the Nineteenth Century," in James Chandler and Kevin Gilmartin (eds.), *Romantic Metropolis: Cultural Productions of the City* (Cambridge: Cambridge University Press, forthcoming). The classic account of the tradition is Raymond Williams, *Culture and Society, 1780–1950* (New York: Harper and Row, 1966).

10. "If we know little of the ancient highlanders, let us not fill the vacuity with Ossian": Samuel Johnson, *A Journey to the Western Islands of Scotland* (Harmondsworth: Penguin, 1984), 119. See Howard Gaskill and Fiona Stafford (eds.), *From Gaelic to Romantic: Ossianic Translations* (Amsterdam: Rodopi, 1988).

11. Matthew Arnold, "The Study of Poetry" (1880), in W. E. Houghton and G. R. Stange (eds.), *Victorian Poetry and Poetics* (Boston: Houghton Mifflin, 1968), 543. For an overview of Burns's posthumous reception see Donald A. Low (ed.), *Robert Burns: The Critical Heritage* (London: Routledge & Kegan Paul, 1974).

12. F. R. Leavis, *The Great Tradition* (New York: New York University Press, 1963), 5, n.2. Georg Lukács, *The Historical Novel* (Lincoln: University of Nebraska Press, 1983), 3–34.

13. See the materials assembled by Peter Duthie in his selection from Baillie, *Plays on the Passions* (Peterborough: Broadview, 2001), 429–39.

14. See, canonically, M. H. Abrams, *The Mirror and the Lamp: Romantic Theory and the Critical Tradition* (New York: Norton, 1958); also Harold Bloom, *The Visionary Company: A Reading of English Romantic Poetry* (New York: Doubleday, 1961).

15. Some landmarks: Geoffrey Hartman, *Beyond Formalism: Literary Essays, 1958–1970* (New Haven: Yale University Press, 1970) and *The Unremarkable Wordsworth* (Minneapolis: University of Minnesota Press, 1987); Thomas Weiskel, *The Romantic Sublime: Studies in the Structure and Psychology of Transcendence* (Baltimore: Johns Hopkins University Press, 1976); Frances Ferguson, *Wordsworth: Language as Counter-Spirit* (New Haven: Yale University Press, 1977); Paul de Man, *The Rhetoric of Romanticism* (New York: Columbia University Press, 1984).

16. James K. Chandler, *Wordsworth's Second Nature: A Study of the Poetry and Politics* (Chicago: University of Chicago Press, 1984); Marjorie Levinson, *Wordsworth's Great Period Poems: Four Essays* (Cambridge: Cambridge

University Press, 1986); David Simpson, *Wordsworth's Historical Imagination: The Poetry of Displacement* (New York: Methuen, 1987); Alan Liu, *Wordsworth: The Sense of History* (Stanford: Stanford University Press, 1989); Alan Bewell, *Wordsworth and the Enlightenment* (New Haven: Yale University Press, 1989).

17. Following the cue of John Barrell, *The Idea of Landscape and the Sense of Place, 1740–1830: An Approach to the Poetry of John Clare* (Cambridge: Cambridge University Press, 1972).

18. Anne Mellor, *Romanticism and Gender* (New York: Routledge, 1993); Gary Kelly, *Women, Writing and Revolution, 1770–1827* (Oxford: Clarendon Press, 1993); Carol Shiner Wilson and Joel Haefner (eds.), *Re-visioning Romanticism: British Women Writers, 1776–1837* (Philadelphia: University of Pennsylvania Press, 1994); Paula Feldman and Theresa Kelley (eds.), *Romantic Women Writers: Voices and Counter-Voices* (Hanover: University Press of New England, 1995).

19. See, e.g., Saree Makdisi, *Romantic Imperialism: Universal Empire and the Culture of Modernity* (Cambridge: Cambridge University Press, 1998), 70–99. Four out of the five case-studies are Scottish in Peter Murphy's *Poetry as an Occupation and an Art in Britain, 1760–1830* (Cambridge: Cambridge University Press, 1993); however, Murphy restates a traditional evaluation of the careers, with Wordsworth providing the foil for Macpherson's, Scott's, and Hogg's varieties of failure to realize an "authentic" poetic vocation; Burns is the partial exception.

20. Jerome Christensen, *Romanticism at the End of History* (Baltimore: Johns Hopkins University Press, 2000), 107–28, 153–75.

21. The term was coined by G. Gregory Smith, in *Scottish Literature: Character and Influence* (London: Macmillan, 1919), 4, and taken up by Hugh MacDiarmid. See Robert Crawford, "Scottish Literature and English Studies," in Crawford (ed.), *The Scottish Invention of English Literature* (Cambridge: Cambridge University Press, 1998), 233–7.

22. Edwin Muir, *Scott and Scotland: The Predicament of the Scottish Writer* (London: Routledge, 1936).

23. David Craig, *Scottish Literature and the Scottish People, 1680–1830* (London: Chatto & Windus, 1961).

24. Cairns Craig, *Out of History: Narrative Paradigms in Scottish and British Culture* (Edinburgh: Polygon, 1996), 82–118. See also Ian Duncan, "North Britain, Inc.," *Victorian Literature and Culture* 23 (1995): 339–50.

25. See the summary by Low, *Robert Burns: The Critical Heritage*, 47–9; Andrew Nash, "The Cotter's Kailyard," and Alan Riach, "MacDiarmid's Burns," in Robert Crawford (ed.), *Robert Burns and Cultural Authority* (Edinburgh: Edinburgh University Press, 1997), 180–97, 198–215; Richard Finlay, "The Burns Cult and Scottish Identity in the Nineteenth and Twentieth Centuries," in Kenneth Simpson (ed.), *Love and Liberty: Robert Burns. A Bicentenary Celebration* (East Linton: Tuckwell, 1997), 69–78.

26. See Mary Louise Pratt, "Women, Literature and National Brotherhood," *Nineteenth-Century Contexts* 18: 1 (1994): 27–47; Catherine Carswell, *The Life*

of Robert Burns (London: Chatto & Windus, 1930). A. L. Kennedy discusses the oppressive gendering of this figure in "Love Composition: The Solitary Vice," in Crawford (ed.), *Robert Burns and Cultural Authority*, 23–39.

27. Patrick Scott Hogg's *Robert Burns: The Lost Poems* (Glasgow: Clydeside Press, 1997), recovering the poet's work in the Radical press, has been followed by a new edition, *The Canongate Burns*, ed. Scott Hogg and Andrew Noble (Edinburgh: Canongate, 2001), and Liam McIlvanney's ground-breaking study, *Burns the Radical: Poetry and Politics in Late Eighteenth-Century Scotland* (East Linton: Tuckwell, 2002).

28. Muir, *Scott and Scotland*, 12.

29. Tom Nairn, *The Break-Up of Britain: Crisis and Neo-Nationalism* (London: Verso, 1981), 114–18.

30. Nairn, *After Britain: New Labour and the Return of Scotland* (London: Granta Books, 2000). General histories in the wake of 1999 include Tom Devine, *The Scottish Nation: A History 1680–2000* (New York: Viking, 1999) and Christopher Harvie, *Scotland: A Short History* (Oxford: Oxford University Press, 2002). Literary-historical overviews include the following: Douglas Gifford, Sarah Dunnigan, and Alan MacGillivray (eds.), *Scottish Literature in English and Scots* (Edinburgh: Edinburgh University Press, 2002); forthcoming projects include a single-authored history by Robert Crawford (Penguin) and a multi-authored, multi-volume history edited by Ian Brown, Thomas Clancy, Susan Manning, and Murray Pittock (Edinburgh University Press).

31. Murray Pittock, *The Invention of Scotland: The Stuart Myth and the Scottish Identity, 1638 to the Present* (London: Routledge, 1991) and *Poetry and Jacobite Politics in Eighteenth-Century Great Britain and Ireland* (Cambridge: Cambridge University Press, 1994); Colin Kidd, *Subverting Scotland's Past: Scottish Whig Historians and the Creation of an Anglo-British Identity, 1689–c.1830* (Cambridge: Cambridge University Press, 1993). See also Pittock's recent *Scottish Nationality* (Houndmills: Palgrave, 2001).

32. Craig, *Out of History*, 112–118.

33. Robert Crawford, *Devolving English Literature* (1992; Edinburgh: Edinburgh University Press, 2000).

34. Susan Manning, *The Puritan-Provincial Vision: Scottish and American Literature in the Nineteenth Century* (Cambridge: Cambridge University Press, 1990); *Fragments of Union: Making Connections in Scottish and American Literature* (Houndmill: Palgrave, 2001); Andrew Hook, *Scotland and America: A Study of Cultural Relations, 1750–1835* (Glasgow: Blackie, 1975).

35. Penny Fielding, *Writing and Orality: Nationality, Culture and Nineteenth-Century Scottish Fiction* (Oxford: Clarendon Press, 1996).

36. See McIlvanney, *Burns the Radical*, 7–37, 220–40.

37. Michael Hechter, *Internal Colonialism: The Celtic Fringe in British National Development, 1536–1966* (London: Routledge, 1975). See, exploring the concept, the set of essays by Matthew Wickman, Ian Duncan, and Charlotte Sussman on "Internal Colonialism" in British and Scottish novels, edited and introduced by Janet Sorensen, in *Eighteenth-Century Fiction* 15: 1 (October 2002): 51–126.

38. Leith Davis, *Acts of Union*; Janet Sorensen, *The Grammar of Empire*. Clifford Siskin, *The Work of Writing: Literature and Social Change in Britain, 1700–1830* (Baltimore: Johns Hopkins University Press, 1998).

39. See, e.g., Fiona Stafford, *The Sublime Savage: A Study of James Macpherson and the Poems of Ossian* (Edinburgh: Edinburgh University Press, 1988); Howard Gaskill (ed.), *Ossian Revisited* (Edinburgh: Edinburgh University Press, 1991); Howard D. Weinbrot, *Britannia's Issue: The Rise of British Literature from Dryden to Ossian* (Cambridge: Cambridge University Press, 1993); Adam Potkay, *The Fate of Eloquence in the Age of Hume* (Ithaca: Cornell University Press, 1994); Adela Pinch, *Strange Fits of Passion: Epistemologies of Emotion, Hume to Austen* (Stanford: Stanford University Press, 1996); Mark Salber Phillips, *Society and Sentiment: Genres of Historical Writing in Britain, 1740–1800* (Princeton: Princeton University Press, 2000).

40. Katie Trumpener, *Bardic Nationalism: The Romantic Novel and the British Empire* (Princeton: Princeton University Press, 1997). See also Ina Ferris, *The Achievement of Literary Authority: Gender, History and the Waverley Novels* (Ithaca: Cornell University Press, 1991), 105–33.

41. James Chandler, *England in 1819: The Politics of Literary Culture and the Case of Romantic Historicism* (Chicago: University of Chicago Press, 1997), 127–74.

42. Trumpener, *Bardic Nationalism*, xiii.

43. Redfield, *The Politics of Aesthetics*, 32.

44. See Richard Sher, *Church and University in the Scottish Enlightenment: The Moderate Literati of Edinburgh* (Princeton: Princeton University Press, 1985), 254.

45. John Brewer, *The Pleasures of the Imagination: English Culture in the Eighteenth Century* (London: HarperCollins, 1997), 44–50, 125–66.

46. See Richard Sher, "The Book in the Scottish Enlightenment," in Paul Wood (ed.), *The Culture of the Book in the Scottish Enlightenment* (Toronto: Thomas Fisher Rare Book Library, 2000), 40–60.

47. Such projects include the ongoing Stirling/South Carolina edition of the works of James Hogg, edited by Douglas Mack and Gillian Hughes (Edinburgh University Press), *A History of Scottish Women's Writing*, edited by Douglas Gifford and Dorothy McMillan (Edinburgh: Edinburgh University Press, 1997), and the electronic archive *Scottish Women Poets of the Romantic Period*, edited by Stephen Behrendt and Nancy Kushigian (Alexander Street Press).

48. Makdisi, *Romantic Imperialism*, 1–22. The phrase is William Blake's.

CHAPTER I

Coleridge, Hume, and the chains of the Romantic imagination

Cairns Craig

Despite being *defined* as an Enlightenment only in 1900 by W. R. Scott,[1] no geography of the Enlightenment could now ignore Scotland's contribution. As Alasdair MacIntyre framed it in *After Virtue*,

The French themselves often avowedly looked to English models, but England in turn was overshadowed by the achievements of the Scottish Enlightenment. The greatest figures of all were certainly German: Kant and Mozart. But for intellectual variety as well as intellectual range not even the Germans can outmatch David Hume, Adam Smith, Adam Ferguson, John Millar, Lord Kames and Lord Monboddo.[2]

Not so, however, with Romanticism. In accounts of the Romantic movement over the last twenty years, Scotland and Scottish writers can be singularly absent. Cynthia Chase's *Romanticism* (1993), a typical collection of critical essays from both sides of the Atlantic,[3] mentions Macpherson and Scott only in footnotes to essays on Wordsworth and Byron, and Burns, Baillie, and Hogg make no appearance at all. Chase's introduction acknowledges Jerome McGann's argument about the extent to which modern criticism has operated with conceptions of literary form and value that themselves derive from Romantic writing: as McGann put it in 1992, using Rene Wellek as the symptomatic critic of Romanticism, "Wellek's position fails to map the phenomena comprehensively because it is a specialized theoretical view derived from the Kantian/Coleridgean line of thought." What Chase does not note, however, and what plays no part in the Romanticism that her essays construct, is McGann's implication that the "Romantic ideology" is also the product of a specifically *national* mapping of Romanticism. McGann's concern is with Byron, who "seems to stand at the very centre of romanticism" when viewed as running "from Goethe and Pushkin to Baudelaire, Nietzsche and Lautreamont"[4] but remains marginal from the perspective of an English Romanticism. Chase suggests that the problem with defining Romanticism is that "Romanticism is *our* past," quoting Paul de Man to the effect that "we carry it within ourselves as the experience of an *act* in which, up to a certain point, we ourselves have participated."[5] She does not, however, reflect on who the "we" is for whom this Romanticism represents "our past."

McGann's choices of significant figures in an *international* Romanticism are particularly pertinent to Scotland, since Macpherson's Ossianic fragments reshape the consciousness of Goethe's Werther as insistently as Scott's works shaped Pushkin's conception of a national Russian literature. The Scotland created by Macpherson and Scott was, of course, one of the ultimate Romantic destinations for European artists – to such an extent, indeed, that modern critics of Scottish culture, such as Tom Nairn, continue to see Scotland as burdened by the false consciousness of its past Romantic glamour.[6] And yet, Scottish culture, so central to Enlightenment, remains marginal to Anglo-American constructions of Romanticism in English. In one respect this is because the "Romanticism" defined by critics such as Chase has a silent and unacknowledged adjective before it – "English" – whose suppression erases the boundaries of a purely regional topography. In another respect, it is perhaps a consequence of the very prominence of the *Scottish* Enlightenment, so that Scottish writers from Macpherson to Scott are interpreted within the framework of Enlightenment values rather than as participants in the development of Romanticism. Indeed, from a Scottish perspective, one might argue that Enlightenment and Romanticism are symbiotically intertwined, a fact obscured by the assimilation of eighteenth-century Scottish culture to European conceptions of Enlightenment.[7]

The marginalization of Scotland in relation to Romanticism has, of course, been significantly challenged by works such as Katie Trumpener's *Bardic Nationalism*,[8] which locates the dynamics of literary change in the development of "national" forms of narrative in Scotland and Ireland: "The period's major new genres . . . its central models of historical scholarship and literary production, and even its notions of collective and individual memory have their origins in the cultural nationalism of the peripheries" (xi). Trumpener's remapping of Romanticism is also a re-evaluation of the hierarchy of genres, displacing the great Romantic lyrics central to "English" Romanticism for the ballad collections, national tales, and historical novels typical of Scottish and Irish writing. For Trumpener, Romanticism and nationalism are two sides of the same historical transformation:

The national tale before *Waverley* presents national character as a synecdoche of an unchanging cultural space; here nationalism is a self-evident legacy, the result of unbroken continuity and a populist community that unites aristocracy and folk. The historical novel draws heavily on this vision of national continuity, but it posits the moment of nationalism at a further stage of historical development: only through the forcible, often violent, entry into history does the feudal folk community become a nation, and only through dislocation and collective suffering is a new national identity forged. (142)

In Chase's collection, on the other hand, the agenda is dictated by the analysis, first, of "a historical context made up of social and political events" (*Romanticism*, 4) – but social and political events whose primarily *English* national provenance is never questioned – and, second, by the relationship of "art and self-consciousness," taking for granted that this is defined by "the connection between English romantic poetry and German Idealist philosophy, established through the mediation of Coleridge," which "has long been a truism of literary scholarship" (8). For all its iconoclasm in shifting Romanticism away from this English–German nexus, however, Trumpener's remapping of Romanticism reveals the lineaments of a much older intellectual landscape, one in which Romanticism in Scotland and Ireland is vitiated by being disablingly retrospective in character, their Romantic national identities "forged" as an evasion of the real history of those nations.[9] For Trumpener, Romantic nationalism is the medium by which the cultural "difference" of marginal cultures can be accommodated to the demands of a modernizing society without disrupting the efficient operation of imperial politics or economics:

The empirewide influence of the Waverley novels lies in their ability to harmonize Scottish materials with British perspectives, as they reconstruct the historical formation of the Scottish nation, the simultaneous formation of the Britain that subsumes it, and a cultural nationalism that survives because it learns to separate cultural distinctiveness from the memory of political autonomy and can therefore be accommodated within the new imperial framework. (*Bardic Nationalism*, 246)

In effect, the Romanticism of "bardic nationalism" enacts the fantasy of a continuing separate identity in a world which does not acknowledge the reality of such identities; it represents a wish-fulfillment that can only be dramatized in the escape from the identity-dissolving present into a past where national identities were still historically relevant.

Translated back into the terms of national literary genres what this does is to leave "English" Romanticism as the Romanticism that is engaged with the present and the future, while Scottish and Irish Romanticisms are displacements into pasts valuable only to the extent that they are irrelevant to the real futures of their societies. Scottish and Irish experience represents "Romanticism-as-evasion" rather than the "Romanticism-as-(potential)-salvation" that continues to underpin the major readings of English Romantic writers. In such constructions, "English" Romanticism is fundamentally embedded in the evolution of modern culture in ways that the evasive Romanticisms of Scotland and Ireland are not. Raymond Williams's early account in *Culture and Society*[10] can stand for many later versions. For Williams, the Romantic artist *may* be shaped by forces that lead to art as "compensation" (*Culture and Society*, 53), as an escape from politics into "natural beauty and personal feeling" (48), but the claim to special insight or knowledge that Romantic art makes is, for Williams, nonetheless justified by its "emphasis on the embodiment in art of certain human values, capacities, energies, which the development of society towards an industrial civilization was felt to be threatening or even destroying" (53). Thus Coleridge, whatever the problems and obscurities of his thinking, remains "an instance, in experience, of the very greatest value" (84) because he represents one of the origins of the very notion of "culture" which it is Williams's business to analyze: "the whole action has passed into our common experience, to lie there, formulated and unformulated, to move and to be examined" (64). "English" Romanticism is thus exonerated of the charge of evasion or nostalgic compensation, because of its teleological place in the development of the culture within which "we" live, whether because, like Williams, one sees it as defining the very terms we use to debate issues of "culture," or because, like Geoffrey Hartman or Paul de Man, one sees it rehearsing the key problems in aesthetic theory with which we still have to wrestle.[11]

Indeed, the critical efforts that have been exerted in recent years on establishing the "commonplace" of the parallels between English Romanticism and German philosophy all participate, explicitly or implicitly, in such teleological justifications of their chosen texts. By reading Wordsworth and Coleridge as the English equivalents of Kant and Hegel, critics who operate in a tradition which sees Kant and Hegel as the crucial turning points of modern thought reflect back upon Wordsworth and Coleridge the philosophical significance accorded to their German contemporaries. And it is part of the fundamental structure of these teleological conceptions of English Romanticism that they should present Romantic thought as producing and being produced by a transcendence of all previous forms of aesthetic thinking, a Hegelian *Aufhebung* that rewrites the very terms in which we can think about the nature of art. James Engell's account of Coleridge in *The Creative Imagination*[12] performs exactly this transition when, having traced in detail the development of the notion of the imagination in both British and German thought, he pronounces that,

In forming his concept of the imagination, Coleridge draws on nearly every other writer who discussed the subject. Despite the fragmentary nature of his own statements – it is hard to find more than a dozen explicit, consecutive sentences at a time on the subject – he states more about the imagination than other Romantic[s] . . . Coleridge distills, connects, and adds to the background with which he was so familiar. (*The Creative Imagination*, 328)

Coleridge's version of the "imagination," in other words, does for the concept exactly what he says the imagination itself does when it "dissolves, diffuses, dissipates, in order to re-create":[13] all past insights are reconstituted in a new version of the imagination which can be grasped only through the very operation of the faculty itself. Engell explains Coleridge's failure to provide full definitions of the creative imagination as intrinsic to the very nature of his subject, since "reason cannot directly comprehend the imagination; or, if it can, according to that principle of subsumption by which every higher power includes the lower ones, then reason cannot express its comprehension of the imaginative power" (*The Creative Imagination*, 347). Imagination, in effect, can only be known through the products of the imagination itself, and can only be truly known when we have Coleridge's conception of the imagination to help us understand it. As Engell puts it in his peroration, the "recognition of Coleridge as at once a culminating and an original figure reveals that we are still somewhere in the mid-course of discovering all that this idea truly means" (366). If we are to have any possible conception of what the imagination "truly means," "we" can only exist within the ambit of Coleridge's (re)definition of it.

The nexus of critical presuppositions and arguments involved in these accounts of Romanticism – its English historical provenance, its crucial relevance to "our" modern conceptions of art, the assumption of a radical transformation of a conceptual framework deriving from Coleridge and German idealism – all contribute – along with the negative presuppositions of the "evasive" or "fantasy" elements in Scottish Romanticism – to a map of Romanticism that makes Scotland a place for the Romantic imagination to visit for scenic effects rather than a place in and through which the Romantic imagination can find expression. It is a nexus of critical presuppositions of which we need to be deeply suspicious, because it seriously misconstrues the historical effectiveness of the aesthetic theories that contribute to a Scottish (and British) Romanticism, theories that are no less "Romantic" by being the very ones that Coleridge rejected in order to define what has come to be seen as the Kantian/Coleridgean version of Romanticism.

The key moment to which Kantian/Coleridgean versions of Romanticism constantly return is the moment in *Biographia Literaria* when Coleridge puts behind him the associationist psychology of Hartley and declares it inadequate to explain the creative power of the mind. The discovery of Kant, Fichte, and Schelling then provides a language – one in which, he declares, "I first found a genial coincidence with much that I had toiled out for myself" (*Biographia Literaria*, 86) – through which his opposition to Hartley can be framed. There is, however, a strange undercurrent that runs through these chapters: Hartley, the stated object of Coleridge's refutation, is constantly and insistently displaced by David Hume, who haunts the chapters like a ghost that cannot be laid nor yet directly confronted. In the crucial chapters in which Coleridge is accounting for the growth of his own thought, the emergence of the German influence is matched by a profound, but profoundly repressed, effort to marginalize the influence of the most significant British thinker of the eighteenth century and of the philosophical tradition that derives from him.

Hume's presence – or, rather, his absence – can first be sensed in chapter v when Coleridge quotes Sir James Mackintosh as having asserted that Hartley stands "in the same relation to Hobbes as Newton to Kepler; the law of association being that to the mind, which gravitation is to matter" (55). It was Hume, however, who had claimed in the *Treatise*, published in 1739,[14] ten years before Hartley's *Observations on Man*, that association represented "a kind of ATTRACTION, which in the mental world will be found to have as extraordinary effects as in the natural" (*Treatise*, 12–13), and almost by a kind of gravitational effect of its own Coleridge's chapter is drawn to conclude with Hume rather than Hartley. At this point, however, Coleridge is engaged not with the truth or falsity of Hume's arguments but with the fact that he believes Hume to have copied his theory of association from Thomas Aquinas – a belief confirmed by his discovery that a Mr. Payne had once possessed volumes of Aquinas belonging to Hume which were "swathed and swaddled" (*Biographia Literaria*, 60) in Hume's commentary.[15] Coleridge, so desperate to defend himself against accusations of plagiarism, dismisses Hume's account not in terms of its intellectual coherence but as though Hume has become the real perpetrator of the crimes with which Coleridge himself was charged. Coleridge then presents his own intellectual development as reaching a crisis "after I had successively studied in the schools of Locke, Berkeley, Leibnitz and Hartley, and could find in neither of them an abiding place for my reason" (79). The absence of Hume from this succession of philosophical engagements – given his earlier presence in Coleridge's narrative and his acknowledged importance to the Kant who would prove Coleridge's salvation – is striking, the more striking since, in 1801, the *Letters* record that after "long wakeful nights" in which "the subject of my meditations ha[s] been the Relations of Thoughts to Things, in the language of Hume, of Ideas to Impressions" (*Collected Letters*, II: 671), he proposed writing a book for Longman "on the originality and merits of Locke, Hobbes, & Hume / which work I mean as a *Pioneer* to my greater work, and as exhibiting a proof that I have not formed opinions without an attentive perusal of the works of my Predecessors from Aristotle to Kant" (II: 707).

Coleridge's perusal of Hume led him to believe that Hume might have correctly identified the key problems in philosophy but that what he produced was "so worthless and so untenable that it induced a more patient and dispassionate huntsman [Kant] to seek the scent again at the point from which his predecessor had flown off, and having again once more caught it on the breeze, he follows it undeterred by the steep and difficult uplands whither it leads him."[16] Hume, indeed, is regularly cited by Coleridge when he wishes to indicate what is unacceptable to his notion of culture; thus, in envisaging the tradition of English letters, Coleridge requires that "England be Sir P. Sidney, Shakespeare, Milton, Bacon, Harrington, Swift, Wordsworth, and never let the names of Darwin, Johnson, Hume *furr* it over!"[17] And in his account of his (unwritten) history of metaphysics in England he declares that he will "confine myself to facts in every part of the work, excepting that which treats of Mr. Hume: – *him* I have assuredly besprinkled copiously from the fountains of Bitterness and Contempt."[18] Hume is so insignificant to Coleridge's intellectual history that he does not merit a mention in the first volume of Richard Holmes's biography, *Coleridge: Early Visions*, and only one footnote in the second, *Coleridge: Darker Reflections*. The latter, however, is significant, since it points to Coleridge's use of the image of the "waterboatman" insect as an analogy for the workings of the imagination, and notes that this image, though "marvellously original," nonetheless "seems to expand on a simile from the philosopher David Hume," a simile in which Hume "remarks on the intrinsic energy of the Imagination," which "is apt to continue, even when its object fails it, and like a galley put in motion by the oars, carries on its course without any new impulse."[19] Coleridge, in other words, introduces the moment of his own discovery of the active power of the imagination and of the inadequacy of Hartley's associationism, by an image which reflects back on and derives from Hume's account of the imagination. The imagination, it should be noted, has almost no role in Hartley's theory, so that Hartleian associationism represents no challenge to the innovation of Coleridge's foregrounding of imagination as "the living power and prime agent of all human perception" (*Biographia Literaria*, 167), while in Hume, on the other hand, associationism is *nothing but* the operation of the imagination. Coleridge's repressed acknowledgment of Hume in the image of the waterboatman is a signal of how much of the intellectual ground that Coleridge wishes now to command by the concept of the imagination was already explicit in Hume, for whom, as the *Treatise* puts it, "the memory, senses, and understanding are, therefore, all of them founded on the imagination" (265).

It is as if, in other words, through the chapters of *Biographia Literaria* relating his own intellectual growth, what Coleridge is trying to achieve is the suppression of the associationism of Hume, with all of the aesthetic, political, and religious consequences that it brought in its train, a suppression rather than a dismissal because he will not confront directly Hume's radical conception of the imagination. The symptoms of Coleridge's evasion can be seen in a series of images in which the associationist conception of the mind is compared with balls on a billiard table. This starts in chapter IV, when Coleridge attributes to Hobbes the notion of "successive particles propagating motion like billiard balls" (58); the image, in fact, does not appear in Hobbes but the reference two pages later to "Hume's essay on association" (60) points perhaps to its real source, and Coleridge's real objection. The billiard ball image then becomes the basis of Coleridge's attack on Hartley's associationism, focusing in particular on Hartley's conception of the mind as related by "vibrations" to objects in the external world:

It is a mere delusion of the fancy to conceive the pre-existence of the ideas in any chain of association as so many differently coloured billiard-balls in contact, so that when an object, the billiard-stick, strikes through the first or white ball, the same motion propagates itself through the red, green, blue, black etc., and sets the whole in motion. No! We must suppose the very same force which constitutes the white ball to constitute the red or black; or the idea of a circle to constitute the idea of a triangle, which is impossible. (*Biographia Literaria*, 63)

There are two problems with this as a *general* attack on associationism. First, Hume's theory, unlike Hartley's, makes no assumptions about the origins of impressions in relation to the external world: associationism does not require the physicalist hypotheses of Hartley and can operate as well in an idealist as in a materialist ontology. By focusing on the already – by

1817 – long-outdated physiology of Hartley's theory,[20] Coleridge allows himself to evade the real epistemological challenge of Hume's theories. Second, Hume does indeed use the analogy of the billiard balls but he uses it in the *Enquiry Concerning Human Understanding*[21] not as an image of the associative process but as an example of the impossibility of predicting, before experience, how things in the world will act: "We fancy, that were we brought on a sudden into this world, we could at first have inferred that one Billiard-ball would communicate motion to another upon impulse; and that we needed not to have waited for the event, in order to pronounce with certainty concerning it" (*Enquiry*, 28). Coleridge adopts Hume's image – an image for the impossibility of knowing a priori the nature of the world – and turns it into an argument for the fact that we cannot, on an associationist account, know the force that governs mental activity. This, however, is precisely the point that Hume himself is making: for Hume, the ultimate grounds of human experience can never be fully known because we can only ever have *empirical* knowledge of their causes. When Coleridge identifies that "to bring in the will, or reason, as causes of their own cause, that is, as at once causes and effects" (*Biographia Literaria*, 64), as the fundamental flaw in associationist theory, he sidesteps the fact that it is precisely such a conception of "cause" that Hume has set in doubt, "cause" having been already revealed by him to be no more than "constant conjunction" – in other words, a special case of association. Equally, one can only pose as a problem the issue of how the will, reason, judgment, and understanding relate to the process of association by ignoring the fact that, for Hume, these are all derivations *from* association rather than possible determinants of it – they are ways of *describing* particular aspects of the associative process, not separate faculties derivable independently of association itself. It is not, of course, that these aspects of Hume's theory are inviolable to criticism: it is simply that Coleridge does not confront them, deflecting his criticism on to the much easier target of Hartley's physiological psychology, as though, in dismissing the latter he had, equally, dismissed the former.

That the spectre of Hume will not be laid by such tactics, however, is revealed in chapter VII, when the ultimate errors of association theory are acknowledged to be its religious rather than its epistemological implications:

The existence of an infinite spirit, of an intelligent and holy will, must on this system be mere articulated motions of the air. For as the function of the human understanding is no other than merely (to appear to itself) to combine and to apply the phaenomena of the association; and as these derive all their reality from the primary sensations; and as the sensations again all their reality from the impressions *ab extra*; a God not visible, audible or tangible can exist only in the sounds and letters that form his name and attributes. (70)

Hume's notorious "atheism" is the direct consequence of his associationism and must, therefore, be overthrown if the process by which "Hume degraded the notion of cause and effect into a blind product of delusion and habit" is not to lead to "the equal degradation of every fundamental idea in ethics or theology" (70). That Hume belatedly but explicitly enters the argument at this point as the object of Coleridge's philosophical ire is clear from the fact that he attempts to save Hartley – the "excellent and pious Hartley" (70) – from any personal contamination by such outcomes, on the basis that "no errors of the understanding can be morally arraigned unless they have proceeded from the heart." Instead, Coleridge turns to condemn those in "an unfortunate neighbour-nation at least, who have embraced this system with a full view of all its moral and religious consequences" and who "need discipline, not argument; they must be made better men before they can become wiser" (71). The "neighbour nation" might, from the context and Coleridge's quotation from his own poetry of 1796, be France, but it might equally be Scotland, since for Coleridge, Hume provides the profound link between all three countries: "But Hume wrote – and the French imitated him – and we the French – and the French us – and so philosophisms fly to and fro – in series of imitated Imitations – Shadows of shadows of shadows of a farthing Candle placed Between two Looking-glasses."[22]

The historical and philosophical suppression involved in this substitution of Hartley for Hume as preparation for the proclamation of the superiority of German idealism is one which has been regularly repeated by much modern criticism, ignoring the fact that Coleridge needed to engage in such a repression not because of the *failure* of those who followed Hume's associationist theories but precisely because of their success, a success reiterated by associationism's key role in the development of nineteenth-century empirical psychology and aesthetics. In this context, John Stuart Mill's account of his salvation from the spiritual wasteland of utilitarianism is regularly cited as indicative of the inadequacies of the associationist theories that underpinned his father's educational practices. The real power of the imagination is supposedly enacted in the younger Mill's recovery from his mental breakdown, with the implication that associationist theories fragment and distort the mind whereas Wordsworthian/Coleridgean theories unite it.[23] This account, however, ignores the fact that Mill never accepted Coleridge's conception of the mind and stuck resolutely to his belief in his father's associationist principles. In the essay in which he declared

Coleridge to be one of the seminal figures of nineteenth-century thought,[24] Mill also declared that "the truth on this much-debated question lies with the school of Locke and Bentham" since there is "no ground for believing that anything can be the object of our knowledge except experience" ("Coleridge," 302–3). In a footnote, he asserted further that "the solution of the problems of the operation of the mind was best to be found in the *Analysis of the Human Mind* by the late Mr. Mill" (346). When Ruskin claimed to have demolished the associationist argument in *Modern Painters*, Alexander Bain was, according to Mill, able to show that Ruskin's own account of art was entirely compatible with associationist principles:

> Mr. Ruskin would probably be much astonished were he to find himself held up as one of the principal apostles of the Association Philosophy in Art. Yet, in one of the most remarkable of his writings, the second volume of "Modern Painters," he aims at establishing, by a large induction and searching analysis, that all things are beautiful or sublime which powerfully recall, and none but those which recall, one or more of a certain series of elevating and delightful thoughts.[25]

In his *Logic*, Mill notes that in Bain's work "the laws of association have been more comprehensively stated and more largely exemplified than by any previous writer," and that Bain provides "incomparably the most complete analytical exposition of the mental phenomena, on the basis of a legitimate Induction, which has yet been produced."[26] As Christopher Turk attests, in *Coleridge and Mill*,[27] Mill's later philosophy, as presented in his *Logic*, "is in fact intended primarily as a foundation for associationism" (75), and is intended to challenge the a priori thinking of Coleridge and his followers by establishing that "the fundamental conceptions of the mind are not intuitive but have the same source in early and forgotten associations as all our other ideas" (75). Associationism was not made redundant by Coleridge's attack on it: indeed, the history of nineteenth-century British aesthetics is shaped by the fact that at every turn the epistemological and aesthetic theories of the a priori school – the school of Coleridge, Carlyle, and Ruskin, of Kantianism and Hegelianism – was met by the associationists in the confidence that they could explain in associationist terms all the processes of the mind and of artistic creativity that the a priori school claimed needed a transcendental justification.

To accept the historical or intellectual validity of Coleridge's overthrow of associationist theories is, necessarily, to accept the redundancy of the Scottish aesthetic tradition to the development of Romanticism, since associationism is fundamental to that Scottish tradition. Even those belonging to the school of Reid, who, in their challenge to the implications of

Hume's theories might seem to be in agreement with Coleridge, nonetheless accepted the central role of association in the mind's workings, and, in particular, the relevance of association theory to aesthetics. Dugald Stewart, for instance, is careful to note that the association of "ideas" must be understood in a Reidian rather than a Humean sense:[28]

I am sensible, indeed, that the expression is by no means unexceptionable, and that, if it be used (as it frequently has been) to comprehend those laws by which the succession of all our thoughts and of all our mental operations is regulated, the word *idea* must be understood in a sense much more extensive than it is commonly employed in. It is very justly remarked by Dr. Reid, that "memory, judgment, reasoning, passions, affections, and purposes; in a word, every operation of the mind, excepting those of sense, is excited occasionally in the train of our thoughts, so that if we make the train of our thoughts to be only a train of ideas, the word *idea* must be understood to denote all these operations." (*Collected Works*, II: 257)

Nonetheless, he is happy to accept that "*An Essay on the Nature and Principles of Taste*, lately published by Mr. Alison" – which is the most rigorously associationist account of aesthetics – means that he can "decline the discussion of a subject which [Alison] had treated with so much ingenuity and elegance" (*Collected Works*, II: 321). Romanticism in Scotland cannot be defined in terms of the development of the transcendental imagination to which Coleridge aspired: it must be understood in terms of the elaboration of the significance of associationist theories both of the mind and of art, theories which shape expectations of the reading experience, notions of the ends of art and of the genres by which such ends can be fulfilled.

The differences between associationist and Kantian/Coleridgean views of art can perhaps best be focused by the notion of the symbol, whose elaboration still plays a crucial role in modern criticism of Romanticism. For Coleridge, the role of the imagination is to mediate between the world of sense and the world of Ideas – ideas understood not as those "general" terms which empiricism believed we derived by comparing individual experiences but Ideas in a Platonic sense, as higher realities which manifest themselves in and through the objects of our senses. As David Aram Kaiser puts it,[29] "For Coleridge, the worldview of empiricism is an 'idea-less philosophy' because it cannot comprehend the real nature of 'Ideas'. In contrast, a worldview informed by the faculty of reason is able to see that 'Ideas' are forces that constitute and guide the material world" (*Romanticism*, 31). The nature of the symbol, therefore, is the point of contact between an eternal idea and a temporal object of the senses, what Coleridge describes as "the translucence of the Eternal through and in the Temporal."[30] For Coleridge, imagination and memory have to be rigorously distinguished – even if they work, in practice, together – because only imagination can escape the "fixities" of the temporal order in order to reveal the transcendental truths of eternity. Within Hume's conception, however, imagination and memory are only quantitatively not qualitatively different:[31] memory is simply the imagination in operation when it retains the apparent order and sequence of ideas or emotions in which they previously occurred rather than producing a new order out of alternative associative connections.

The Kantian/Coleridgean conception of the imagination is one which seeks – or, indeed, already assumes – the possibility of certainty, of our direct awareness of an ultimate truth – in the end, of the eternal truth of the Logos incarnated in the historical – and symbolic – being of Christ. Humean associationism presents a very different and much more anguished conception of the imagination since, for Hume, the imagination is both the foundation of all our experience and, at the same time, its inevitable dissolution. Only through the workings of the imagination can we discover a stable world – "I am naturally led to regard the world, as something real and durable, and as preserving its existence, even when it is no longer present to my perception" (*Treatise*, 197) – but that stable world is, in the end, a "fiction":

The smooth passage of the imagination along the ideas of the resembling perceptions makes us ascribe to them a perfect identity. The interrupted manner of their appearance makes us consider them as so many resembling, but still distinct beings, which appear after certain intervals. The perplexity arising from this contradiction produces a propension to unite these broken appearances by the fiction of a continu'd existence. (*Treatise*, 205)

The real that can only be discovered in and through the imagination is, in exactly the same constructive act, dissolved into what we know can only be a "fiction," a series of associations held together, like the mind, in "a heap or collection of different perceptions, and supposed, tho' falsely, to be endow'd with a perfect simplicity and identity" (207). Suppositions of the imagination's truth – the world is real and available to me – and suppositions of its falsehood – the world is simply a heap of falsely connected perceptions – are both equally compelling. "This deficiency in our ideas," Hume notes,

is not, indeed, perceiv'd in common life, nor are we sensible, that in the most usual conjunctions of cause and effect we are as ignorant of the ultimate principle, which binds them together, as in the most unusual and extraordinary. But this proceeds merely from an illusion of the imagination; and the question is, how far we ought to yield to these illusions. (267)

The Humean imagination, unlike the Kantian/Coleridgean one, continually subverts rather than affirms its own truth: even "if the consideration of these instances makes us take a resolution to reject all the trivial suggestions of the fancy, and adhere to the understanding, that is, to the general and more establish'd properties of the imagination; even this resolution, if steadily executed, wou'd be dangerous, and attended with the most fatal consequences" because "the understanding, when it acts alone, and according to its most general principles, entirely subverts itself, and leaves not the lowest degree of evidence in any proposition" (267). From this contradiction we can only escape by submitting ourselves again to an illusion, to "that singular and seemingly trivial property of the fancy, by which we enter with difficulty into remote views of things" (268).

Applied to aesthetic theory, Hume's associationism produces similar contradictions. We can only experience the work of art through the stimulation of our own associations but we know that what we experience is not the work of art itself but patterns derived from the activity of our own minds. The power of the Humean model lies in the fact that anything can be the object of aesthetic contemplation and any observer is capable of aesthetic experience by following his/her own associative trains. In doing so, however, what is produced is not the experience described by Coleridge in which "necessity and free-will are reconciled in the higher power of an omnipresent Providence," one "that predestinates the whole in the moral freedom of the integral parts,"[32] but the experience of a profound sense of contingency, of the random and the accidental, of the fragility by which we are bound to the objects of our aesthetic contemplation. Francis Jeffrey, in his account of Alison's theories in *The Edinburgh Review* of 1811, points to exactly this consequence of association theory:

Take, for example, the scenery so beautifully, and yet imperfectly, described by Mr. Scott, on the borders of Loch Katrine. The images which it is calculated to suggest, will agree, perhaps, in being ideas of seclusion – of a life set free from the restraints of the world, and hidden from its observation – of sympathy with the simple joys and animating toils of its natives – and of awe and veneration for the power which has left the traces of its might on the cliffs and mountains: but the particular train of images, by the help of which those general impressions may be moulded into distinct objects of emotion, is evidently altogether loose and undetermined, and must depend on the taste, dispositions and information of every different beholder.[33]

The intense subjectivism of such an outcome is modified by the fact that associations generated from identical sources – such as having read the same poem – may produce a common set of memories that can, for instance,

infuse particular landscapes with the sense of a shared associative significance. The importance of *landscape* in Romantic art lies precisely in the
fact that the forms of Romantic art – the national tale and the historical
novel as much as the meditative lyric or the descriptive poem – populate
a national landscape with memorable characters and events to provide a
common storehouse of associative potential through which, at a later point,
people will come to view that landscape as not only *aesthetically* interesting
but as uniting them through the associative process in a communal – a national – memory. It is, however, the fragility of those communal memories,
the ease with which, through time, they will be forgotten and return to
having a purely subjective significance that is the anguish of (associationist)
Romantic art – and the anguish that afflicts Romantic nationalisms in their
desperate effort to maintain the associative power of their common culture. From Macpherson's *Ossian* to Walter Scott's *Lay of the Last Minstrel*,
Scottish poets dramatize this double significance: the bard holds the last
memories of "his tuneful brethren," now "all dead," but one last time allows
imagination to defy forgetfulness:

> Each blank in faithless memory void,
> The poet's glowing thought supplied.[34]

The poem proceeds to reinscribe in a printed text the song supposedly about
to be erased from common memory, but the threat of erasure remains – the
common memory will, in the end, revert to a personal series of associations
that will die with their possessor. Each aesthetic experience is the act of
recollection from an imagined past of some memory that is on the boundary of disappearing for ever out of our potential trains of associations –
a threat underlying Romantic nationalisms' desperate efforts to retain the
associative contexts of past national cultures, and the profound mourning
over their loss.

If European Romanticism can be dated back to Macpherson's *Ossian*,
then Romanticism in general as much as Romanticism in Scotland is the
exploration of this Humean double bind. *Ossian's* infamous status as a fake
needs to be reread as a demonstration of the problematics of an imagination which reconstructs the past out of memories that are themselves
transformed by their imagining to make it impossible for us ever to come
in contact with any past which we can be certain is real – a very different
kind of "fantasy" of the past than the "Romanticism-as-evasion" model
might suggest. It is from the non-transcendental symbols of the associationist tradition, symbols which are no guarantee of an eternal Idea but
the creatures of an all too temporal associative chain, that the dynamics of

the development of Romantic art in Scotland derive. Far from being at the margin of Romanticism, far from being made redundant by Coleridge, that Scottish tradition was to shape profoundly the development of British and Irish Romanticism not only from the 1760s to the 1820s, but from Hallam's defence of Tennyson in 1830[35] through Pater's *The Renaissance*[36] in 1873 to Yeats's effort to repopulate the Irish landscape with Celtic associations in the 1890s.[37]

The anguish of the desire for certainty that is subverted by the very power, the power of the imagination, that could be its only source, the Humean anguish that runs through all the works of science as much as of art, is perhaps most intensely prefigured by Adam Smith in the conclusion to his "Essay on Astronomy," where he is describing the force of Newton's conception of the universe:

And even we, while we have been endeavouring to represent all philosophical systems as mere inventions of the imagination, to connect together the otherwise disjointed and discordant phenomena of nature, have insensibly been drawn in, to make of language expressing the connecting principles of this one, as if they were the real chains which Nature makes use of to bind together her several operations.[38]

The most powerful, the most convincing account of the phenomena of the universe that we have ever devised is only an "as if," deceiving us into believing it to be a description of the "real chains" of Nature, rather than simply chains of the imagination.

NOTES

1. W. R. Scott, *Francis Hutcheson: His Life, Teaching and Position in the History of Philosophy* (Cambridge: Cambridge University Press, 1900).
2. Alasdair MacIntyre, *After Virtue* (2nd edn, London: Duckworth, 1985), 37.
3. Cynthia Chase, *Romanticism* (London: Routledge, 1993).
4. Jerome McGann, "Rethinking Romanticism," *ELH* 59 (1992): 736.
5. Paul de Man, *The Rhetoric of Romanticism* (New York: Columbia University Press, 1984), 50; quoted in Chase, *Romanticism*, 1.
6. See, for instance, Nairn's continued debate with the ghost of Walter Scott in *After Britain* (London: Granta, 2000), 230:

   Walter Scott was the most influential literary representative of the old posture. Like many other voices of the long facing-both-ways era, he learned to set off ineffectual (hence emotionally exaggerated) regret against a "level-headed" (and all too effective) acceptance. Boring-bastard heroes were required for that job, and he was notoriously good at inventing them. More alarmingly, such traits soon came to be incorporated into Scottish "national character" and were eventually awarded ethnic status.

7. See Aidan Day, *Romanticism* (London: Routledge, 1996), especially chapter 1.
8. Katie Trumpener, *Bardic Nationalism: The Romantic Novel and the British Empire* (Princeton: Princeton University Press, 1997).
9. This view was given its classic statement in Edwin Muir's *Scott and Scotland* (London: Routledge, 1936), and became the burden of the long-running debate in Scottish cultural criticism over Tartanry and Kailyard.
10. Raymond Williams, *Culture and Society* (Harmondsworth: Penguin, 1958; 1961).
11. Geoffrey Hartmann, "Romanticism and Anti-Self-Consciousness," insists, "This is as crucial a matter today as when Wordsworth and Coleridge wrote" (Chase, *Romanticism*, 52).
12. James Engell, *The Creative Imagination: Enlightenment to Romanticism* (Cambridge, MA: Harvard University Press, 1981).
13. Samuel Taylor Coleridge, *Biographia Literaria or Biographical Sketches of my Literary Life and Opinions*, ed. George Watson (London: Dent, 1956), 167.
14. David Hume, *A Treatise of Human Nature*, ed. L. A. Selby-Bigge (Oxford: Clarendon Press, 1888).
15. The same well-recollected Mackintosh was not considered by Coleridge so trustworthy in his letter to Mr. Wedgewood on February 18, 1801, in which he praises Hume's attack on Locke's notion of "innate ideas" and says he would not have pursued his own criticisms "had I not heard Mr. Mackintosh affirm in his Lectures, that 'the Doctrine of Innate Ideas (a doctrine unknown to the ancients) was first introduced by Des Cartes, & fully overthrown by Locke'. Mr. M. must have made a mistake"; *Collected Letters of Samuel Taylor Coleridge*, ed. Earl Leslie Griggs, 6 vols. (Oxford: Clarendon Press, 1956–71, II: 681).
16. Alice D. Snyder, *Coleridge on Logic and Learning, with Selections from the Unpublished Manuscripts* (New Haven: Yale University Press, 1929), 91 and 95.
17. *The Notebooks of Samuel Taylor Coleridge*, ed. Kathleen Coburn, 6 vols. (London: Routledge & Kegan Paul, 1962), II: 2598.
18. *Collected Letters*, "To Samuel Purkis, Feb 17, 1803," II: 490–1.
19. Richard Holmes, *Coleridge: Darker Visions* (London: Harper Collins, 1998), 397n. The quotation from Hume is from *Treatise of Human Nature*, Book 1, Part IV, Sect. II, 198.
20. It was already edited out of Joseph Priestley's abridged version of Hartley's *Observations on Man* in 1775.
21. David Hume, *An Enquiry Concerning Human Understanding*, ed. L. A. Selby-Bigge (Oxford: Clarendon Press, 1966).
22. *Letters*, To Robert Southey, October 15, 1799, I: 538.
23. It is often forgotten that Mill only read Wordsworth and Coleridge after recovering from his depression and that it was sentimental fiction that began the recovery. See A. O. J. Cockshut, ed., *The Autobiography of John Stuart Mill* (Krumlin, Halifax: Ryburn Publishing, 1992), 77.
24. John Stuart Mill, "Coleridge," in J. B.Schneewind (ed.), *Mill's Essays on Literature and Society* (New York: Collier-Macmillan, 1965).
25. J. S. Mill, "Review of Bain's Psychology," *Dissertations and Discussions*, 4 vols. (London: John W. Parker and Son, 1859–75), III: 135.

26. John Stuart Mill, *Collected Works*, vol. VIII, *A System of Logic Ratiocinative and Inductive: Being a Connected View of the Principles of Evidence and the Methods of Scientific Investigation*, ed. J. M. Robson (London: Routledge and Kegan Paul, 1974), 853n.

27. Christopher Turk, *Coleridge and Mill* (Aldershot: Avebury, 1988).

28. Sir William Hamilton, ed., *The Collected Works of Dugald Stewart*, vol. II: *Elements of the Philosophy of the Human Mind* (Bristol: Thoemes Press, 1994), 1.

29. David Aram Kaiser, *Romanticism, Aesthetics and Nationalism* (Cambridge: Cambridge University Press, 1999).

30. Samuel Taylor Coleridge, *The Statesman's Manual, The Collected Works of Samuel Taylor Coleridge*, 16 vols., vol. VI, ed. R. J. White, *Lay Sermons* (Princeton: Princeton University Press, 1972), 30.

31. See Jan Wilbanks, *Hume's Theory Of Imagination* (The Hague: Martinus Nijhoff, 1968):

> We must never lose sight of the fact that the materials of the imagination are, in Hume's view, the same as those of all other types of thinking; that the having of ideas (or images) is something which is common to memory, imagination, and reason. It is not something peculiar to imaginative activity . . . Hume holds that if one is imagining then one is having ideas; he does not hold that if one is having ideas then one is necessarily imagining. (63)

32. Coleridge, *Statesman's Manual*, 31–2.

33. *The Edinburgh Review* (May 1811): 28.

34. Sir Walter Scott, "The Lay of the Last Minstrel," *The Poetical Works of Sir Walter Scott*, ed. J. Logie Robertson (London: Henry Frowde, Oxford University Press, 1913), 2.

35. Henry Hallam (ed.), *Remains in Verse and Prose of Arthur Hugh Hallam* (London: J. Murray, 1863), 162.

36. Walter Pater, *The Renaissance* (London: Macmillan, 1873).

37. See, for instance, W. B. Yeats, "Art and Ideas," *Essays and Introductions* (London: Macmillan, 1961), 349:

> Among the little group of poets that met at the Cheshire Cheese I alone loved criticism of Arthur Hallam's sort . . . Yet all the while envious of the centuries before the Renaissance, before the coming of our intellectual class with its separate interests, I filled my imagination with the popular beliefs of Ireland, gathering them up among forgotten novelists in the British Museum or in Sligo cottages. I sought some symbolic language reaching far into the past and associated with familiar names and conspicuous hills that I might not be alone amid the obscure impression of the senses.

38. Adam Smith, *Essays on Philosophical Subjects*, ed. W. P. Wightman and J. C. Bryce (Indianapolis: Liberty Fund, 1982), 105.

CHAPTER 2

The pathos of abstraction: Adam Smith, Ossian, and Samuel Johnson

Ian Duncan

Samuel Johnson's *A Journey to the Western Islands of Scotland* (1775) represents the most famous of English encounters with Scotland at the zenith of
its so-called Enlightenment, a phenomenon that goes unnoticed in the
book. Recent criticism has interpreted Johnson's notorious search-and-
destroy critique of "Ossian" within a larger historical agenda, the imperial
restructuring of British nationality after 1707 and 1745.[1] Johnson wields
the discourses of Enlightenment – social history, political economy, anthropology, linguistic theory – even as he declines to recognize the authors
and institutions that are currently producing them in Lowland Scotland.
"The real imperialism of the *Journey*," writes Katie Trumpener, "lies in its
insistent appropriation, occupation, and emptying out" of the ideological
themes of eighteenth-century Scottish writing.[2]

Yet the tone of the *Journey* is more melancholy than triumphant: "We
came thither too late to see what we had expected, a people of peculiar
appearance, and a system of antiquated life."[3] Johnson's disappointment,
sounded across a range of topics, inflects the scientific project that compensates for a lost world of primitive encounters: the opportunity to observe
at first hand the historical transformation of a traditional society. The state
of the Highlands in the wake of the '45 affords Johnson, as it afforded
the Scots literati, with a case-study in wholesale social change. The center of the *Journey* consists of an extended philosophical essay in which
Johnson weighs the material and cultural values of loss and gain in the
transit of modernization. He finds himself gazing into the breach between
historical stages: military conquest followed by a legislative dismantling
of traditional social bonds have opened the country to the influx of capital. As landlords abandon patriarchal obligation for rent-racking, their
demoralized tenants emigrate in droves. The Highlands occupy a historical interim in the form of a vacancy, a desert, which horrifies Johnson
because it portends a world without people – a scenery of national extinction. Johnson finds his commitment to a destiny of economic and

cultural improvement undermined by a persistent apprehension that this may not constitute the country's future after all, any more than it does the present.

Johnson installs this Scottish desert, as Trumpener suggests, by emptying out a flourishing cultural present. The tonality of pathos hints at the defensive repression of a threat. His depiction of Scotland as a wasteland encodes a response to – a revenge upon – a modernist philosophical tradition that Johnson views as undertaking a kind of metaphysical desertification of knowledge and belief. David Hume functions as the hypothetical antagonist or intellectual devil of the *Journey*, which never once refers to him, despite his preeminence among the Enlightenment literati. Hume is master of the peculiarly Scotch cognitive fallacy that recurs throughout Johnson's text: the skeptical evacuation of a historically and metaphysically real relation between world and subject, and its substitution by a delusive work of the imagination. Johnson reduces this logic to a withering formula in his closing critique of *Fingal*, modern Scotland's epos of the desert and of cultural extinction: "If we know little of the ancient highlanders, let us not fill the vacuity with Ossian" (*Journey*, 119). In this chapter I shall argue that Macpherson's Ossianic poetry develops an intensively subjective and temporal rendering of a logic of abstraction that is characteristic of eighteenth-century Scottish writing. Johnson's attack on Ossian masks a philosophically principled engagement with this logic of abstraction and what he understands to be its false metaphysics.

Johnson describes a modern Scotland fatally severed from an authentic past or future. Modernity makes its appearance as a formal category in the Scottish Enlightenment human sciences, in philosophical history and its accessory discourses. Two orders of history work together, reinforcing and naturalizing one another, to produce the figure of modernity as the effect of a temporal rupture – a breach with the past, a disconnection from origins. The empirical narrative of national history related a series of drastic political and cultural disjunctions: the Reformation, Union of Crowns, Union of Parliaments. Eighteenth-century historiography repudiated Scotland's past as violent, fanatical, abject – ideologically antithetical to post-Union civil society.[4] Meanwhile, the narrative of conjectural history projected a universal scheme of human development along a succession of distinct socioeconomic stages, each one of which cancels the one before, terminating in the modern formation of "commercial society." The principle of disconnection governs the phenomenological as well as socio-historical basis of modernity in Scottish writing, from Hume's deconstruction of the metaphysical foundations of continuity and causality in the *Treatise of Human Nature* to the various poetic and antiquarian "revivals" of a lost ancestral nation.

The disjunction from origins constitutes a common (we might call it Romantic) matrix of representation – what Susan Manning calls "a grammatical and conceptual space"[5] – for a variety of terms in which recent critics have sought to characterize modernity. Besides those I have already mentioned – the historicist scheme of a radical break between past and present, the metaphysical disconnection from a cause – these include the following. First: the relation of subjectivity not to the world itself, nor to ideas, but to representation, in the detour of cognition through a system of signs – for example, the claim "that society constitutes a system," visible in the representation of political economy.[6] Second: the predication of such a system on the abstraction of space and time (with attendant effects of homogenization, standardization, and instrumentalization), as analyzed by Henri Lefebvre and a tradition of commentary following Walter Benjamin.[7] And third: the thesis (made familiar by Marshall McLuhan and Benedict Anderson) that print culture, the medium of these abstractions, conditions a peculiarly modern form of subjectivity.[8] Peter Osborne has made the case for understanding modernity as a phenomenology, "a structure of historical consciousness," rather than as "an empirical category of historical sociology."[9] Although I shall be emphasizing the subjective term, the structure of consciousness, in the discussion that follows, these frames by no means exclude each other – especially in eighteenth-century Scotland, where we can read the simultaneous emergence of modernity as an empirical category of historical sociology *and* as a structure of historical consciousness.

We can read it in the ostensibly antithetical literary projects – both of them massively influential – of James Macpherson and Adam Smith: the poetic fabrication of a legendary national past, the scientific invention of political economy. In contrast to the materialist certainties promised by *The Wealth of Nations*, it would be the fate of the *Poems of Ossian* to be dismissed as a merely metaphysical confection, the opposite of historical reality – as, worse than a fiction, a forgery. Putting the case this way, it is not difficult to begin interpreting a dialectical relation between the modern real and the fake antique, or to see them as inflecting another opposition, between objective knowledge and subjective fantasy.

It is interesting that a tradition of commentary should have discovered an equivalent opposition within Smith's own intellectual career – the so-called "Adam Smith problem," an alleged ethical contradiction between the sympathy-promoting *Theory of Moral Sentiments*, a treatise on modern subjectivity, and the "selfish" political economy of *The Wealth of Nations*.[10] Both these texts propose, however, a structural dynamic of *exchange* as a fundamental principle of human nature, so that modern commercial society can be justified as human nature's fulfillment rather than its corruption. The same principle – this time, it is linguistic rather than economic or sympathetic exchange – informs the *Lectures on Rhetoric and Belles Lettres*, Smith's pioneering prescription for the formation of a modern, British, professional subjectivity through techniques of literacy that are historically specific to the medium of print.[11] Eighteenth-century Scottish print culture was largely constituted in the imperial dialect of English: a linguistic hegemony that kept visible, rather than concealed, a historical alienation, by reiterating the figure of the break of modernity – as an effect of reading – on the surface of daily life. Abstraction, the character of a reflective relation between subjectivity and representation, or the relay of cognition through a system of signs, is a key effect of these techniques of literacy. Before considering Smith's account of subjectivity, however, let us look at his "objective" vision of the economic forces of modernity in *The Wealth of Nations*.

What is radical in Smith's account of modernity becomes clear when we compare it with a rival version, Adam Ferguson's *An Essay on the History of Civil Society* (1767). Ferguson registers the threat of an erosion of "national spirit" in commercial society. In certain pre-modern societies – hunting clans, republican city-states – each man can represent, entire in himself, the body politic, as he fulfills the various functions of economic producer, citizen, and warrior. This relation to a social totality provides the medium of national spirit. Contra Hobbes, it is not savagery but modernity that renders man "a detached and a solitary being."[12] "The mighty engine which we suppose to have formed society [i.e., the individualist agency of competitive desire] only tends to set its members at variance, or to continue their intercourse after the bands of affection are broken" (*Essay*, 24). Two processes work together to produce this condition. One is economic, the "separation of arts and professions" (Ferguson's version of Smith's "division of labour"), which may increase wealth and refinement but dissolves the individual's relation to a collective whole, until "society is made to consist of parts, of which none is animated with the spirit of society itself" (207). The internal subdivision of economic and social relations tends to coincide with a second process, the political enlargement of the national territory. Although he never specifies it, Ferguson seems to have in mind the modern condition of Scotland in the new "United Empire":

But if nations pursue the plan of enlargement and pacification, till their members can no longer apprehend the common ties of society . . . [they may], like the inhabitants of a conquered province, be made to lose the sense of every connection, but that of kindred or neighbourhood; and have no common affairs to transact, but those of trade: Connections, indeed, or transactions, in which probity or friendship may still take place; but in which the national spirit, whose ebbs and flows we are now considering, cannot be exerted. (208)

In proportion as territory is extended, its parts lose their relative importance to the whole. Its inhabitants cease to perceive their connection with the state, and are seldom united in the execution of any national, or even of any factious, designs. Distance from the seats of administration, and indifference to the persons who contend for preferment, teach the majority to consider themselves as the subjects of a sovereignty, not as the members of a political body. (256–7)

Ferguson predicts the disintegration of a rational public domain, essential to political liberty, which relies upon the synchronization of individual intelligence with the corporate will. "Its parts lose their relative importance to the whole": that synecdochal equivalence, modeled on the organic integrity of the body, generates the ethical totality of "national spirit."

In *The Wealth of Nations* (1776) Smith reformulates Ferguson's vision of modernization as a structural amplification and complication of social relations. Here, though, commercial society represents not simply an enlargement of prior formations by aggregation, but a geometrical and "metaphysical" gain in complexity – and thus, not fragmentation and atomization, but the multiplication of connections and mediations, binding together a potentially global totality.[13] Smith identifies the foundation of commercial society in the "propensity in human nature . . . to truck, barter, and exchange one thing for another."[14] In other words, Smith's scheme does not rely on the figure of the singular body as totality. Quite the contrary, as we see in the analysis of the division of labour that occupies the first chapter of *The Wealth of Nations*. In the second half of the chapter, Smith turns from the analysis of productive labour to disclose the condition of the object in a commercial society, adapting Locke's analysis of property in the second *Treatise of Government*. Where Locke characterizes the transformation of a natural resource into property in terms of an arithmetical aggregation, through labour, of other resources – "a strange *Catalogue of things*"[15] – Smith represents economic improvement in terms of a mystical plenitude. Far more than in Locke's description, "society constitutes a *system* visible only to the moral philosopher cum political economist."[16] The philosopher's vision illuminates even the humblest object in a commercial empire, such as the "coarse and rough" woolen coat of the day-labourer, with an aura of almost infinitely extensive and intricate relations of production:

Observe the accommodation of the most common artificer or day-labourer in a civilized and thriving country, and you will perceive that the number of people of whose industry a part, though but a small part, has been employed in procuring him this accommodation, exceeds all computation. The woollen coat, for example, which covers the day-labourer, as coarse and rough as it may appear, is the produce of the joint labour of a great multitude of workmen. The shepherd, the sorter of the wool, the wool-comber or carder, the dyer, the scribbler, the spinner, the weaver, the fuller, the dresser, with many others, must all join their different arts in order to complete this homely production. How many merchants and carriers, besides, must have been employed in transporting the materials from some of those workmen to others who often live in a very distant part of the country! How much commerce and navigation in particular, how many ship-builders, sailors, sail-makers, rope-makers, must have been employed in order to bring together the different drugs made use of by the dyer, which often come from the remotest corners of the world! (*The Wealth of Nations*, 22–3)

Smith's opening chapter culminates in a virtual representation of his system – a spatial, synchronic totality consisting of an unimpeded flow of production, circulation, and exchange. Wealth has become a curiously imaginary condition, the effect of a global network of relations that remains invisible to the subject on the ground, although it is legible in the register of the political economist. What appears present to the senses – the primitive simplicity of a rough woollen coat – is an illusion. Reality inheres in a phantasmagoric glamour of complicities and connections, in a sublime, dynamic system rather than in solid bodies or objects. It is (and so Smith displaces the work of weaving from the labourer's coat to his own representation of it) textual and figural.

Modernity thus takes on the imaginary or spectral character of a relation to representations rather than to life itself. The position of the subject in an invisible, sublime system of relations of production, exchange, and accumulation can generate a psychology of paranoia as well as triumphalism, as in Smith's image (much later on) of the rich man, "at all times surrounded by unknown enemies, whom, though he never provoked, he can never appease, and from whose injustice he can be protected only by the powerful arm of the civil magistrate continually held up to chastise it" (710). Relations among persons, in which transactions of exchange are handclasps and speech acts, give way to a more nebulous intercourse. The powerful arm of the civil magistrate is the juridical counterpart of that more famous trope, the "invisible hand" of market forces: the body politic has become a sublime body dissociated from individual agency or consciousness. The difference between a local market, in which people may haggle and bargain face to face, and the invisible, potentially boundless market of world empire ("agoraphobia," after all, means fear of the populous expanse of the marketplace) remains latent rather than active in *The Wealth of Nations*. All that is solid does not, quite yet, melt into air: Smith may still rely upon the materiality of place to stabilize the flux of capital. Limitations imposed by distance, terrain, and transport technology secure the bounds of a market that would otherwise be universal and undifferentiated.

The Theory of Moral Sentiments (1759), Smith's treatise on the psychic disciplines of modernity, analyzes the subjective equivalences of the economic principles of exchange-value and the division of labour that constitute commercial society. Covering what Smith, following Hume, calls "the void of human life"[17] (in other words, everyday life as a domain emptied of metaphysical structures), *sympathy* is the mimetic technology of subject formation that founds the social self in the act of imaginary exchange. Sympathy turns out to be constituted, not through "the reflection of any sentiment of the sufferer," but through the spectator's own "consideration of what he himself would feel if he was reduced to the same . . . situation" (*The Theory of Moral Sentiments*, 12). A work of the imagination, sympathy cannot be sustained by those "passions which take their origin from the body," but moulds itself upon "the shape and configuration of the imaginations" of others (27–9). Far from being simple or spontaneous, this imaginary assumption is complex, studied, and laborious.[18] The technique is both aesthetic and forensic, involving the ordering of subjective impressions. The often arduous work of judgment must convert the spectatorial gaze into the transaction of feeling. For this, the spectator becomes a *reader*, attentive above all to the narrativity (rather than simply the spectacularity) of the situation:

In all such cases, that there may be some correspondence of sentiments between the spectator and the person principally concerned, the spectator must, first of all, endeavour, as much as he can, to put himself in the situation of the other, and to bring home to himself every little circumstance of distress which can possibly occur to the sufferer. He must adopt the whole case of his companion with all its minutest incidents; and strive to render as perfect as possible, that imaginary change of situation upon which his sympathy is founded. (21)

The temporality of this imaginary work, with its successive stages of observation, reflection, and identification, is distinctively a temporality of reading.

We regulate our own conduct, conversely, by imagining the point of view of the other, internalizing the figure of a "fair and impartial spectator" (110). Society is a "mirror" (110) in which "I divide myself, as it were, into two persons": defendant and judge, agent and spectator (113). Nor does the actual other in the sympathetic transaction remain an object in the field of vision. The work of sympathy requires reciprocity – although of a strangely negative kind. Violent outbursts of feeling disgust us, according to Smith, because they make us aware of the gap between the other person's sensations and the capacity of our imagination to reproduce them. Sympathy arises, instead, when we are spared the embarrassment of this revelation of the imagination's weakness. The man who remains cheerful in misfortune earns our sympathy insofar as he "makes no demand upon us for that more exquisite degree of sensibility which we find, and we are mortified to find, that we do not possess" (48). In order for us to sympathize with him, in other words, he has first to have sympathized with us. In one of Smith's more baroque examples, the torture victim "commands our highest admiration" when he represses cries of agony that he knows would only upset us: "His firmness enables him to keep time with our indifference and insensibility" (31). That is to say, he conceives of us in terms of the abstract, negative moral medium of "propriety," sympathy's effectual cause and end. In this sentimental economy, not a surplus of sensibility but its scarcity generates the sympathetic flow. Sympathy is an aesthetic technique for managing alienation in a community characterized by a public space of encounters among strangers. Its function is to maintain a collective, neutral, abstract field of insensibility, called propriety, which constitutes the moral atmosphere of a civil society fearful of the potential violence of individual passions.

The self as well as the other is thus produced in a sequential correspondence of imaginary figures, an interactive serial fiction. In an admirably subtle account of *The Theory of Moral Sentiments*, David Marshall emphasizes the theatricality of Smith's model:[19] but even the figure of theatre may imply an excessively clear distinction between actors and spectators, and a condition altogether more stable than is yielded in Smith's analysis of the modern self as an ongoing project of representation in a textual system of intersubjective relations.

Adam Ferguson's ideal of a civil society guaranteed by a part-to-whole correspondence between a corporate body and its members is scarcely a possibility, let alone an occasion for nostalgia, in Smith's regime of representation, where division itself, in the field of exchange, is the generative

principle of subjectivity.[20] Such nostalgic effects as do turn up in Smith
usually accompany an imported generic register – for instance, the modern
epic topos (from Ariosto to Milton) of the obsolescence of heroic virtue
in conditions of mechanized warfare. Late in *The Wealth of Nations*, the
modernist trope of an abstracted, invisible causality invests the modern
battlefield:

the noise of fire-arms, the smoke, and the invisible death to which every man
feels himself every moment exposed, as soon as he comes within cannon-shot, and
frequently a long time before the battle can be well said to be engaged, must render
it very difficult to maintain any considerable degree of... regularity, order, and
prompt obedience, even in the beginning of a modern battle. In an antient battle
there was no noise but what arose from the human voice; there was no smoke,
there was no invisible cause of wounds or death. (699)

Smith must resort to a grammar of negation to recall the Homeric battlefield, with its vanished effects of visual transparency, oral immediacy, and
a visible causality of death in the clash of arms and bodies.

Perhaps we should not be surprised to find the descriptive rhetoric of
Smith's modern battle informing the age's most notorious version of "an
ancient epic poem," James Macpherson's "translations" of the third-century
Gaelic bard Ossian:

As a hundred winds on Morven; as the streams of a hundred hills; as clouds fly
successive over heaven; or, as the dark ocean assaults the shore of the desert: so
roaring, so vast, so terrible the armies mixed on Lena's echoing heath. – The groan
of the people spread over the hills; it was like the thunder of night, when the cloud
bursts on Cona; and a thousand ghosts shriek at once on the hollow wind.[21]

In a recent discussion of the modernity of Ossian, Adam Potkay comments
on the "obscurity and tact" with which the poems render heroic violence:
all is metonymically depersonalized, disembodied, dispersed in "columns
of mist." Potkay interprets this rhetoric as part of an ideological technique
by which Macpherson projects a contemporary "ethos of politeness" onto a
screen of ancestral heroism. Primitive virtue provides the legitimating frame
for a modern ideal of conduct, rendered as though in its natural state.[22]
Acute as this explanation is of the appeal of the Ossian poems, perhaps it
finds in them an excessive – sheerly ideological – positivity. Peter Womack
has argued that the poems represent "an imaginary primitive world which
is wholly structured and saturated by the categories of [modernization],"
but – crucially – as the effect of their absence or negation.[23] I shall argue
along these lines that the affective power of Ossian derived as much from
the representation of modernity as a peculiar temporal relation, a kind of

negative dialectic, between past and present, as from the primitive framing of a modern ideology of conduct.

"The 'Works of Ossian' aspired to be, and for half a century or so actually were, the sacred texts of pure subjectivity":[24] for this they make not only the past but the present into a spectral condition, devoid of life and body. This condition includes the notorious inauthenticity of the epos and our relation to it as readers, focused – or rather diffused – through the crucial, mediating subjectivity of the Bard, Ossian himself. The poems' aesthetic charge lies in the process rather than content of their ideology-making, in the pathetic reflective fading of a concrete social reality, rather than in the ideal of manners that hangs in its wake. The historical premise of this heroic world is its extinction – and it is Macpherson's representation of extinction as a cultural phenomenon, the passing of a "whole way of life," that constitutes the reference-point of the epic's modernity. (Homer and Vergil imagine the physical destruction of Troy, but Trojans and Achaians share the same culture.) "Carril of other times," the chief exhorts his bard, "raise thy voice on high, and tell the deeds of other times"; for "lovely are the words of other times" (*The Poems of Ossian*, 61–2): the Ossianic epos is founded on the temporal negation of modernity.

Nor does the alterity of "other times" establish the kind of dense allegorical relation to the present provided by (for instance) Spenser's Faerie. The central Ossianic trope of dematerialization performs a metonymic dispersal of a solid and busy world of labour, commerce, reproduction, all social relations except imaginary "patriarchal" ones founded on violence and loss, into a curiously fluid space composed of a limited set of recurrent scenic or rather atmospheric topoi: mist, stream, moonshine, echoing mountain, deserted heath. It is the evacuated image of that full and thriving space of commerce projected by Adam Smith. Womack argues that Macpherson's strategy is one of radical subjectivization: scenes and objects dissolve into a "climate of moods."[25] The climate is dominated, more exactly, by a single mood, the elegiac – as commentators have noted from the start.[26] Ossianic melancholy absorbs even sympathy, Smith's moral technique of intersubjectivity, into its elegiac logic. Hugh Blair, Macpherson's most eloquent champion, praised the poems' disciplinary lesson: "That the most compleat victory over an enemy is obtained by that moderation and generosity which convert him into a friend."[27] Along these lines *Fingal* rewrites the distressing end of the *Aeneid*, substituting elegiac reconciliation for revenge. The hero remembers a murdered maiden and spares his vanquished enemy, turning the female victim into a sacrificial foundation for male friendship and a masculine assumption of feminine sympathetic and life-giving virtues.[28] Yet the function of sympathetic recall appears to be the perpetuation, the enshrinement, of melancholy, rather than its cure. "The impulses of reminiscence" generate not only the motives of this action but its end, as the work of sympathy converts elegy into the modernist utterance that Jahan Ramazani has called "self-elegy."[29] "Take now my hand in friendship," says the defeated Swaran to his conqueror, Fingal:

> Let thy bards mourn those who fell. Let Erin give the sons of Lochlin to earth. Raise high the mossy stones of their fame. That the children of the north hereafter may behold the place where their fathers fought. And some hunter may say, when he leans on a mossy tomb, here Fingal and Swaran fought, the heroes of other years. Thus hereafter shall he say, and our fame shall last for ever.
>
> Swaran, said the king of the hills, to-day our fame is greatest. We shall pass away like a dream. No sound will be in the fields of our battles. Our tombs will be lost in the heath. The hunter shall not know the place of our rest. Our names may be heard in song, but the strength of our arms will cease. O Ossian, Carril, and Ullin, you know of heroes that are no more. Give us the song of other years. Let the night pass away on the sound, and morning return with joy. (*The Poems of Ossian*, 101)

Audition, we shall find, is a kind of sensory ghost that haunts the act of reading, and the reader cannot help hearing "mourning return with joy": what the bard has elsewhere called the "joy of grief," well noted by Blair (*The Poems of Ossian*, 61, "A Critical Dissertation," 396). The site of mourning, the mossy tomb, will be dematerialized to "the song of other years."

The quintessentially dejected Cuchullin gives perhaps the most extensive recital of a mourning that modulates into self-mourning. This declension extends to the voice that relays the song of other years: the bardic medium itself. Responding to Fingal's exhortation, the narrator Ossian reiterates the self-elegiac turn:

> Raise, ye bards of other times, raise high the praise of heroes; that my soul may settle on their fame; and the mind of Swaran cease to be sad.
>
> They lay in the heath of Mora; the dark winds rustled over the heroes.
>
> – A hundred voices at once arose, a hundred harps were strung; they sung of other times, and the mighty chiefs of former years.
>
> When now shall I hear the bard; or rejoice at the fame of my fathers? The harp is not strung on Morven; nor the voice of music raised on Cona. Dead with the mighty is the bard; and fame is in the desart no more. (*The Poems of Ossian*, 102)

We can scarcely imagine that Swaran ceased to be sad, or that he would have wished to be deprived of the joy of grief. Strikingly, "the bard" appears as a figure condemned to a boundless temporal displacement. Although this is supposed to be the bard speaking, Ossian himself, he proclaims the death of the bard whose voice he waits to hear: "When now shall I hear the bard? . . . Dead with the mighty is the bard." We ask in turn: does the voice of the bard speak in the past or the future? What temporality does he inhabit?

Throughout the Ossianic poems we read the past mourning itself *as past in the future*, a reflection that renders the present tense of textuality – the scene and moment of our reading – as a peculiarly dissevered and spectral condition. Reading, we find ourselves at home in an abyss of temporal recessions and a melancholy that, like all luxuries, pretends to constitute its own necessity. The bard is dead, but his song revives in our reading of it; yet the song remains silent, the voice absent, as we view its mute apparition, a printed text. Notoriously, Macpherson represented the Ossianic poems as translations. Walter Benjamin, citing Rudolf Pannwitz, called upon translation to perform a kind of linguistic reverse-colonization – an alienation not of the "original" but of the host language, so that while the former may keep its foreign home, the latter finds itself in internal exile.[30] A translation, we might say, is the ghost of an original – only here the ontological status of the original would be a notoriously vexed question. Sceptics such as Johnson called upon Macpherson to furnish the original of Ossian, in the corporeal form of a manuscript: to provide physical evidence of an original, organic link between text and human body. But none was forthcoming. Macpherson did not command the theoretical defence of an oral culture, which the contemporary prestige of literacy rendered a conceptual blank, a condition of lack.[31] Translation thus becomes a trope for the text's historical dematerialization – the effacement of its conditions of production in concrete acts of enunciation and transmission. The poems project their oral origins as a negative temporal relation of textuality to itself: "the song of other years," a phantom cultural past realized in the present tense of its extinction. Not just the world within the poem, receding at its moment of utterance into a yet remoter anteriority, but the world around it falls under the shadow. Macpherson's translation, obliterating the Gaelic original in order to recreate it as a dead poetic language embalmed in English prose, also effectually obliterated a modern tradition of Gaelic poetry that enjoyed a remarkable – and politically contentious – mid eighteenth-century revival.[32]

The controversy over the authenticity of Ossian pushed the paradox of the poems' textuality to the further remove of literalization, restoring as a condition of inauthenticity the materiality the poems everywhere sublimated rhetorically. Macpherson's prefaces and notes suppress the historical and social relations of the text's production, such as the editor's gathering of manuscript and oral sources, his negotiations with informants, and his selection, combination, and transformation of topics. The apparatus occludes, in short, translation as a dynamic material process, a traversal of heterogeneous social and linguistic sites. For this it substitutes a cultural field of reference which locates the historicity of the Ossianic poems in their illustration of the customs and manners of the heroic epoch of Gaelic society. This ethnographic field of culture depends on a conjectural circularity: details from the poem are adduced as evidence of a world in which the poem has its origins – reinforcing the effect of that world's insubstantiality, its ghostliness. Already, then, the "inauthenticity" of Ossian exposes at its inception the logical problematic of the concept of culture defined by Christopher Herbert: "the disconcerting possibility that all the interlinked signifiers of a given culture *signify nothing but one another*, in an eternal circular or labyrinthine traffic of 'meaning' which never attains an authentic signified."[33] Proponents of the poems' authenticity, such as Blair, would repeat the conjectural circuit – arguing, for example, that the apparent anachronisms of polite conduct and delicacy of sentiment were effects of the institutional situation of the bards, "highly respected in the state, and supported by a public establishment," and so cultivating in turn the manners of the society that honoured them ("A Critical Dissertation," 350).

The Ossianic poems do not represent a "primitive society," however, except as a negative reflection of the present. They constitute an elegiac fantasy in which the subject broods upon ghostly origins and imagines its own modernity – in solace rather than complaint – as a condition of inauthenticity and obsolescence. This blank space, the desert of oral-cultural origins projected upon our site of reading, quickly became the theoretical crux of the Ossian controversy. The defenders of Ossian, notably Blair, argued that the primitive desert was in fact a fertile field, where virtue, sensibility, and figurative language flourished. Rehearsing an influential argument, Blair maintains that poetry belongs to primitive rather than refined cultural stages, and he sketches an economic rationale: "Figurative language owes its rise chiefly to two causes; to the want of proper names for objects, and to the influence of imagination and passion over the form of expression" ("A Critical Dissertation," 345). Imagination and passion characterize the subjectivity of an "unsettled state of life," prone to the succession of "new and strange" objects and "sudden changes of fortune" (345). The psychic surplus of this (very modern-sounding) phenomenology of continuous estrangement and excitement over a limited stock of proper names for things produces the peculiar linguistic excess based on lack that is figuration: "Men never have used so many figures of style, as in those rude ages, when, besides the power of a warm imagination to suggest lively images, the want of proper and precise terms for the ideas they would express, obliged them to have recourse to circumlocution, metaphor, comparison, and all those substituted forms of expression, which give a poetical air to language" (346). A material and linguistic homelessness lies at culture's wild origins. The labour of rational cultivation, making a home in the world, produces a better fit between words and ideas, with the joint resources of "copiousness" and "precision," but as the linguistic gap is closed, passion and imagination fade. The theoretical promise of Ossian, and of oral culture generally, is that it will recapture the excitement and yearning of that primal estrangement between subject and object, word and world, language and idea. But as Blair expounds the matter, that origin slips away into a further anteriority, as he finds his argument imitating the Ossianic trajectory: "In one remarkable passage, Ossian describes himself as living in a sort of classical age, enlightened by the memorials of former times, which were conveyed in the songs of bards; and points at a period of darkness which lay beyond the reach of tradition" (352).

The affective power of the Ossian poems and the foundation for their historic importance (their appearance in the early 1760s effectively inaugurates European Romanticism) consist in their intensive opening of that "form of historical consciousness" that Osborne, following Benjamin, finds characteristically "modern": "an abstract temporal structure which [totalizes] history from the standpoint of an ever-vanishing, ever-present present":

Modernity is a form of historical time which valorizes the new as the product of a constantly self-negating temporal dynamic. Yet its abstract temporal form remains open to a variety of competing articulations. In particular, by producing the old as remorselessly as it produces the new . . . it provokes forms of traditionalism the temporal logic of which is quite different from that of tradition as conventionally received.[34]

I have been suggesting that Macpherson's "invention of tradition" instantiates a temporal logic that is exemplarily modern, not least in its scandalous equivocation between the archaeological reconstruction, or simulation, of an absolute past and the reflection of a present emptied of everything except the pathos of its own struggle to possess itself.

Samuel Johnson, fixated on the topos of the desert, understood this Ossianic logic all too clearly. He described Macpherson's project, in the unforgiving phrase already quoted, as the discovering and covering up again of a "vacuity": "If we know little of the ancient highlanders, let us not fill the vacuity with Ossian" (*Journey*, 119). The partisans of Ossian, in another scathing formulation, "remember names, and perhaps some proverbial sentiments" – a Humean pattern of customary associations – "and, having no distinct ideas, coin a resemblance without an original" (118). With an elegiac intensity at least equal to Macpherson's, Johnson also associated oral origins with evanescence and mortality: but as a consequence of an excessive physical substantiality rather than otherwise, in the fact that orality is not just located in the body but confined there.

At first Johnson pays attention to stories of a wild ancestral past: "Narrations like this, however uncertain, deserve the notice of a traveller, because they are the only records of a nation that has no historians, and afford the most genuine representation of the life and character of the ancient highlanders" (68). But, as the *Journey* proceeds, the instability of oral information grows oppressive: "such is the laxity of Highland conversation, that the inquirer is kept in continual suspense, and by a kind of intellectual retrogradation, knows less as he hears more" (69). The primitive condition waiting at the end of this retrogradation is not just ignorance but oblivion and death. Throughout the *Journey*, intimations of personal mortality and of a larger, historical extinction darken one another. For Johnson a culture of speech and hearing is locked into the lifespan of the body, with no historical hope of transcendence. "In nations, where there is hardly the use of letters, what is once out of sight is lost for ever" (79). Sight, the privileged sense of reason and cognition, fails without the technology of letters to fix it. Books "may be a while neglected or forgotten; but when they are opened again, will again impart their instruction: memory, once interrupted, is not to be recalled." In a thoroughly Ossianic figure, "Tradition is but a meteor, which, if once it falls, cannot be rekindled" (113). The body and its faculties are by themselves too frail to sustain the burden of culture, since all their operations are underwritten by mortality:

He who has not made the experiment, or who is not accustomed to require rigorous accuracy from himself, will scarcely believe how much a few hours take from certainty of knowledge, and distinctness of imagery; how the succession of objects will be broken, how separate parts will be confused, and how many particular features and discriminations will be compressed and conglobated into one gross and general idea. (139)

This could almost be a description of Macpherson's Ossianic rhetoric, which rhapsodizes just such a surrender to the confusions, disjunctions, and dissolutions of a death-bound human temporality.

Against this, in the famous set piece among the ruins of Iona, Johnson rehearses abstraction as a rational and contemplative discipline: "Whatever withdraws us from the power of our senses; whatever makes the past, the distant, or the future predominate over the present, advances us in the dignity of thinking beings" (141). Such a claim can only be made out of the insistence on systematic physical observation and mensuration; on, in fact, the discipline of literacy, and the security of universal, abstract sign-systems. An oral language and culture are bound (in Johnson's modernist account) to the eternally vanishing present moment, cut off from history: "the Earse merely floated in the breath of the people, and could therefore receive little improvement" (116). Orality is the figure of blindness (obscurity and ignorance) and of breath (evanescence, mortality). Against this, Johnson imagines cultivation as the inscription of a blank world with visible signs: tree-plantation, agriculture, and road-building join literacy and numeracy to compose a system that totalizes the field of the visual.[35] It is not simply that the visual "overwhelms the whole body and usurps its role";[36] this textualization of the world redeems human life from the perishable body by reconstituting it as culture, which can be transmitted across generations. Hence perhaps, in contrast to his skepticism towards Ossian, Johnson's curious and poignant readiness to believe in "second sight" – a mode of vision that surmounts the limits of the body and the gaps of time and space, as hearing cannot.

A more reliable version of the plenitude of vision – of a world constituted wholly through the act of reading – appears at the end of the narrative, in Johnson's visit to the Edinburgh college for the deaf and dumb. Lynch and Trumpener read the episode as a culminating, utopian scenario of colonization: spelling and arithmetic codify a universal, instrumentalizing reason.[37] Once more, though, let us attend to the pathos, rather than triumphalism, with which Johnson imagines a totalization of vision in the absence of hearing (although not of speech):

[The pupils] not only speak, write, and understand what is written, but if he that speaks looks towards them, and modifies his organs by distinct and full utterance, they know so well what is spoken, *that it is an expression scarcely figurative to say, they hear with the eye* . . . Orthography is vitiated among such as learn first to speak, and then to write, by imperfect notions of the relation between letters and vocal utterance; but to those students every character is of equal importance; for letters are to them not symbols of names, but of things; when they write they do not represent a sound, but delineate a form. (151; my emphasis)

"Form" bears the charge of a Platonic vocabulary. For Johnson audition enacts a linguistic fall, a fatal split between sign and idea and world, now healed in a discipline of pure writing – a primordial grammatology – available to those innocent of the sirenic delusions of the ear. Johnson reverses and redeems the logic of abstraction for a wistfully imagined metaphysical recovery. Only by short-circuiting the detour through the corruptible body might we be able to inhabit an original, authentic relation with a transcendental system.

NOTES

1. See Deidre Lynch, "'Beating the Track of the Alphabet': Topography, Lexicography, and Johnson's Visions of the Ideal," *ELH* 57: 2 (1990): 357–405; Martin Wechselblatt, "Finding Mr. Boswell: Rhetorical Authority and National Identity in Johnson's *A Journey to the Western Islands of Scotland*," *ELH* 60 (1993): 117–48; Pat Rogers, *Johnson and Boswell: The Transit of Caledonia* (Oxford: Clarendon Press, 1995); Katie Trumpener, *Bardic Nationalism: The Romantic Novel and the British Empire* (Princeton: Princeton University Press, 1997), 67–71, 77–100; Leith Davis, *Acts of Union: Scotland and the Literary Negotiation of the British Nation, 1707–1830* (Stanford: Stanford University Press, 1998), 89–99.
2. Trumpener, *Bardic Nationalism*, 100.
3. Samuel Johnson and James Boswell, *A Journey to the Western Islands of Scotland and The Journal of a Tour to the Hebrides*, ed. Peter Levi (Harmondsworth: Penguin, 1984), 73. Subsequent references to this edition will be given in the text.
4. See Colin Kidd, *Subverting Scotland's Past: Scottish Whig Historians and the Creation of an Anglo-British Identity, 1689–c.1830* (Cambridge: Cambridge University Press, 1993).
5. Susan Manning, *Fragments of Union: Making Connections in Scottish and American Writing* (Houndmills: Palgrave, 2002), 228 – referring to "the tension between union and fragmentation in Anglo-Scots philosophy and aesthetics."
6. Mary Poovey, *A History of the Modern Fact: Problems of Knowledge in the Sciences of Wealth and Society* (Chicago: University of Chicago Press, 1998), 217.
7. On "abstract space": Henri Lefebvre, *The Production of Space*, trans. D. Nicholson-Smith (Oxford: Blackwell, 1991), 49–50, 285–7. On "homogeneous, empty time": Walter Benjamin, *Illuminations: Essays and Reflections*, trans. Walter Zohn, ed. Hannah Arendt (New York: Schocken Books, 1968), 261–4, and Benedict Anderson, *Imagined Communities: Reflections on the Origin and Spread of Nationalism* (London: Verso, 1983), 28–31.
8. Marshall McLuhan, *The Gutenberg Galaxy: The Making of Typographic Man* (Toronto: University of Toronto Press, 1962), 244–50; Anderson, *Imagined Communities*, 30–49.
9. Peter Osborne, *The Politics of Time: Modernity and Avant-Garde* (London: Verso, 1995), 3, 29.
10. For a refutation of the "problem" (no longer much current) see Richard F. Teichgraber, *"Free Trade" and Moral Philosophy* (Durham, NC: Duke University Press, 1986).

11. See Ian Duncan, "Adam Smith, Samuel Johnson, and the Institutions of English," in Robert Crawford (ed.), *The Scottish Invention of English Literature* (Cambridge: Cambridge University Press, 1998), 37–54.
12. Adam Ferguson, *An Essay on the History of Civil Society*, ed. Fania Oz-Salzberger (Cambridge: Cambridge University Press, 1995), 24. Subsequent references to this edition will be given in the text.
13. John R. R. Christie argues that Smith's historical account of material, linguistic and cognitive relations unfolds a "steadily mounting trajectory of metaphysical complexity": "Adam Smith's Metaphysics of Language," in A. F. Benjamin, G. N. Cantor, and J. R. R. Christie (eds.), *The Figural and the Literal: Problems of Language in the History of Science and Philosophy, 1630–1800* (Manchester: Manchester University Press, 1987), 202–29 (211).
14. Adam Smith, *An Enquiry into the Nature and Causes of the Wealth of Nations*, ed. R. H. Campbell and A. S. Skinner (Oxford: Clarendon Press, 1976), 25. Subsequent references to this edition will be given in the text.
15. John Locke, *Two Treatises of Government*, ed. Peter Laslett (Cambridge: Cambridge University Press, 1967), 316.
16. Poovey, *A History of the Modern Fact*, p. 217. For a different account of Smith and "the production of abstract space," see Poovey's *Making a Social Body: British Cultural Formation, 1830–1864* (Chicago: University of Chicago Press, 1995), 27–35.
17. Adam Smith, *The Theory of Moral Sentiments*, ed. D. D. Raphael and A. L. Macfie (Oxford: Clarendon Press, 1976), 41. Subsequent references to this edition will be given in the text.
18. Nicholas Phillipson emphasizes how social experience is "complex and demanding," sympathy "demanding and self-conscious," in Smith's account: "Adam Smith as Civic Moralist," in Istvan Hont and Michael Ignatieff (eds.), *Wealth and Virtue: The Shaping of Political Economy in the Scottish Enlightenment* (Cambridge: Cambridge University Press, 1983), 184.
19. David Marshall, *The Figure of Theatre: Shaftesbury, Defoe, Adam Smith and George Eliot* (New York: Columbia University Press, 1986), 167–92.
20. Janet Sorensen argues that Smith's account of language formation is divided between two paradigms, the cultural and the natural, the latter of which identifies the body as the source of certain linguistic effects: *The Grammar of Empire in Eighteenth-Century British Writing* (Cambridge: Cambridge University Press, 2000), 144–5, 158–9.
21. James Macpherson, *The Poems of Ossian*, ed. Howard Gaskill (Edinburgh: Edinburgh University Press, 1995), 77. Subsequent references to this edition will be given in the text.
22. Adam Potkay, *The Fate of Eloquence in the Age of Hume* (Ithaca and London: Cornell University Press, 1994), 196–200; developing an argument made by John Dwyer, "The Melancholy Savage: Text and Context in the Poems of Ossian," in Howard Gaskill (ed.), *Ossian Revisited* (Edinburgh: Edinburgh University Press, 1991), 164–206.
23. Peter Womack, *Improvement and Romance: Constructing the Myth of the Highlands* (Basingstoke: Macmillan, 1989), 108.

24. *Ibid.*, 99.
25. *Ibid.*, 78–9.
26. For a description of the critical tradition see Fiona Stafford's "Introduction," *The Poems of Ossian*, v–viii.
27. Hugh Blair, "A Critical Dissertation on the Poems of Ossian" (1763), repr. in *Poems of Ossian*, 359. Future references to this edition will be cited in the text.
28. For this recurrent topos and its contexts see Potkay, *The Fate of Eloquence*, 201–7.
29. Jahan Ramazani, *Poetry of Mourning: The Modern Elegy from Hardy to Heaney* (Chicago: University of Chicago Press, 1994), 30, 119–29.
30. Benjamin, "The Task of the Translator," in *Illuminations*, 80–1.
31. On the complicated contexts of Ossianic orality in eighteenth-century Scotland, see Penny Fielding, *Writing and Orality: Nationality, Culture, and Nineteenth-Century Scottish Fiction* (Oxford: Clarendon Press, 1996), 9–10.
32. "*Fingal* erased, then presented anew the rich tradition of Scots Gaelic literature with a single opus": Davis, *Acts of Union*, 83. For the linguistic and cultural politics of the eighteenth-century Gaelic revival, see Sorensen, *Grammar of Empire*, 50–62, 172–96.
33. Christopher Herbert, *Culture and Anomie: Ethnographic Imagination in the Nineteenth Century* (Chicago: University of Chicago Press, 1991), 11–21 (19).
34. Osborne, *The Politics of Time*, 23, xii. See Ina Ferris's chapter in this volume for a fuller discussion of this temporal model.
35. See Lynch's account of the disciplines that textualize the visual field in the *Journey*, "'Beating the Track of the Alphabet'," 387–9.
36. Lefebvre (citing Guy Debord), *The Production of Space*, 286.
37. Lynch, "'Beating the Track of the Alphabet'," 392–3; Trumpener, *Bardic Nationalism*, 94–6.

CHAPTER 3

Antiquarianism, the Scottish Science of Man, and the emergence of modern disciplinarity

Susan Manning

"It is evident," Adam Smith wrote in the second section of his "History of Astronomy,"

> that the mind takes pleasure in observing the resemblances that are discoverable betwixt different objects. It is by means of such observations that it endeavours to arrange and methodise all its ideas, and to reduce them into proper classes and assortments. Where we can observe but one single quality, that is common to a great variety of otherwise widely different objects, that single circumstance will be sufficient for it to connect them all together, to reduce them to one common class, and to call them by one general name.[1]

The epistemological, linguistic, and historiographic endeavors of the Scottish Enlightenment pursued what we may construe as syntactic questions: they investigated the nature and texture of connections between fields of inquiry which together contributed to the totality of the "Science of Man."[2] Dugald Stewart would retrospectively describe the "utility" of the "philosophy of the human mind" as lying in the "*mutual connexion between the different arts and sciences*"; he drew the pedagogical conclusion that "the human mind in its highest state of cultivation" would be the product of a general nurturing of all the faculties, rather than the contracted "pedantry of a particular profession."[3] In this chapter I shall consider the complete imbrication of this project with the problematics of empiricism, and the Science of Man's heroic failure totally to subdue the proliferation of information to a connected grand narrative with recognizable public value. These conflicts come to a focus in the refractory relationship between antiquarian evidence and "philosophical" narrative in Scottish Enlightenment historiography, a power struggle that engaged issues of territoriality and disciplinarity consequent on the Science of Man's reconceptualization of the field of knowledge. In the final section I shall argue that the ridicule attached to antiquarianism became a means of encountering a consequential aspect of the new overarching "Science" which was becoming apparent

to its proponents by the third quarter of the eighteenth century, whose
implications threatened to unravel the coherence of the project itself and
are imprinted on the structure of the modern academy.

Bishop Berkeley's *Principles of Human Knowledge* (1710) anticipated Scottish
philosophy's alignment of epistemological and historiographic perspectives
on the status of matter. Addressing the question of whether material extension can be shown to have independent existence, or whether it must be
regarded as a quality of perception, Berkeley deplored how

the vague and indeterminate description of Matter or corporeal substance, which
the modern philosophers are run into by their own principles, resembles that
antiquated and so much ridiculed notion of *materia prima*, to be met with in
Aristotle and his followers. Without extension solidity cannot be conceived; since
therefore it has been shewn that extension exists not in an unthinking substance,
the same must also be true of solidity.[4]

"Antiquated notions" were ridiculous, in this schema, to the extent that,
failing to link material extension to perception, they resisted synthesis of
things and thought.

There was a long genealogy for a caricatured devotion to the matter of
"antiquity." *A New Dictionary of the Terms ancient and modern of the Canting Crew* (1699) defined the antiquary as a "curious Critick in old Coins,
Stones and Inscriptions, in Worm-eaten Records and ancient Manuscripts;
also one that affects and blindly doats, on Relicks, Ruins, old Customs,
Phrases and Fashions."[5] Antiquaries, in the common eighteenth-century
view, were entirely other-directed: they catalogued and accumulated objects, delighting in singularity. Their relationship to the matter of their
inquiries was subjective, affective, and – crucially – unconceptualized. The
stylistics of the antiquarian imagination were characterized, like that of
Swift's philosophers in the Grand Academy of Lagado, by preoccupation
with nouns and naming: they were at once the aborigines of historiographic
discourse, and the sifters amongst its wreckage, who produced as "evidence"
what philosophers – and historians – attempted to articulate as structured
experience.[6] Like children or senescent elders, antiquaries were represented
as naïve nominalists, whose primitive nature was expressed in verbose utterance, the failure to submit expression to the principles of understanding.
Ridiculous, they were also (in the earlier sense of the term) *ludicrous*, playful,
fantastic: the miscellaneous trinketry of their collections drew whimsical
arabesque traces in the margins of historiography.

For eighteenth-century Scots, the ambivalent standing of antiquarianism was inseparable from the cultural politics of post-Union Scotland. In 1778 Samuel Johnson and James Boswell dined in London at Allan Ramsay's house, in company with "Dr. Robertson the historian"; they "talked of antiquarian researches."[7] Boswell himself had at an earlier stage made "collections . . . upon the antiquities of Scotland," and had encouraged his friend John Johnston of Grange to "Be much of an Antiquarian," too.[8] Two years after this dinner, however, he recorded "a ridiculous account of the [inaugural] meeting" of the "Society of the Antiquaries of Scotland"; to avoid becoming associated with its activities, he "wrote next day a card . . . evading the Society."[9] The doubleness is indicative, politically as well as personally. The Society of Antiquaries of Scotland was granted a Royal Charter in 1783 designating its province as "antiquities as well as natural and civil history in general."[10] It was, evidently, an enterprise closely aligned with the aims of Scottish Enlightenment historiography, supported by such eminent Edinburgh literati as Lords Kames and Hailes, Sir William Forbes and the Reverend Hugh Blair. Undoubtedly, its founder, the Earl of Buchan, was over-ambitious for the Society of Antiquaries at an early stage, and laughably self-aggrandizing: Walter Scott's informal epitaph suggested that his "immense vanity, bordering on insanity, obscured, or rather eclipsed, very considerable talents."[11] But the personal eccentricities of Buchan are as insufficient to account for the ridicule as are those of Boswell himself. The Society was dogged by controversy from its foundation: the University of Edinburgh and the Faculty of Advocates, in particular, regarded the granting of the Charter as a challenge to their hegemony in cultural and scientific affairs in Scotland. Although in practice there was a large overlap in membership, the subsequent incorporation of the "Philosophical Society" as the Royal Society of Edinburgh institutionalized the bifurcated opposition of "philosophers" and antiquarians. From its earliest days, the Scottish Society of Antiquaries was subject to a concerted attempt to marginalize – and to portray as marginal – its activities.

The issue was a political as much as it was a historiographic or a philosophic one; a factional or party-based reading of the animosity between the "philosophical" historians of the Establishment and their "antiquarian" counterparts is inescapable. Too invested in detail and too keen to foist it intemperately on the reader's attention, the antiquaries of Buchan's camp were characterized in terms borrowed from the Earl of Shaftesbury as "mere scholastics," lacking in "civility": "what wonder is it if the monstrous product of such a jumbled brain be ridiculous to the world?"[12] The most significant threat posed by the antiquarians' empirical and taxonomic

activities – themselves methodologies of Enlightenment – was their resistance to the grand narratives of philosophic history and its imaginative
synthesis of the branches of human inquiry. The Edinburgh institutional
controversy betokened by Boswell's self-contradicting moves towards dissociation and adherence gave local habitation to an already emergent struggle
for dominance between rival possessions of the past that seems to have
carried particular poignancy and disquiet in a Scottish context. Its foundation was an anxiety about the relation between narrative and its evidential
base. Dugald Stewart cited Livy on the task of "conquering the rudeness of
antiquity by the art of writing" in praise of Robertson's achievement with
inherently barbarous materials in his *History of Scotland*:

[T]he influence of Scottish associations, so far as it is favourable to antiquity, is
confined to Scotchmen alone, and furnishes no resources to the writer who aspires
to a place among the English classics. Nay, such is the effect of that provincial
situation to which Scotland is now reduced, that the transactions of former ages
are apt to convey to ourselves exaggerated conceptions of barbarism, from the
uncouth and degraded dialect in which they are recorded.[13]

This reformulates in national terms the antiquated, ridiculous adherence
to irreducible matter that shadowed Berkeley's Idealist speculations. National inflection of the epistemological argument persisted through the various interrogations of the split between "corporeal substance" and thought
which characterised the Science of Man, one of whose key planks was
the new practice in historiography retrospectively described by Dugald
Stewart as "Philosophical" or "Conjectural" History.[14] Conjectural history
had two distinguishing features: employing as building blocks the empirical evidence uncovered by antiquarian research, it construed connected
narratives of the rise and progress of individual societies; to this it added
a presumption (also known as "stadialism") that all societies, beginning in
barbarity, would pass through a similar sequence of organizational stages
on their progress to "Civil Society." It was established, that is, on the belief
that available empirical evidence about one society's past enabled the historian to fill imaginatively the evidential gaps in another society's "story." A
theory of the universality of social process in and through time – because
of the unvarying constitution of human nature – supplied the rationale for
conjectured connection even where empirical evidence was lacking.

The structural analogy between this and two other constitutive fields of
inquiry of the Science of Man, the epistemological and the linguistic, is crucial. Hume made them equally, and inseparably, foundational. His writing
aligned the grammar of human imagination itself with other taxonomies in

Scottish Enlightenment thought, as essentially empirical and nominative. Setting out his synthesizing project in the *Treatise of Human Nature* in 1739, with all the brashness of a young man in his twenties who has discovered the key to all mythologies, he affirmed that "all the sciences have a relation, greater or less, to human nature"; all are "in some measure dependent on the science of Man; since they lie under the cognizance of men, and are judg'd of by their powers and faculties."[15] Instead, therefore, of pursuing further the "tedious lingring method" pertaining to one or other branch of inquiry (the old Humanist disciplines of the *Trivium* and *Quadrivium*), "taking now and then a castle or a village (the petty, knowledge-based specialisms) on the frontier," he boldly proposed

to march up directly to the capital or center of these sciences, to human nature itself; which being once masters of, we may every where else hope for an easy victory. From this station we may extend our conquests over all those sciences, which more intimately concern human life, and may afterwards proceed at leisure to discover more fully those, which are the objects of pure curiosity. There is no question of importance, whose decision is not compriz'd in the science of man. (*Treatise*, 4)

The metaphor of territorial colonization is suggestive. Repositioning Aristotle's identification of philosophy as the essential meta-discipline, the universal inquiry that brought together all the fields of learning, the grandly synthetic project of the Science of Man was also an enterprise of cultural renewal.[16] It rewrote post-Union Scotland back on the world stage by aggressively locating the theatre of mind at the centre of intellectual endeavor and asserting the subordination of all other realms of inquiry to it.

But the case is more complicated. Immediately proceeding to unwrite the confident comprehensiveness of its opening assertion, the *Treatise* asserts that "the soul, as far as we can conceive it, is nothing but a system or train of different perceptions . . . united together, but without any perfect simplicity or identity." Interrogating consciousness, all the inquirer can catch is a succession of elements: "every thing, that exists, is particular: And therefore it must be our several particular perceptions, that compose the mind. I say, *compose* the mind, not *belong* to it. The mind is not a substance, in which the perceptions inhere" (*Treatise*, 414 [Hume's italics]). Empirical investigation is, apparently, the only epistemological tool we have, but it is an insufficient, if not a treacherous one, offering a heap of fragments in place of a coherent story. In this predicament, the syntactic powers of imagination are alone constitutive of the irreducible sense of human identity and the architects of its "history." Hume's argument

makes the nature of this imagined grammar of "relations" which permit
the mind's easy transition from fragmentary perception to a sense of identity crucial: this is the connective tissue of selfhood. The universal "uniting
principles" of simple ideas, the building blocks of thought, are association,
contiguity, and sympathy; their ubiquity is "the cause why," as the *Treatise*
put it, "languages so nearly correspond to each other" (12–13). The connection between the structure of language and the structure of thought
become increasingly central to the epistemological argument in Thomas
Reid's writing, and from Hume's "universal principles" of sympathy and
association Henry Homes, Lord Kames went on to theorize the purpose
of literature (and, subsequently, History) as armchair exercises of moral
sentiments, opportunities to educate the sympathies. Both subjects were,
that is, about forging finer, more subtle and coherent, imaginative stories
of connectedness which made things mean in a universe apparently constituted by atomized empirical perceptions.[17] The grandest narrative of all
was that of the progression to civility, the conjunction of the personal and
social states in post-Union Britain.

Following Hume, all the empirical inquiries of Scottish Enlightenment
thought were distinguished by a close and operative analogy between the
structure of mind and that of language. Again the preoccupation is inseparable from the cultural politics of post-Union Scotland. It is at least
arguable that Hume, Kames, and their compatriots articulated issues of
personal identity and the experience of consciousness in terms of the structures of language, because the words of their experience – the things that
told their identity – were culturally marked in anglophone post-Union
Britain. "North Britons" were acutely self-conscious of the fact that they
were identifiable, and identified, by their distinctive non-English use of the
language. Lists of Scotticisms (of which there were many, including Hume's
own) were quasi-antiquarian exercises, fragmentary taxonomies of language
rendered peculiar and remarkable by its separation from the grammatical,
syntactic, and expressive connections of use. But these collections took on
additional significance as monitory catalogues of remainders, the last words
of a moribund culture. Proscription and preservation were paradoxical near
neighbours in lexical impulses to collect and collate an archaic idiom whose
very absence of cultural authority was its most authenticating feature.

With this in mind, we can reconnect the linguistic issue with a paradox
of eighteenth-century antiquarianism which made it at once a highly empirical *and* a counter-Enlightenment drive – an inbuilt contradiction which
carried particular currency in Scottish thought, where the analogy between
cultural and linguistic development was axiomatic. Because if the naming of

things was at the end of history, it was, equally, at its beginning. The earliest manifestation of language, in Adam Smith's account, was the accumulation of nominative forms: "the simpler the language the less it will . . . be capable of various arrangement: and lastly it will be more prolix."[18] Hugh Blair's lectures established hieroglyphs – writing *with* things – as a landmark in the stadialist history of writing. Though they found a place in developmental schema, hieroglyphs (according to the theory) could not develop or evolve, they could only multiply. In the context of the primary subject of the Science of Man, human nature, they offered only the most basic of aggregative testimonies, a taxonomy rather than a narrative. In the conjectural framework of the progress from savagism to civilization multiplication of examples came before distinction or conceptualization. It was not until the emergence of the verb, affirming existence and agency ("be-ing") that the presence of a judging, discriminating and structuring consciousness could be inferred in language-use.[19] That is, the persistence of a "language of things" (whether numismatic or philological) conceptualized in antiquarian recovery as both pre- and post-cultural, at once underpinned and implicitly challenged the connecting activities and progressive presence of verb-driven action in the linguistic, grammatical, and historiographic hierarchies established in Scottish Enlightenment writing. Certainly, as Mark Phillips has recently described, antiquarianism contributed to the "reconceptualization of social knowledge" as part of the Scottish "Science of Man" project, but I would argue that it continued to inhabit a contested position at the margins of a self-consciously new historiography, despite the fact that its enumerative investigations represented an earlier stage in the same empirical methodology as that of its "philosophical" rival.[20] Antiquarian procedures facilitated a rather suspect form of engagement with history, recently described as "affectionating" the past, in which the recovery of family "relics," local landmarks, and memorabilia evoked sentimental and proprietorial responses, often of a very personal nature.[21]

Antiquaries' engagement with instantiation at the expense of conjecture, their investment in the immediate pleasures of the particular, without investigation or sublimation of that pleasure, made them vulnerable, in the cultural currency of the eighteenth century, to charges not only of incivility but of "enthusiasm", defined as incapacity to link things to thought: "All passions . . express themselves in a very loose and broken manner . . . The higher the Rapture the more broken is the expression" (Smith, *Rhetoric*, 139–40). In Humean terms, antiquaries failed to register the power of memory and imagination in creating a continuous picture of reality; their activities lacked self-reflection, punctuation, and perspective. The objectivity of their empiricism was compromised by the enthusiasm which motivated it. They concerned themselves with the past as recuperable only in ruined form, not as part of a chain of progress. With their clutter of detail, collectors of the past sought quixotically to instantiate all the links in the great chain of thoughts, to fill up the gaps in the story that otherwise are filled (necessarily, in Hume's or Smith's schemes) by the connecting power of imagination. Antiquarians distrusted conjecture, and wanted evidence, as a prophylactic against spaces for uncertainty. The associative taxonomy of the antiquarian collections, like those of natural philosophy and language, was at once primordial and post-historical: things, like words, were the building blocks of history, and its ruined remnants.[22] The more they found, the more they were caricatured as obsessives fixated on individual manifestation and resistant to conjectural procedures; self-styled "true" antiquaries like Joseph Ritson or David Herd employed empirical minutiae as weapons of legitimacy in a war of authenticity. Their activities diverted the operations of the imagination from tracing a successive train of thought to endlessly associative arabesques on discrete objects or events, unparsed by an executive verbal progression. Without the self-reflexive perspective, their enthusiasm was "intemperate," mired in the moment, and inimical to the synthesizing sweep of the Science of Man.

So we find an image of the cluttered, clotted prose of the antiquarian – neither decorous nor witty, too object-filled, too close to its subjects – like his mind, not sufficiently composed. "[T]he repose and tranquillity of the imagination," wrote Smith, "is the ultimate end of philosophy."[23] Antiquarians were portrayed as busy, restless souls constantly worrying after the next sample, the missing piece of the jigsaw; unable, as Samuel Johnson put it in another context, to find "repose in the stability of truth."[24] Ridiculing the gigantism of Clarendon's *History of the Rebellion*, Smith specifically objected to the padding of narration by an overgrowth of detail as a stylistic flaw which hindered the direction of a reader's imagination. "Crouding in so many trifling circumstances he has swelled the history of 18 years at most to the size of 3 folio volumes" (*Rhetoric*, 116). The "Dryasdust" syndrome – detail pursued to the furthest reaches of argument – proved to have enormous power to choke the smooth running of the cogs of what Mark Twain would later call the "History Mill."[25] At the beginning of the nineteenth century, Francis Jeffrey would contrast the antiquary's "stupid amazement [at] the singular and diversified *appearances* of human manners and institutions," with John Millar's architectural vision in teaching "his pupils to refer them all to one simple principle, and to consider them as necessary links in the great chain which connects civilized with barbarous society."

Millar's meta-disciplinary achievement was to perceive the embryo of Civil Society in the disinterred remnants of antiquity: "While the antiquary pored with childish curiosity over the confused and fantastic ruins that cover the scenes of early story, *he* produced the plan and elevation of the original fabric, and enabled us to trace the connections of the scattered fragments, and to determine the primitive form and denomination of all the disfigured masses that lay before us."[26] As ever, the issue of connection is central to the argument between antiquarians and historiographers, as it is to empiricism itself.

The rivalry and animosity between antiquarians and philosophic historians over ownership of the past are inscribed into an indicative stylistic development in historiographic and philosophic composition which allows us to extend Hume's territorial metaphor to the visual and typographic domain of the printed page. Footnotes and endnotes in their "modern" form came into being, according to Anthony Grafton, around the turn of the eighteenth century, gradually replacing the marginal gloss.[27] Functionally an element of the material text, but displaced to its peripheries, this semi-exiled commentary became "a way of speaking in two voices at once."[28] Footnotes or endnotes punctuate a reader's encounter with the progressive thrust of narrative: interpretation is supplemented, but also brought to a stop, by "information."

In his life of William Robertson, Stewart cites Hume's being "plagued" with Gibbon's notes at the end of the volume; on breaking off reading to turn to them, "you often find nothing but a reference to an authority. All these authorities ought only to be printed at the margin or the bottom of the page."[29] Notes containing illustrative material were acceptable in "philosophical" historiography only within a certain "measure" – which itself was increasingly set according to the political, religious, and national agendas of the conjectural historians themselves. "Where a writer finds it necessary to enter into speculation and discussion, the whole of his argument should undoubtedly be stated at once, and not broken down into fragments, which the reader is to collect from different parts of the book." Stewart's authority here was Adam Smith, whose awareness that supporting apparatus within historiography might commit narratological treason led him to "consider every species of note as a blemish or imperfection; indicating, either an idle accumulation of superfluous particulars, or a want of skill and comprehension in the general design" (*Life of Robertson*, 96, 93). In the hierarchical historiography generated by the Science of Man, the "evidence" of the antiquary found a humble role in the hinterland of conjectural narratives of societal progression. But marginality itself proved treacherous: once this evidential detail began to engage the affections in its own right, to claim attention for itself at the expense of the master narrative it served, it undermined the very position it was designed to defend:

In no species of writing is it agreeable to have the attention so frequently withdrawn from the text; but in historical writing it is impossible to devise a more effectual expedient for counteracting the effects of the author's art. The curious research and the epigrammatick wit so often displayed in Mr Gibbon's notes, and which sometimes render them more amusing than even the eloquent narrative which they are meant to illustrate, serve only to add to the embarrassment occasioned by the unfortunate distribution of his materials. (*Life of Robertson*, 94–5)

"Embarrassment" comprehends the meaning not only of hampering or impeding, but also of complication: of obstructing or confusing a straight line of thought. Ritson's attacks on Thomas Warton's *History of English Poetry*, as Mark Phillips has noted, "took the form of antiquarian commentary": a series of footnotes, in essence, that broke up the authority of Warton's narrative and challenged its claim to authenticity.[30] The distracted, embarrassed, state induced into the reading experience by "excessive" recourse to notes and marginalia replicated the way the "broken" expression of an enthusiast dismembered continuous, synthetic thought.[31] From a marginal position, that is, antiquarian information was perceived to exercise a strangely disruptive influence on the master narrative to which it was appended.

Hume's and Robertson's misgivings about Gibbon's footnotes and Smith's dislike of all "extraneous" matter appended to connected argument clarify the issue of territoriality (and therefore of disciplinarity) raised by Hume's metaphor for the Science of Man. Addressing the question of how much factual evidence should be introduced into the narration of conjectural history as an issue of decorum, Smith established a sharply hierarchical demarcation of textual space: "When a historian brings anything to confirm the truth of a fact it is only a quotation in the margin or a parenthesis and as this makes not part of the work it can not be said to be a part of the didactick" (*Rhetoric*, 90). Meaning and instruction (the "didactick") reside clearly in the realm of narrative. But the evidential, as Jacques Derrida points out, cannot be separated from argument: the separate space of marginalia has its own limiting – and therefore meaning-making – function of alterity. "Philosophy has always insisted upon this: thinking its other. Its other: that which limits it, and from which it derives its essence, its definition, its production."[32] In this sense antiquarianism, the alternative text drawing attention to itself in the margins or the back of the volume, is the "other" of Enlightenment historiography, the double agent on its boundaries which disdains the Science of Man's synthesizing self-reflective enterprise in favor of immersion in the delight of detail. It reorganizes narratological principles from a single temporally and syntactically defined trajectory towards the hoards of pre-syntagmatic particulars from which they are drawn.

Antiquarians were the misers of historiography. As the antiquarian's delight in the detail of his collection impeded narrative progress in history, so the miser's accumulated hoard of coins was anathema to the circulating economic and sympathetic currencies of Civil Society. When, on behalf of the Highland Society, Henry Mackenzie produced a *Report* on the authenticity of the Ossianic poems in 1805, he likened the effects of "recovering" the ancient poetry of Scotland to putting a miser's hoard back into circulation: in both cases, the identifying features of the "things" are lost when they become goods of exchange in the public domain: "Language is changed from its use in society, as coins are smoothed by their currency in circulation. If the one be locked up among a rude, remote, and unconnected people, like the other when it is buried under the earth, its great features and general form will be but little altered."[33] To preserve intact the features which made them valuable, in other words, the antiquary's finds had, in this view, necessarily to remain private, withdrawn from the economic sphere. So, in Scott's tale "The Two Drovers" (1827), Robin Oig guards his family affiliations with the legendary Highland cateran Rob Roy Macgregor "like the miser's treasure, the secret subject of his contemplation," not a thing for conversational exchange with strangers. Robin's "history" dies with him, its value intact, and only its external manifestations available for glossing by an English judge's summative stadialist reconstruction of the Highlander's fatal act.[34]

Scott's novels used notes deliberately to "withdraw" the reader's sympathetic engagement from the narrative towards competing arts of narration and sources of authority. His amateur antiquarian Laurence Templeton, dedicating the narrative of *Ivanhoe* to "The Rev. Dr Dryasdust, F. A. S.," indicted Scott's earlier novel *The Antiquary* (another work preoccupied with the recovery and authenticity of buried "currency") as "unjustifiably expos[ing] to the public [the details of] the private and family affairs of your learned northern friend Mr Oldbuck of Monkbarns." Templeton's own fiction was validated by the "singular Anglo-Norman MS" of Sir Arthur Wardour (another character from *The Antiquary*), supplemented by antiquarian glosses which punctured and punctuated the narrative's

illusion of verisimilitude.[35] Scott himself (like many country gentlemen)
would later turn his home Abbotsford into a veritable Aladdin's cave of
relics, reliques, and antiquarian bric-à-brac. The material survival of the
past crowds its walls, tables, and showcases in unsyntaxed profusion. These
private collections, like the miserly hoards of Ossianic verse or Highland
genealogy, also represented the cultural past of the nation in process of
production, accumulated but not yet catalogued. In Scott's narratives they
became the constituents of a national story as much about ruin and loss
as about progress and connection, qualifying the plot's embodied stadialist historiography. The unfinished catalogue of the Abbotsford Museum
was *Reliquae Trottcosiensis, or the Gabions of the late Jonathan Oldbuck Esq.*
Oldbuck was both fictional character (the eponymous "antiquary" of the
novel) and the pseudonymous space through which Scott mildly ironized
Abbotsford's manifest realization of his own antiquarian obsessions.[36]

The peculiar jargon and obsession with singularity of antiquarian discourse
which became instantly recognizable identifiers in caricature were pernicious to the Science of Man's ideology of transferable methods, its attempt
to make connections beyond the professionally specific idiom of the various branches of human inquiry. Antiquaries brought to prominence the
resistance of objects and of words: their stubborn capacity to survive the
dissolution of contextual syntax, on the one hand, and on the other their
refusal to yield themselves completely to the hypotactic grammar of the
conjectural history which relied on them for its primary evidence. They
offered, that is, a challenge to the politics of knowledge and representation
silently embedded in the Science of Man. The taxonomic and fragmented
language of things offered by antiquarians lacked the connecting parts of
articulated speech that made a single coherent narrative possible, and the
"progression" into the anglophone homogeneity of Civil Society inevitable –
which is not to say that antiquarians did not frequently also assume the
connecting mantle of the conjectural historian, as (for example) Thomas
Percy did in the stadialist ballad history he constructed around the *Reliques
of Ancient Poetry*, or Scott in the two new essays appended to the *Minstrelsy
of the Scottish Border* in the collected *Poetical Works* of 1830.[37]
     It is not, however, far-fetched to suggest that ridicule of the antiquary's
activities carried the cultural anxieties of the Scottish Enlightenment's progressive narrative and universalizing paradigm.[38] When collections of evidence ceased to constitute a marginal confirmation of thought and invaded
the sanctum of the text, when the nominative barbarians overwhelmed

the temple of philosophy with seductive detail, the highly developed
Scriblerian tradition of ridicule was invoked to counteract their "pedantry."
The sheer diversity and particularity of information generated by the empirical projects of Enlightenment threatened to overwhelm the conceptual basis of an empire of consciousness united by its capacity to forge
imaginative connection and to generate cultural capital for post-Union
North Britain from a synthetic progressive "British" historiography (as, for
example, Hume did in his stadialist *History of England* or Macpherson in
*A History of Great Britain, from the Restoration to the Accession of the House
of Hannover* [*sic*]). At this point – Macpherson's *History* was published in
1775 – Adam Smith introduced a crucial new characteristic benchmark of
the state of civil society: the division of labor.

The greatest improvement in the productive powers of labour, and the greater
part of the skill, dexterity, and judgment with which it is any where directed, or
applied, seem to have been the effects of the division of labour. The effects of the
division of labour, in the general business of society, will be more easily understood,
by considering in what manner it operates in some particular manufactures. It
is commonly supposed to be carried furthest in some very trifling ones... in
those trifling manufactures which are destined to supply the small wants of but
a small number of people, the whole number of workmen must necessarily be
small....[39]

The Wealth of Nations opens with a breathtaking perspectival swoop from a
synoptic to an atomistic view; within a couple of sentences the conjectural
historian has refocused attention from the universal pattern to the smallest
detail of its structure. "Design and Contrivance is what chiefly interests
us," Smith had instructed in his earlier *Lectures on Rhetoric* (90); when
the articulation of narrative was embarrassed by the weight of instance, he
turned his attention to reformulating the relationship between the syntactic
principles which made society cohere and the "trifling" constituents of the
process. The Science of Man's empirical methodology inherently tended
to fragment into separate areas of study defined by bodies of information.
    The discourse of specialization in a market economy was rapidly adopted
to the politics of disciplinarity. In this domain, however, increasing special-
ism was explicitly accompanied by anxiety about its fissile effects on the
field of knowledge and attempts to institute new hierarchies of knowledge.
By 1813 the most articulate heir of the Scottish Enlightenment seemed possessed by a sense of the intellectual bankruptcy of the empirical method.
Francis Jeffrey's important retrospective review of de Staël's *De la littérature*

reflected gloomily on the disintegration of the unifying empire of the liberal arts by Smithian economic principles of division:

Men of general information and curiosity seldom think of adding to the knowledge that is already in the world; and the inferior persons upon whom that task is consequently devolved, carry it on, for the most part, by means of that minute subdivision of labour which is the great secret of the mechanical arts, but can never be introduced into literature without depriving its higher branches of all force, dignity, or importance. One man spends his life in improving a method of dyeing cotton red; another in adding a few insects to a catalogue which nobody reads; – a third in settling the metres of a few Greek Choruses; – a fourth in decyphering illegible romances, or old grants of farms; – a fifth in picking rotten bones out of the earth; – a sixth in describing all the old walls and hillocks in this parish; – and five hundred others in occupations equally liberal and important: each of them being... profoundly ignorant of every thing out of his own narrow department, and very generally and deservedly despised by his competitors for the favour of that public which despises and supports us all.[40]

Jeffrey's analysis, carried in contributions to *The Edinburgh Review* across the early years of the nineteenth century, placed antiquarian endeavor as a consequence of this division of literary labor on analogy with mechanical production, in which historians no longer sought the big pictures, the central narrative, of conjectural history, but contented themselves with filling in details on a map of knowledge now divided up into territorially demarcated disciplines constantly skirmishing on the boundaries.

Men learn, instead of reasoning. Instead of meditating, they remember; and, in place of the glow of inventive genius... nothing is to be met with, in society, but timidity on the one hand, and a fastidiousness on the other – a paltry accuracy, and a more paltry derision – a sensibility to small faults, and an incapacity of great merits – a disposition to exaggerate the value of knowledge that is not to be used, and to underrate the importance of powers which have ceased to exist.[41]

Imagination has seceded from the observational method. It seems to have been one of the ironies of the Science of Man that its strong commitment to universality and methodological synthesis resulted in the devolution of areas of intellectual inquiry into discrete professional tracks. Sociology, anthropology, and the separation of the branches of "natural philosophy" into the modern sciences owe their emergence directly to comprehensive investigation of (in Stewart's words) "the phenomena resulting from the faculties and principles of the mind," but having separated, they rapidly diverged from its principles.[42] Extending the territorial metaphor for the empire of thought, Stewart theorized a synergy between the "*materia prima*" unearthed by the antiquarians and the conjectural enterprise of the historians:

"The detached facts which travels and voyages afford us, may frequently serve as land-marks to our speculations; and sometimes our conclusions a priori, may tend to confirm the credibility of facts, which, on a superficial view, appeared to be doubtful or incredible."[43] Notwithstanding the closeness of their integration in Smithian economics, the specialist activities of the antiquarian were at odds with the public circulation of the product of his labor as the currency of historiography.

Most obviously of all, antiquarians tended not to be interested in consolidating the status of their activity by demonstration of its scientific principles, or its utility. In their own way equally resistant to disciplinarity, their empirical methods were motivated by private pleasure – that impulse which Hume himself had shown to be at once fundamental to philosophical pursuits and inimical to their codification. Warton's Preface to his *History of English Poetry* opposed "useful intelligence" to "the observance of arrangement"; the delight, and the devil, is in the detail, for an antiquarian sensibility.[44] When the margins threatened to invade the centre, the "dread empire" of these Dunce-like antiquarians, restoring Chaos with their "uncreating words," acted as an irritant to the Science's of Man's neo-Ciceronian anxiety about non-utilitarian knowledge.[45] These pleasures were, ominously for the ethos of civic humanism, private rather than public ones. The diarist John Aubrey noted in 1685:

I was from my childhood affected with the view of things rare; which is the beginning of philosophy . . . I was carried on with a strong impulse to undertake this taske: I knew not why, unles [*sic*] for my owne private pleasure. Credit there was none; for its gets the disrespect of a man's neighbours. But I could not rest quiet till I had obeyed this secret call.[46]

This is the delight of the miser: the "private pleasure" of collection defies the economic and sympathetic imperatives of exchange which underpin the smooth circulation of civil society. There is a teasing connection here with Hume's dramatization in the *Treatise* of the philosopher returning to his study to find his private speculations "cold, and strain'd, and ridiculous" after a good meal and the "solid" convivial pleasures of friendship and backgammon.[47] Hume's *Treatise* recognizes the role of the passions (desires and aversions) in the production of all knowledge; developing this into a theory of ethics, Smith made sympathy (and the natural sensibility that enables its operation) *the* interdisciplinary counter, the shared transferable instrument of knowledge and understanding, the one factor bound to neutralize and overwhelm intellectual skepticism. But – and this is the crux – what is elided in the gap between Hume's dramatized and Smith's theorized account is the extent to which passions – pleasures – may be asocial and private. This is the paradox that potentially sets sensibility and sociability at odds, and allows pleasure to escape the governing utilitarian ethos. Hume's narrator links the ridiculousness of *his* pastime to its failure to connect with the socializing narrative of sympathy, and to the strange private pleasure, quite separate from utility, that its pursuit nonetheless continues to afford. The power of philosophy itself, in his account, is emotional not effectual. Scott wrote that Warton had failed to write "a distinct and connected history of our poetry," because he was "*too deeply enamoured*" of "our poetical antiquities."[48] Although the philosopher's speculations were at the opposite end of the conceptual spectrum from those of the antiquary (mired as he was in the accumulation of examples rather than the analysis of process) both activities exhibited the failure of the evidential and conjectural to connect, of mind to integrate with material, of "things" to unite and circulate. Fundamentally, it raised the specter which the Science of Man sought always to keep at bay: that of the power of solipsistic pleasure to undermine social connection, the ethics of sympathy (based on "exchange" or transferability of sentiment), and the public imperatives of Civil Society.[49]

The procedures of antiquaries like Scott's Jonathan Oldbuck and his predecessors held out against a psychologized and developmental version of reality but encouraged sympathetic associations of a more wayward – because more private and personal – kind. Their accumulative, associative, paratactic activities, whether as collectors of coins or of ballads, made it clear that objects survived their connective tissue, whose reconstruction depended on conjecture. Antiquaries furnished a "natural history" of culture in fragmented form, the juxtaposed "things" from which imagination might construe both authorized *and* illegitimate pasts. Returning to Hume, we might say that the diminished relations between things in antiquarian retrieval disrupted their temporal connections as part of a currency of progress: "we have no *just standard*, by which we can decide any dispute concerning the time, when they acquire or lose a title to the name of identity."[50] Narratology was primary in conjectural history – it related the details of past, present, and to come through sympathetic association, and became thereby a teacher of universal principles. But in Hume's epistemology sympathy, occurring spontaneously and at the moment of stimulus, was at once a principle of communication (*Treatise*, Book II) and a conjunction without "story" forged in the private theatre of the mind (Book I). It attached sensibilities directly to objects as nostalgic icons of pleasure that resisted empirical recuperation and public circulation.

However, despite its melodramatic overtones, the play enacted in the *Treatise's* "theatre of the mind" is not a tragedy but a comedy, perhaps even a farce, as the "universe of the imagination" stubs its toe against the all too solid satisfactions of appetite. "The foundation of Ridicule," as Smith put it with some emphasis in his lectures on rhetoric, "is either when what is in most respects Grand or pretends to be so or is expected to be so, has something mean or little in it or when we find something that is realy [*sic*] mean with some pretensions and marks of grandeur." These, as he pointed out, are the principles of the mock-heroic; incongruity lies at the heart of the ridiculous, "the odd association of grand and mean or little ideas" (*Treatise,* 43, 44). In this sense, antiquarianism, placing the marginal at the center of attention, may have functioned as a kind of joke, a historiographical mock-heroic unwriting the epic imperialism of the Science of Man into the miserly barbarisms and secret pleasures of disciplinary pursuits whose public self-justification lay in utility and specialist expertise.

NOTES

1. Adam Smith, "The History of Astronomy," *Essays on Philosophical Subjects,* ed. W. P. D. Wightman and J. C. Bryce (Oxford: Clarendon Press, 1980), 37–8.
2. See Susan Manning, *Fragments of Union: Making Connections in Scottish and American Writing* (London: Palgrave, 2002), Introduction.
3. Dugald Stewart, *Elements of the Philosophy of the Human Mind,* 4th edn, 2 vols. (London: T. Cadell and W. Davies, 1811), 1: 17, 1: 21–2. Alexander Broadie has drawn the connection between the Science of Man project and the emergent tradition of generalism in Scottish education, well in advance of the nineteenth-century features noted by G. E. Davie's *Democratic Intellect* (Edinburgh: Edinburgh University Press, 1961). See Broadie (ed), *The Scottish Enlightenment: An Anthology* (Edinburgh: Canongate, 1997), 42–3.
4. Bishop Berkeley, *The Principles of Human Knowledge* (1710), ed. G. J. Warnock (London and Glasgow: Fontana/Collins, 1962; 1981), part I, paragraph II (70).
5. (London, 1699), quoted by Joseph M. Levine, *The Battle of the Books: History and Literature in the Augustan Age* (Ithaca and London: Cornell University Press, 1991), 337.
6. See, on this point, John Moreland, *Archaeology and Text* (London: Duckworth, 2001), 62.
7. *Boswell's Life of Johnson,* ed. George Birkbeck Hill, rev. L. F. Powell, 6 vols. (Oxford: Oxford University Press, 1931;1971), III: 331, 333.
8. *Ibid.,* II: 92; *Correspondence of James Boswell and John Johnston of Grange,* ed. Ralph S. Walker, 2 vols. (London, 1960), I: 49.
9. J. W. Reed and F. A. Pottle (eds.), *Boswell, Laird of Auchinleck, 1778–1782* (New York: McGraw-Hill, 1977), 271.

10. William Smellie, "Historical Account . . .", *Archaelogia Scotica* (1782), quoted by Ronald G. Cant, in "David Steuart Erskine, 11th Earl of Buchan: Founder of the Society of Antiquaries of Scotland," *The Scottish Antiquarian Tradition: Essays to Mark the Bicentenary of the Society of Antiquaries of Scotland and its Museum, 1780–1980* (Edinburgh: John Donald, 1981), 15.

11. *The Journal of Sir Walter Scott*, ed. W. E. K. Anderson (Oxford: Clarendon Press, 1972), 550.

12. Anthony Ashley Cooper, Third Earl of Shaftesbury, "Sensus Communis, an Essay on the Freedom of Wit and Humour," *Characteristics of Men, Manners, Opinions, Times* (1711), ed. Lawrence E. Klein (Cambridge: Cambridge University Press, 1999; 2001), 32–3. Shaftesbury's derision adds a class-based animosity to the political grounds of opposition.

13. Dugald Stewart, *Account of the Life and Writings of William Robertson* (1801), in Robertson, *The History of Scotland*, 2 vols. (London: T. Cadell, 1791), 1: 28–9. Subsequent references are in the text.

14. In his "Account of the Life and Writings of Adam Smith" (1793), reprinted in Smith, *Essays on Philosophical Subjects*, 293.

15. David Hume, *A Treatise of Human Nature*, eds. David Fate Norton and Mary J. Norton (Oxford: Oxford University Press, 2000), 4. Subsequent references are in the text.

16. It is worth noting that the term "Science of Man" was already in use amongst French *philosophes* in the early eighteenth century; Hume silently appropriates it, possibly from Malebranche.

17. For an expanded version of this account, see Manning, *Fragments of Union*, chapter 1.

18. Smith, *Lectures on Rhetoric and Belles Lettres*, ed. J. C. Bryce (Oxford: Clarendon Press, 1983), 8, 13. Subsequent references are in the text.

19. Michel Foucault, *The Order of Things: An Archaeology of the Human Sciences* (New York: Vintage, 1973), 103–5.

20. Mark Salber Phillips, *Society and Sentiment: Genres of Historical Writing in Britain 1740–1840* (Princeton: Princeton University Press, 2000), 7. My information, though not my interpretation and argument, is indebted to this fine study at various points.

21. See Jayne Elizabeth Lewis, *Mary Queen of Scots: Romance and Nation* (London: Routledge, 1998), esp. 109–16.

22. Susan Stewart's account of the object-centred psychology of the eighteenth century, *On Longing: Narratives of the Miniature, the Gigantic, the Souvenir, the Collection* (1993; rpt. Durham, NC: Duke University Press, 1999) is foundational here, and throughout this chapter.

23. Smith, "The History of Astronomy", 61.

24. "[T]he mind can only repose on the stability of truth", *Johnson's Preface to Shakespeare*, ed. P. J. Smallwood (Bristol: Bristol Classical Press, 1985), 4.

25. Mark Twain, *A Connecticut Yankee at King Arthur's Court*, ed. M. Thomas Inge (Oxford: Oxford University Press, 1999), 30.

26. Review of John Millar's *An Historical View of the English Government, The Edinburgh Review* 3 (October 1803): 157 (italics added). See also Susan Manning, "Walter Scott, Antiquarianism and the Political Discourse of the Edinburgh Review," in Massimiliano Demata and Duncan Wu (eds.), *British Romanticism and the Edinburgh Review: Bicentenary Essays* (Basingstoke: Palgrave, 2002), 102–23.
27. Anthony Grafton, *The Footnote: A Curious History*, quoted by Kevin Jackson, *Invisible Forms: A Guide to Literary Curiosities* (London: Macmillan, 1999), 157.
28. Hugh Kenner, *The Stoic Comedians: Flaubert, Joyce and Beckett* (Berkeley: University of California Press, 1962), 40, cited in Jackson, *Invisible Forms*, 143.
29. Stewart, *Life of Robertson*, 95–6.
30. Phillips, *Society and Sentiment*, 269.
31. See Sam Smiles, *The Image of Antiquity: Ancient Britain and the Romantic Imagination* (Yale: Yale University Press, 1994), 8: "in the later eighteenth century antiquarian research moves in from the margins to compete with traditional historiography in establishing and evaluating the prehistory of these islands[;] then, losing ground before the more rigorous development of archaeological method in the nineteenth century, antiquarianism survives as an increasingly amateur approach to the past."
32. Jacques Derrida, *Margins of Philosophy*, trans. Alan Bass (Brighton: Harvester Press, 1982), xi.
33. *Report of the Committee of the Highland Society of Scotland, Appointed to Inquire into the Nature and Authenticity of the Poems of Ossian, Drawn up, according to the Directions of the Committee, by Henry Mackenzie, Esq.* (Edinburgh: Archibald Constable and Co., and London: Longman, Hurst, Rees & Orme, 1805), 147.
34. Walter Scott, *Chronicles of the Canongate* (1827; rpt. Oxford: Oxford University Press, 1912), 3.
35. See, for example, Scott, *Ivanhoe*, ed. Graham Tulloch (Edinburgh: Edinburgh University Press, 1998), 12, 38–9. "Turner" refers to the historian Sharon Turner (1768–1847), admiringly cited in Templeton's "Dedicatory Epistle." (*Ibid.*, 8).
36. Here, as elsewhere in this chapter, I am indebted to Maureen McLane's perceptive comments on earlier versions.
37. It is important to reiterate that antiquarian and Enlightened approaches were not incompatible. For this chapter's purpose of trying to understand those aspects of antiquarian practice which resisted incorporation in the comprehensive circulation of the grand narrative of the Scottish Enlightenment, and attracted its ridicule, I neglect the many ways in which antiquarians aligned their activities with Humean or Smithian principles of circulation, sympathy, and progress, and became the willing foot-soldiers of history. Indeed, in many cases (Scott being the most obvious example), one author's work may combine strategies deriving from both approaches.
38. Sigmund Freud, "Jokes and the Comic," *Jokes and their Relation to the Unconscious*, trans. James Strachey, ed. Angela Richards (London: Penguin Books, 1960; 1976), 249.

39. Adam Smith, *An Inquiry into the Nature and Causes of the Wealth of Nations* (1776), eds. R. H. Campbell, A. S. Skinner and W. B. Todd, 2 vols. (Oxford: Clarendon Press, 1976), 1: 13–14.
40. Francis Jeffrey, Review of Mme. De Stael, *De la Littérature . . .* , *The Edinburgh Review* 21 (February 1813): 20–1.
41. "The Life of Colonel Hutchinson", *The Edinburgh Review* 13 (October 1808): 1–25 (21).
42. Stewart, *Elements of the Philosophy of the Human Mind*, 1:18–19.
43. Stewart, *Life and Writings of Adam Smith*, in Smith, *Essays on Philosophical Subjects*, 93.
44. Phillips, *Society and Sentiment*, 168.
45. Alexander Pope, *The Dunciad*, ed. John Butt (London: Methuen & Co. Ltd., 1963), Book III, line 340 (425).
46. Quoted by Stuart Piggott, "The British Antiquaries," *Ancient Britons and the Antiquarian Imagination: Ideas from the Renaissance to the Regency* (London: Thames and Hudson, 1989), 20.
47. Hume, *Treatise*, 175.
48. Review of Ellis's *Specimens of the Early English Poets*, 1804, in Scott, *Periodical Criticism*, in *The Miscellaneous Prose Works of Sir Walter Scott*, 28 vols. (Edinburgh: Robert Cadell, 1834–44), 1: 4–5 (italics added).
49. We should, however, note that Hume's narrative of solipsistic alienation and private pleasure, in the concluding Part of Book 1 of the *Treatise*, invokes a highly "socialized" rhetoric of imagination to engage its readers' sympathies. The natural history of the "universe of the imagination" is foundational in the Science of Man.
50. Hume, *Treatise*, 171.

CHAPTER 4

Melancholy, memory, and the "narrative situation" of history in post-Enlightenment Scotland

Ina Ferris

> *. . . time or succession is always broken and divided.*
> David Hume, *A Treatise of Human Nature* (1739)

In a memorable prolepsis in her *Letters from France* (1790) Helen Maria Williams anticipates "grateful" generations in the future flocking to the Champs de Mars, site of the Festival of the Federation in Paris on July 14, 1790, an event which epitomized for Williams, as for many others, the liberal promise of the Revolution. Elaborating the imagined scene, Williams presents the visitors eagerly pointing to and searching out the spots "where they have heard it recorded" that various participants in the festival took their places, and then stops to comment: "I think of these things, and then repeat to myself with transport, '*I* was a spectator of the Federation!'"[1] The redundancy of this declaration – she and her readers already know she was a spectator – underlines the paradoxical point of the rhetorical maneuver: in anticipating a time when she no longer *is*, Williams not only assures herself that she has been but does so by transforming a central experience of her own life into a vital memory for those who will come after. Reiterating her presence at the scene, she inscribes herself into a larger narrative of historical continuity that confirms and extends her own present-tense narrative of contemporary witness. For Jules Michelet, however, who came over fifty years after and who equally valorized the Festival of the Federation, the Champs de Mars appeared a very different scene from the one conjured by Williams. In the preface to his *History of the French Revolution* (1847–53) he presents himself wandering alone into the silent square of "parched grass" and "arid plain," now the only remaining trace of a revolution largely erased from cultural memory by a "forgetful generation."[2] Other events and institutions (e.g. the Empire, the church, the monarchy) have left concrete monuments in the city, Michelet notes, but "the Revolution has for her monument – empty space" (*History*, 4). Even more devastating, this space is now a racetrack modeled on English fashion, so

that what Williams imagined as a site of patriotic remembrance has degen-
erated into "the theatre of . . . vain amusements, borrowed from a foreign
land" (4). Far from generating an optimistic narrative of national continuity and celebration, then, the revolution triggers for Michelet a melancholy
awareness of disjunction and loss, and he writes its history in an attempt to
counteract the national drift of memory he has witnessed. His monumental
History of the French Revolution is thus a work of recompense but it is also
powerfully a work of mourning, and what is mourned is not so much the
loss of the past as the loss of someone to *talk to* about the past. As the
preface makes apparent, it is the "empty space" in the present that haunts
the melancholy historian. Nor is it incidental that Michelet concludes the
preface by recording his grief at the death of his father, "him who so often
narrated the scenes of the Revolution to me" (13).

I cite these moments on the Champs de Mars because they draw vivid
attention to the personal figure of the historian, thereby highlighting the
often overlooked status of history as an enunciation.[3] More particularly,
they present modern history as a writing produced by an "I" intensely
aware of the passage of generations and fueled by desire for what we might
call "the narrative situation" (most simply, the desire for a situation in which
one can tell an interested someone else that something happened). Thus
Williams, imagining herself inside the narrative of grateful generations in
the future, deploys the trope of those generations to justify her current
telling; while Michelet inserts his narration in the "empty space" of the
revolution in the hope of gaining a hearing from the forgetful generation.
Neither move is unusual – appeals to or complaints about other generations
are a longstanding feature of European discourse, literary and otherwise –
but in the historical genres of the late eighteenth and early nineteenth
centuries the trope of generations took on a new resonance.[4] In the wake of
Enlightenment models and revolutionary experience the venerable literary
trope became historicized, attached to a specific historical temporality rather
than to the general temporality of common mortality.

For a Romantic historiography, coming after the philosophical history
articulated most powerfully by the Scottish Enlightenment, the passage
of and gap between generations became a *historical* problem as it had not
been for earlier classical and humanist forms of history. Where the uniform
and non-progressive temporality of the latter allowed for the ready trans-
fer of values across generations – the "exemplary" function of the past –
the rewriting of historical process as linear but non-synchronous progress
blocked the kind of relation and recognition permitted by the older historical genres. History writing thus became "sentimental" not just in the sense

of deploying rhetorics of emotion and affect to help consolidate national or class formations in ways that have drawn recent critical attention but also in Friedrich Schiller's more philosophical sense of the sentimental mood: that equivocal, self-conscious mood of modernity which recognizes itself as free and knowing but also as belated and lacking wholeness.[5] To think about Romantic historicism in this way is to shift attention from history as the celebrated "recovery" of the past (its conventional signature in the period) to history as anxiety about a diminished present.[6]

The history mindedness of turn-of-the-century Scotland, expressed most influentially for Europe not so much in the histories of Hume and Robertson as in the novels of Walter Scott, moved into the foreground anxieties about social connection that always – and explicitly – shadowed the confidence of Enlightenment analyses of the "state" of societies moving through historical time. James Chandler has drawn attention to the complexity of the whole notion of "the state" of society (as both concept and genre) for the Romantic inflection of the Enlightenment model, but what he stresses is the fascination with correlation and relation opened up by the double line of time posited by philosophical history: the even calendrical time of the world ("civilization") and the uneven national time of particular states ("stages"). This model allows for the correlation of different national states or stages because all can be located within the same state of the world, and the intersection of the two lines produces a particular "historical situation."[7] As the mathematical language of correlation suggests, this model (despite the language of time) is essentially spatial: a flattening out of time across space, as in a map. Herein in fact lie its powers of relation, and the important point is that these powers are not simply analytic but affective. As Julie Ellison notes, the Scottish Enlightenment "crafted the culture of *systems* that is so important to the modern individual's feeling of being meaningfully related to remote locations and cultures."[8] Ironically, however, it did less to generate feelings of meaningful relation to recent times close to hand, for the Scottish philosophers equally posited the modern commercial age (in the succinct phrase of Adam Ferguson) as "this age of separations."[9]

The "separations" of what was known as "polished society" bore down on individual and collective subjectivities from two directions: temporally, in the way in which one stage replaced another in successive, as opposed to dialectical, fashion (hence they did not, in theory, incorporate earlier phases so as to allow for recognition across stages); spatially, in the way that the principle of the division of labour eroded what were often called "the bands of society." In relation to the representation of historical time, the important point is that even when philosophical history allowed for some blurring of stages, it drew a very firm line between modern and pre-modern, between past and present. "Writing speaks of the past only in order to inter it," Michel de Certeau acerbically notes in his critique of "the historiographical operation," and one does not need to share his logocentrism or anti-historiographic bias to take the point.[10] Enlightenment thought was clearly invested in understanding itself as operating in a present that had left behind forms of order belonging to a clearly distinct past, so that the writing of figures like Adam Ferguson and David Hume decisively situates itself in a "civil" present set off from a "superstitious" or "savage" past. It thus exemplifies the sense of time distinctive of the modern temper, what the Germans call a sense of "new time" (*Neuzeit*). Modernity, Peter Osborne has stressed in his discussion of *Neuzeit*, is distinguished from all prior epochs in perceiving itself as a radical break with the past. This positing of a break allows it to set up a differential between itself and all prior times, and it does so in a way that makes it the measure of all times, bearer of universal standard time.[11]

But this "new time," Romantic history writing reminds us, is itself broken, not only broken off from the past but broken inside itself as well, founded upon the division of labor that segmented and severed formerly integral activities (e.g. Smith's famous example of the making of pins in the opening chapter of *The Wealth of Nations*). It was the division of labor Ferguson had in mind when he spoke of his own time as "this age of separations." Like Adam Smith, Ferguson saw the division of labor as the productive principle of commercial society, but (more so than Smith) he brooded over its corrosive social effects. The ultimate effect of "the separation of professions," he concluded in *An Essay on the History of Civil Society* (1767) was "to break the bands of society . . . and to withdraw individuals from the common scene of occupation, on which the sentiments of the heart, and the mind, are most happily employed" (218). Thus separated from one another, he argues, the members of polished society find themselves without either a common discourse ("every individual is supposed to possess . . . his peculiar skill, in which the others are confessedly ignorant" [218] or common sentiment, notably without "the glowing sentiments of public affection" [219]). Ferguson's is not, it should be noted, a pacific or pastoral vision of such "glowing sentiments," for his vigorous notion of citizenship builds out of classical republican notions of the masculine *via activa*. In his text centripetal movements of social concord exist in essential — and often openly contradictory — tension with centrifugal movements of debate and agitation, a friction Ferguson regarded as necessary to keep at bay the threat of luxury and torpor he saw as constantly threatening modern polities.[12]

In the scenario presented by philosophical history, then, subjectivity, whether individual or collective, became flattened, placed in a chronotope in which both the line of historical time and the horizontal bands of community were losing purchase as well as dimension. Memory thinned out and social sentiments shrank, reducing the material out of which consciousness (and thus, according to empirical psychology, identities) were largely formed. Moreover, as has been much noted, the Scottish theory of history as systematic process tended to discount individual particulars in favor of generalities and impersonal forces, while its central "law of unintended consequences" had very doubtful consequences for longstanding religious and political assumptions about individual agency, will, and action.[13] Process, Hannah Arendt notes in speaking of the modern historical model, has "engulfed every tangible thing, every individual entity that is visible to us, degrading them into functions."[14]

It is in response to this matrix of concerns, concerns generated both by and within the self-reflective processes of Enlightenment reason, that the historical genres of early nineteenth-century Scotland assume their specificity. Scotland itself, widely perceived by the turn of the nineteenth century as the most radically changed part of the British polity, appeared to be modernity's paradigmatic testing ground. Indeed, it came to stand as the emblematic scene of modern history, and Scott presents it in this way in the Postscript to the first of his historical fictions. "There is no European nation," he declares in an often quoted passage from *Waverley* (1814), "which, within the course of half a century or little more, has undergone so complete a change as this kingdom of Scotland."[15] The change has been so complete, Scott states, as "to render the present people of Scotland a class of beings as different from their grandfathers, as the existing English are from those of Queen Elizabeth's time" (*Waverley*, 340). Suggestively, he tropes the speeded-up process of historical change as the production of a gulf in just two generations, thereby bringing its consequences home to the intimate space of the familial body ("different from their grandfathers"). By contrast, historical change in England is articulated in the abstract language of impersonal collectivity ("the English") and conventional historical periodization ("Queen Elizabeth's time"). The point is reiterated in the "Dedicatory Epistle" to *Ivanhoe* (1819), the first of the Waverley series set outside Scotland, when the English Templeton recalls a comment by the Scottish antiquarian Dryasdust: "within these thirty years, such an infinite change has taken place in the manners of Scotland, that men look

back upon the habits of society proper to their immediate ancestors, as
we do on those of the reign of Queen Anne, or even the period of the
Revolution."[16]

While the accelerated tempo of historical change on Scottish soil is a
matter of some authorial satisfaction, Scott's insistent dating of the change
("'tis sixty years since," "within these thirty years," "within the course of
half a century") calls attention as much to loss and disorientation as to
success and achievement. "Such of the present generation as can recollect
the last twenty or twenty-five years of the eighteenth century," he notes,
will be "fully sensible" of the distance between the point "from which
we set out" and that at which Scotland has now arrived (*Waverley*, 340).
Even as Scott confirms this distance as the sign of progress, however, he
immediately turns to that which has "almost entirely vanished" in the
process, identifying it as the motive of his own narrative (*Waverley*, 340).
The "sixty" or "thirty" or "twenty" years to which he refers thus periodize
loss, and in so doing transform the common fate of generations into a
specifically historical problem for contemporary Scotland. Scott's friend
John Ramsay of Ochtertyre makes the point even more clearly in his memoir
of *Scotland and Scotsmen in the Eighteenth Century*, composed between 1785
and 1810, when he invokes the revival of Scottish letters in the eighteenth
century in the opening pages of his text. "It must . . . be deeply regretted,"
Ramsay declares, "that in a matter hardly eighty years old, it should already
be next to impossible to trace a number of particulars respecting its rise and
progress."[17] Transmission relays have clearly failed, and memories continue
their rapid fading. Indeed, Ramsay now wishes he had turned earlier to
his own project of retrieval and recording: "Had I myself undertaken this
work thirty years ago, I might have had much excellent information which
is now irrevocably lost" (*Scotland*, 1: 2).

As the fabled site of "ancient manners" and lost Jacobite causes, the
Highlands stood as the most dramatic instance in the period of forms of
life eradicated by modernizing policies and processes. But they also figured
in the more unsettling modality of the "almost" ("almost total extinction"
[*Waverley*, 340]), a modality not so readily converted into the "romance"
or "tradition" that, as often noted, helped to underwrite a modern North
Britain.[18] More to my point than the Jacobite motif glamorized by Scott
and others is the more submerged theme of the Clearances, the problem
not so much of past as of passing things, which engendered a certain fal-
tering in the poise of philosophical history as a traumatic instance of those
"separations" shadowing its account of the smooth rationality of historical
processes. Unlike the Jacobite rebellions, the depopulation of the Highlands

consequent on the transformation of its economy after the 1760s was an ongoing and visible process in the early nineteenth century, one that effected a fundamental change in the constitution of everyday life and in the "sentiments" infusing social order. So John Ramsay emphasizes that in the last thirty or forty years the sentiments of Highland proprietors have "entirely changed," alienating both gentlemen tenants and common tenants. "The rising generation," he comments, "can hardly form an adequate idea of the anguish and distress which their fathers felt when chieftains began to look cold upon the cadets of their family, and to set at naught their pretensions, founded on a long series of affectionate services and attachment" (*Scotland*, II: 526, II:531).

A similar sense of break and attenuation in the social bond informs Anne Grant's ethnography of Highland culture in *Essays on the Superstitions of the Highlanders of Scotland* (1811). A text motivated by the conviction that it is almost "too late" to produce such an ethnography, it includes an extended condemnation of the "perverted" chiefs who have forced their people into exile for "paultry profits."[19] Foregrounding the forced removal from habitual location, she stresses the emotional cost: "It is in their feelings, chiefly, that they suffer" (*Essays*, 155). "There are a thousand peculiarities belonging to that mode of life," Grant explains, "which cannot be separated from it, without the extinction of all enjoyment" (158). For his part, Walter Scott, famously reticent about the Clearances, concludes his long ethnographic article on the Highlands in the *Quarterly Review* in 1816 with a sardonic twist. Following a cautious condemnation of the "unrelenting avarice" of some chiefs in the present, he then moves out of the vocabulary of moral philosophy governing his analysis to evoke a future scene when, "in the hour of need," a summons to war reaches an empty glen and remains unanswered. This sentimental appeal to British self-interest takes a turn, however, when he presents the emigrants throwing back the conventional Highland lament of departure in ironic "re-echo": "We return – we return – we return – no more!"[20]

It is not that such commentators stood in critical relation to the Enlightenment model of historical process; on the contrary, all subscribed to it in a fundamental way. "To prohibit the extension of sheep-farms would be like fighting with nature" (*Scotland*, II:536), Ramsay flatly declares, but the pages he devoted to worrying the issue demonstrate that *general* adherence to the model did not preclude a sense of local discomfort. The historical genres emerged out of that tension. Registering an asymmetry between the systematic and the particular (emotionally rather than cognitively in the first instance), observers like Ramsay or Scott turned to writing to articulate (in both senses) the gaps and ironies thus glimpsed. Erosion, the temporality of disappearing, tended to be a prime trigger, and it was so in part because erosion moved into the foreground the anxieties of a modality of historical consciousness that had only recently begun to take shape in the culture. The late eighteenth century increasingly witnessed what Mark Phillips calls "the reframing of common life as a domain of pervasive historical change"(*Society and Sentiment*, 320). Such "reframing" meant that aspects of private life earlier considered unhistorical ("natural") assumed historical meaning and moved into public discourse. But this respositioning also meant that everyday changes or, rather, changes in the everyday began to impinge on subjectivity in new and unsettling ways. No longer simply "natural" processes, the erosions of "manners" and cultural memory assumed weight as losses of precisely historical being. The ironic outcome was that historians, who had established the historicity of "manners" to begin with, now emerged as the figures who would salvage the historical weight of cultural beings by counteracting the erosion of memory in the generations currently on the (historical) ground. Scott thus addressed *Waverley* both to "elder persons," whose memories of youth it would recall, and to "the rising generation," for whom the tale "may present some idea of the manners of their forefathers" (*Waverley*, 341).

In such an understanding of the act of historical writing, history emerges less as a form of knowledge of the past (although the period saw the beginnings of the professionalization of history as a modern knowledge genre) than as a mode of connection in the present posited on the historian's own alienation. "I am a borderer . . . between two generations," writes Chrystal Croftangry, who stands in many ways as Scott's most exemplary historian, "and can point out more perhaps than others of those fading traces of antiquity which are daily vanishing."[21] Like the Romantic poet famously defined by Wordsworth, Scott's Romantic historian exists in the comparative mode ("more perhaps than others"), but where the poet discerns more acutely than others the "primary laws" structuring concrete experience, the historian is more attuned than others to what is passing away. The condition of his knowledge – the generic condition of history – is what we might call "homelessness," recalling Siegfried Kracauer's contention that the historical consciousness is essentially an exilic one. It is only in a state of "homelessness," he argues, that the historian can commune with "the material of his concern."[22] Anticipating his point, Scott casts his most elaborated figure of the history-teller as an atopic figure without hereditary place or generational bonds. Having cast away his paternal inheritance, Croftangry moves into exile and redeems himself, but – in a negative turn on the familiar

Christian parable – his homecoming years later finds him unrecognized and unwelcomed.

Scott repeatedly underlines this point. Upon his return to Edinburgh, Croftangry rushes to meet the benevolent lawyer who had extricated him from his difficulties only to find the aged man sadly overtaken by senility; returning to the even earlier site of the lost paternal estate, he encounters an old family servant who fails to recognize him or, even worse, pretends she does not. The motif extends to Croftangry himself, who cannot make a connection with his younger self: "I did not seem to be the same person" ("Chronicles," 60). Even when he mingles with the few former friends left in Edinburgh, he finds that "all community of ties between us had ceased to exist," for they "held their life in a different tenor from what I did" (42). Abandoning standard models of belonging, Croftangry moves himself into the dubious zone of the Canongate, where he wanders about and takes up antiquarian studies, exchanges tales with his Highland housekeeper, and treasures the company of anecdotalists, notably the elderly Mrs Bethune Baliol, whose memory stretches back to before 1745 and who bequeaths to him a manuscript containing tales he will include as part of his "chronicles." Something like a ghost and something like Orpheus, he passes between realms, and it is this movement that defines his being.

Scott's most suggestive fable of history-telling and modern memory is attached to this figure. In the frame to *The Fair Maid of Perth* (1828), Croftangry tells a mischievous tale of the meeting between an English tourist and a Scottish stain in Holyrood House. It is the kind of story natives like to tell on tourists, and Scott indulges himself in some nationalist anti-English fun, but at the same time the tale sharply focuses what was at stake for him in the writing of his histories. Croftangry recounts how, while he was wandering the halls of Holyrood House one day, the housekeeper of Queen Mary's Apartments, Mrs. Policy, was showing around a tourist from London. The visitor, "the brisk, alert agent of a great house in the city," fidgeted through her stories, even that of Rizzio's murder, until she pointed to the bloodstains on the floor "in support of her narrative." The tourist, it turned out, sold Scouring Drops, "and a stain of two hundred and fifty years' standing was interesting to him, not because it had been caused by the blood of a Queen's favourite, slain in her apartment, but because it offered so admirable an opportunity to prove the efficacy of his unequal Detergent Elixir." Dropping to his knees, the Englishman proclaims: "Why, if it had been five hundred, I have something in my pocket will fetch it out in five minutes." Energetically, he begins scrubbing the floor, whereupon Mrs. Policy screams and begins to pull at him. Croftangry rushes in and has great difficulty persuading the assiduous representative of modern commerce that "there were such things in the world as stains which ought to remain indelible, on account of the associations with which they are connected."[23]

Beneath the fun, the story stands as a serious gloss on the way in which the modern time of development collapses all time into itself. For this time, stains are simply blotches to be removed as efficiently as possible ("five minutes"). By contrast, the time of the history-tellers in this scene appears as distinctly resistant to the modern, blocking its erasure in order to retain within its frame the signs of the differentiated being of the past. In its view, stains are traces to be preserved for the density they add to the present ("associations with which they are connected"). Historical thought, Paul Ricoeur has observed, is "a knowledge by traces," the pursuit of the vestiges of past forms of life.[24] But the key point for Scott's scene is not so much the pursuit of vestiges as their function within the present as signs of former passage: "the trace indicates 'here' (in space) and 'now' (in the present), the past passage of living beings" (*Time and Narrative*, 120). The trace thus thickens the time of "is" by layering into it the tenses of "has been," and Croftangry's whole narrative enterprise is driven by the impulse to preserve such layering. The "pursuit" it actually triggers at this point, however, is not a pursuit of the living beings whose passage it signals but a pursuit of discursive argument, as Croftangry goes on to defend the authenticity of the bloodstain. Eschewing the conventional province of historical reason (why did "that" happen?), Croftangry produces a display of (semi-comic) antiquarian reason and its material logic (how could this mark actually have been preserved?).

The point of this, as the play of irony throughout the scene suggests, is to block nationalist mystification as much as modernizing erasure. Ambiguity governs the comic confrontation, deflating any sense of the trace as privileged access to the past, let alone to national origins. Not only is the stain itself of dubious provenance, but some stains, after all, *should* be removed. For those in the place it has become a quasi-relic, but it is only "quasi" because it too appears within a modern time and a modern economy which is characterized, on the one hand, by the absence of the sacred and, on the other, by the ubiquity of fabrication. The stain is, quite literally, a tourist spot even if those in the place choose to understand it otherwise. Thus Croftangry compares Mrs. Policy's response to the visitor's scouring to that of the Abbess of St. Bridget's "when a profane visitant drank up the phial of brandy which had long passed muster among the relics of the cloister for the tears of the blessed saint" (*Fair Maid*, 8). Equally dubious are the series of portraits of the Scottish monarchs in the adjoining gallery, their uniform noses tweaking the claim to unbroken Scottish lineage and the whole iconic process of national myth-making. Neither stain nor portrait, Scott makes clear, offers access to an authentic "other" time or direct communion with the dead.

All the same the fascination of the stain is that it holds out the promise of some sense of connection with the life of Mary Stuart, who famously intrigued and baffled eighteenth-century historians from Hume and Robertson onwards. As a sign of Mary, however, the stain figures opacity, pointing to that which remains undecipherable to the categories of historical explanation. Hers is "this most singular of all tragedies" in the words of Mrs. Baliol, Croftangray's interlocutor in the scene (*Fair Maid*, 13), who urges him to supplement William Robertson's famous account of Mary in his landmark *History of Scotland* (1759). Croftangry declines, but Scott himself had already impinged on Robertson's ground in *The Abbot* (1820), and his late introduction to the novel invokes the rubric of impenetrable "mystery" in relation to the unhappy queen: "Queen Mary, so interesting by her wit, her beauty, her misfortunes, and the mystery which still does, and probably always will, overhang her history."[25] While Scott may have had in specific mind the revival of the debate over Mary's guilt in the murder of Darnley,[26] his overhanging mystery has as much to do with Mrs. Baliol's point of singularity: Mary Stuart presents something unassimilable to the general rule of tragedy and, a fortiori, to that of history. It is notable that when Dugald Stewart, heir to the moral philosophers in early nineteenth-century Edinburgh, comes to the question of the queen of Scots in his memoir of Robertson, he expresses a profound lack of interest on the grounds that her case does not yield useful generalizations: "It is a subject which I have never examined with attention, and which, I must confess, never excited my curiosity. Whatever judgment we form concerning the points in dispute, it leads to no general conclusion concerning human affairs, nor throws any new light on human character."[27]

What finally matters in the scene of the stain is that it confirms a connection between between Croftangry and Mrs. Policy, establishes a line of communication based on a shared commitment to the local that allows each to act as responsive audience for the other. The dislocations of history are offset (if only temporarily) by the achievement of the "narrative situation" to which I referred at the outset of this essay. It is thus not a matter (as in Stephen Greenblatt's famous declaration) of speaking *with* the dead but of speaking with others *about* the dead and being heard.[28] Appropriately enough, Scott at one point thought of titling Croftangry's collection of tales *Conversations of the Canongate* rather than *Chronicles of the Canongate*,[29] and his original choice underscores the centrality of the trope of conversation in mediating authorial voices and readerly spaces in the Waverley Novels. Repeatedly, the paratexts of the fictions assume the form of letters or dialogues and invoke the recollection of sites and scenes of conversation and exchange, defining the act of narration as an extension of the sociability on which the Scottish school of moral philosophy founded its model of individual identity. Dead beings, as much as live ones, seem able to participate in this process, for many of Scott's novels are ushered into the world as literal "remains" of the dead. Crucially, Scott consistently presents these dead in the context of living conversation, effecting a reanimation not so much of their bodies as of their sociality, even when that sociality is as minimal, as in the case of the solitary Old Mortality recalled by Peter Pattieson in the novel of the same name. More characteristic is Pattieson's introduction of Dick Tinto in the first chapter of *The Bride of Lammermoor*. "The memory of Tinto is dear to me," he writes, "from the recollection of the many conversations which we have had together," and he then goes on to reconstruct one of those conversations.[30] Given the fact of his own death, the conversation is doubly ghostly, and as the Waverley Novels continue to germinate, this sense of a haunting of the present becomes ever more insistent, culminating in the curiously fugitive figure of Croftangry (who too recalls conversations with the dead and transcribes "remains" for his readers). Such haunting is very much to Scott's point. As the encounter over the stain suggests, the time of modernity is a flat, unhaunted time, and it is in relation to the unfolding of this time (and the narratives it underwrites) that Scott's scene comes to resonate into our own time as a parable of a local antiquarian sensibility within modern historical consciousness.

When Croftangry and Mrs. Policy "rescue" the infamous stain from erasure, they perform an act of antiquarian stickiness vis-à-vis general history. Theirs is an antiquarian rather than traditional sensibility, even though it overlaps with the traditional in its local focus (Scott's antiquaries have little interest in antiquities beyond their purview) and in the positive significance it assigns to the world of matter. However, Croftangry and Mrs. Policy do not operate in unofficial, communal or distinctively oral terms, identifying themselves with an official albeit deserted site of national story wherein they reproduce, with more or less irony, what has been handed down in this site. Their stickiness ensues from their insistence on fixing story to specific place – literally, to a spot – for this testifies to an antiquarian refusal of portability and transportability, an unwillingness to understand objects (including story-objects) outside the material site of origin. Certainly theirs is a textual imagination – antiquarians in Scott are constantly writing and publishing – but at the same time texts too tend to become physical objects – part of the "stuff" of the past requiring preservation – and not primarily containers of extractable codes of signification. Hence Croftangry jokes about reserving his grandfather's rather tedious family memoir until he is admitted to the Bannatyne Club when he will publish a handsome edition, and Scott adds a serious note at this point informing the reader that this society (of which Scott was in fact president) "has already rescued from oblivion many curious materials of Scottish History" ("Chronicles," 46).

Friedrich Nietzsche famously identified this retentive drive – the desire to preserve "materials" from "oblivion" – as the source of both the positive and negative power of antiquarian history. Rooted in local place, the anti-quarian soul for Nietzsche restricts and drains vital expansive energies even as its commitment to its own place endows it with a certain social value in preserving "for those will come after" a connection with the habitus of their predecessors. "Loving," "reverent," and "loyal" as it may be, the antiquarian soul for Nietzsche regresses from the human, retreating into the ancestral "furniture"only to become itself absorbed into the "nest" it has built, something thing-like and "mummified."[31] As the frequently satirized figure of antiquaries in Scott suggests – one need only name Dr Dryasdust – he would well have understood the modern philosopher's point. But he also understood antiquarianism as a rehumanizing of souls dislocated by the "separations" of modern history. For all their folly (perhaps because of their folly), rootless figures like the half-pay officer Captain Clutterbuck of *The Monastery* (1820) find in turning "local antiquary" (Clutterbuck becomes expert on the ruined abbey in the area) not only a purpose for formerly empty days but a way of making common converse with those among whom they had formerly lived at a distance. And such a view of antiquarianism, in both its negative and positive implications, seems to me to bear in an important way on our own current situation as readers and critics committed to "doing history."

In his recent study of Romantic and contemporary historicism in *England in 1819*, James Chandler argues that the current historical turn in Romantic studies recapitulates the Romantic genre of "the state" (the state of the na-tion, the state of affairs) and thereby repeats at a distance the robust political and interventionary desires of public genres in the early nineteenth cen-tury. The same historical turn, it seems to me, also repeats at a distance the antiquarian gambit of the same period, which acted as dialectical counter-Enlightenment's purchase on modernity, resisting the time of development and the move forward in favor of what Jean-François Lyotard has termed an "advance backwards."[32] It seems no accident that the whole subject of antiquarianism has begun to return to the serious critical stage.[33] In the current fascination with the mundane details of past cultures like the records of circulating libraries, the habits of female shopping, the physical property of books, the role of turnips in agriculture, and so on, we witness the emergence of a new antiquarianism. Current critical practice may define itself in the more up-to-date idiom of "case study" or "materialist analysis" in order to distinguish itself from the macro-ambitions of general history and the unifying drive of the old national history, but this new antiquarianism seeks something of the same stickiness achieved by the old, a similar purchase on resistant matter.

In the attraction to the local, the overlooked, and the ephemeral, current Romantic scholars are in general doing what could be called history in the minor key, an activity for which "antiquarianism" might be another name.[34] And they engage in this practice for reasons similar to those of Romantic predecessors like Scott, looking to the minor to counter the major. But in our own accelerated *Neuzeit* the Romantic antiquarian's sense of belatedness and melancholy has become aggravated, not least by the printed word's loss of cultural centrality, which makes more difficult than for earlier antiquarians the question of address and audience for the texts we like to produce. Self-consciously circulating in between past and future in this intervalic moment, students of the printed word occupy a situation emptied of a sense of "those who will come after" in a way that Scott's antiquaries did not, quite. Accordingly, for current literary scholars the question of "the narrative situation" (of someone to speak to) has taken on a deeper melancholic note, and one of the crucial functions of the more bracing "political turn" in Romantic studies has been precisely to help offset or allay that melancholy. Returning to the paradigmatic Scottish scene of modern historical consciousness thus allows us to rethink the stakes of the writing of history, including literary history, by reminding us that historical discourse is not simply a representation *of* something but a representation *to* someone. In the terrain between the "of" and the "to" made visible by the emergent historical genres of Romanticism, we can discern the operation of a pragmatics of history that bears in important ways on our own practice.

NOTES

1. Helen Maria Williams, *Letters Written in France* (1790; rpt. Oxford: Woodstock Books, 1989), 108.
2. Jules Michelet, *History of the French Revolution* ed. Gordon Wright, trans. Charles Cocks (Chicago and London: University of Chicago Press, 1967) 4.

3. Linda Orr is one of the few to draw explicit attention to the significance of the enunciative pole of historiography. She highlights Michelet's preface in "Intimate Images: Subjectivity and History – Staël, Michelet and Tocqueville," in Frank Ankersmit and Hans Kellner (eds.), *The New Philosophy of History* (Chicago and London: University of Chicago Press, 1995), 89–107.

4. In referring to "historical genres," I follow Mark Phillips, who argues in his important study of Enlightenment historiography that the historical project of the period found expression in a whole set of genres and should not be restricted to the one commonly termed "history"; *Society and Sentiment: Genres of Historical Writing in Britain 1740–1840* (Princeton: Princeton University Press, 2000). This is not to discount either the period debate about what counted as history proper nor the struggle among different genres for authority in the historical field.

5. Friedrich Schiller, *On the Naive and Sentimental in Literature*, trans. Watanabe-O'Kelly (Manchester: Carcanet New Press, 1981). On "sentimental historiography" and the Scottish Enlightenment, see J. C. Hilson, "Hume: The Historian as Man of Feeling," in J. C. Hilson, M. B. Jones, and J. R. Watson (eds.), *Augustan Worlds: Essays in Honour of A. R. Humphreys* (Leicester: Leicester University Press, 1978), 205–22; Jerome Christensen, *Practicing Enlightenment: Hume and the Formation of a Literary Career* (Madison: University of Wisconsin Press, 1987); Jayne Elizabeth Lewis, "Mary Stuart's 'Fatal Box': Sentimental History and the Revival of the Casket Letters Controversy," *The Age of Johnson* 7 (1996): 427–73. For the most wide-ranging analysis of sentiment and history in the period, see Phillips, *Society and Sentiment*.

6. On Romantic history as recovery and reconstruction, see in particular Stephen Bann, *The Clothing of Clio: A Study of the Representation of History in Nineteenth-Century Britain and France* (Cambridge: Cambridge University Press, 1984) and *Romanticism and the Rise of History* (New York: Twayne Publishers, 1995).

7. James Chandler, *England in 1819: The Politics of Literary Culture and the Case of Romantic Historicism* (Chicago and London: University of Chicago Press, 1998), see especially Part One, chs. 2 and 4.

8. Julie Ellison, *Cato's Tears and the Making of Anglo-American Emotion* (Chicago and London: University of Chicago Press, 1999), 12. Ellison goes on to note it is no accident that Enlightenment Scotland should also have produced "that classic of masculine sensibility," Henry Mackenzie's *The Man of Feeling*.

9. Adam Ferguson, *An Essay on the History of Civil Society* (New Brunswick and London: Transaction Publishers, 1980), 183.

10. Michel de Certeau, *The Writing of History*, trans. Tom Conley (New York: Columbia University Press, 1988), 101.

11. Peter Osborne, *The Politics of Time: Modernity and Avant-Garde* (London: Verso, 1995), 8–16.

12. In the section "Of National Felicity," for example, Ferguson places "public felicity" (based on "peace and unanimity") against "the principles of political life" (the "rivalship" of communities and the "agitations of a free people"),

and he draws direct attention to the problem he has generated: "How shall we reconcile these jarring and opposite tenets? It is, perhaps, not necessary to reconcile them" (*Essay*, 61).

13. On this point see, for example, David Allan, *Virtue, Learning and the Scottish Enlightenment: Ideas of Scholarship in Early Modern History* (Edinburgh: Edinburgh University Press, 1993), especially ch. 4; John Dwyer, *Virtuous Discourse: Sensibility and Community in Late Eighteenth-Century Scotland* (Edinburgh: John Donald, 1987); Mary Poovey, *A History of the Modern Fact: Problems of Knowledge in the Sciences of Wealth and Society* (Chicago and London: University of Chicago Press, 1998), ch. 5.

14. Hannah Arendt, *Between Past and Future* (London: Faber, 1961), 63.

15. Sir Walter Scott, *Waverley; or, 'Tis Sixty Years Since*, ed. Claire Lamont (Oxford: Oxford University Press, 1986), 340.

16. Scott, *Ivanhoe*, ed. Ian Duncan (Oxford: Oxford University Press, 1996), 14.

17. John Ramsay, *Scotland and Scotsmen in the Eighteenth Century*, 2 vols. (1888; rpt. Bristol: Thoemmes Press, 1996), I: 1–2. Ramsay, incidentally, was one of the sources for the antiquary Jonathan Oldbuck in Scott's *The Antiquary*.

18. Among numerous recent studies, see in particular Robert Crawford, *Devolving English Literature* (Oxford: Clarendon Press, 1992); Leith Davis, *Acts of Union: Scotland and the Literary Negotiations of the British Nation, 1707–1830* (Stanford: Stanford University Press, 1998); Colin Kidd, *Subverting Scotland's Past: Scottish Whig Historians and the Creation of an Anglo-British Identity, 1689–c.1830* (Cambridge: Cambridge University Press, 1993); Murray Pittock, *The Invention of Scotland: The Stuart Myth and the Scottish Identity, 1638 to the Present* (London: Routledge, 1991); Howard D. Weinbrot, *Britannia's Issue: The Rise of British Literature from Dryden to Ossian* (Cambridge: Cambridge University Press, 1993); Peter Womack, *Improvement and Romance: Constructing the Myth of the Highlands* (London: Macmillan, 1989). See also Hugh Trevor-Roper's landmark "The Invention of Tradition: The Highland Tradition of Scotland," in Eric Hobsbawm and Terence Ranger (eds.) *The Invention of Tradition* (Cambridge: Cambridge University Press, 1983), 15–41.

19. Anne Grant, *Essays on the Superstitions of the Highlanders of Scotland*, 2 vols. (London, 1811), I:9, II: 151.

20. Scott, "Culloden Papers," *Quarterly Review* 14 (January 1816): 333.

21. Scott, "Chronicles of the Canongate," *Two Drovers and Other Stories*, ed. Graham Tulloch (Oxford: Oxford University Press, 1987), 91–2.

22. Siegfried Kracauer, *History: The Last Things Before the Last* (New York: Oxford University Press, 1969), 84.

23. Scott, *The Fair Maid of Perth*, *Waverley Novels*, Centenary Edition, 25 vols. (Edinburgh, 1871), XXII: 7–8.

24. Paul Ricoeur, *Time and Narrative*, vol. III, trans. Kathleen Blarney and David Pellauer (Chicago and London: University of Chicago Press, 1988), 120. In the context of another argument about history and the novel, Everett Zimmerman makes suggestive use of Ricoeur's notion of the trace as frame for his discussion of the historical problematic engaged by eighteenth-century fiction; *The*

Boundaries of Fiction: History and the Eighteenth-Century British Novel (Ithaca: Cornell University Press, 1996), 6, 235–6.

25. Scott, *The Abbot, Waverley Novels*, XXII: 6.
26. On the revival of the controversy over Mary Stuart in the eighteenth century, see Jayne Lewis, "Mary Stuart's 'Fatal Box.'"
27. Dugald Stewart, "Account of the Life and Writings of William Robertson," *The Works of William Robertson, D. D.* (London, 1835), vi.
28. I refer to the much quoted opening line of Stephen Greenblatt's *Shakespearean Negotiations: The Circulation of Social Energy in Renaissance England* (Berkeley and Los Angeles: University of California Press, 1988), 1.
29. Scott, *Letters of Sir Walter Scott*, ed. Herbert Grierson *et al.*, 12 vols. (London: Constable: 1932–7), X:72.
30. Scott, *The Bride of Lammermoor*, ed. Fiona Robertson (Oxford: Oxford University Press, 1991), 20.
31. Friedrich Nietzsche, *On the Advantage and Disadvantage of History for Life*, trans. Peter Preuss (Indianapolis: Hackett Publishing, 1980), 19–21.
32. Jean-François Lyotard, *The Inhuman: Reflections on Time*, trans. Geoffrey Bennington and Rachel Bowlby (Stanford: Stanford University Press, 1991), 3.
33. Katie Trumpener's *Bardic Nationalism: The Romantic Novel and the British Empire* (Princeton: Princeton University Press, 1997) is perhaps the most influential of such recent studies. Scott himself has long attracted attention as an antiquarian, but for the new interest in this subject, see Yoon Sun Lee, "A Divided Inheritance: Scott's Antiquarian Novel and the British Nation," *ELH* 64 (1997): 537–67, and Richard Maxwell, "Inundations of Time: A Definition of Scott's Originality," *ELH* 68 (2001): 419–68.
34. In a suggestive new essay Marshall Brown also argues for a concept of "minor" history as a way of retemporalizing a critical practice that has come to favor spatial categories, although his analogies are musical rather than antiquarian, "Rethinking the Scale of Literary History," in Mario Valdes and Linda Hutcheon (eds.), *Rethinking Literary History* (Oxford: Oxford University Press, forthcoming).

CHAPTER 5

Scott, the Scottish Enlightenment, and Romantic Orientalism

James Watt

In a *Quarterly Review* essay of 1816, Walter Scott drew attention to the similarities between the "purely patriarchal" manners of Scottish Highland clans and Afghan or Persian mountain tribes; such "curious points of parallelism," he claimed, served "to show how the same state of society and civilisation produces similar manners, laws, and customs, even at the most remote periods of time, and in the most distant quarters of the world."[1] The early decades of the nineteenth century saw the heyday of what has been termed "Scottish Orientalism," as a range of writers invoked the stadial theory of the Scottish Enlightenment in order to compare the condition of European and Asian societies, and to consider the future development of British India.[2] The authority enjoyed by such stadial perspectives on the East was nonetheless short-lived, and by the 1820s articles that were skeptical about the universal applicability of philosophical history began to appear even in the journal that had hitherto supplied one of its main platforms, *The Edinburgh Review*.[3] This chapter will begin by providing a brief overview of Scottish writing about India in the period, before going on to examine the distinctive brand of Romantic Orientalism offered by two of the later novels of Sir Walter Scott. *The Surgeon's Daughter* (1827) and *The Talisman* (1825) are often seen to represent a falling away from the standard of Scott's earlier fiction, as he struggled to break new ground. The significance of these novels becomes much more apparent, though, when they are read alongside other contemporary works dealing with the East, and when they are read in the context of competing efforts to explain the differences between cultures or peoples. Although it is difficult to translate such playful and disruptive works into more readable ideological terms, these remarkable novels eschew the increasingly influential language of racial essentialism, and complicate the mythology of oriental despotism, while at the same time focusing on the ramifications of cultural contact and exchange.

94

Connections between Scotland and India were well established even before Henry Dundas was made President of the East India Company's Board of Control in 1784. By the mid eighteenth century, Scots were prominent in the Company's armies, and at different levels of Indian administration, while by the early 1800s Scots who had been educated at the University of Edinburgh, especially, were widely involved in the fast-developing field of oriental scholarship.[4] The most famous example of Scottish Orientalism in this period is also probably the least typical – James Mill's *The History of British India*, published in 1817. Mill's *History* was clearly rooted in Scottish Enlightenment social theory, since it accepted that there were general or universal laws governing the development of civilizations from "rudeness" to "refinement." Following the example set by writers such as John Millar or Adam Smith, Mill claimed that it was possible to assess the progress of different societies by common criteria, and therefore to form a "scale of civilization" on which "the relative positions of nations can be accurately marked."[5] Mill, however, seldom drew analogies between East and West, and rarely used the evidence provided by modern India to conjecture about the European past, emphasizing instead, for example, that "the Hindus of the present day" only offered a perspective on the lives of *other* Hindus.[6] Given its scathing references to previous accounts of "the wonderful learning, wonderful civilization, and wonderful institutions of the Hindus," indeed, Mill's *History* has most often been interpreted as an attack on the "orientalist" position associated primarily with Sir William Jones.[7] Regardless of its grounding in stadial theory, therefore, Mill's *History* has come to be best known as a work that heralded the advance of utilitarianism, offering a hostile account of Indian, and especially Hindu, customs and manners as a means of defining the agenda for reform. For Mill, the Hindu population of India had "passed but a small number of stages in the career of civilization," and – "stationary for many ages" – remained at a manifestly low level of development.[8]

The example of Mill's *History* demonstrates that works founded on the principles of stadial theory could potentially underwrite claims of essential "Western" superiority, since Western Europe was always assumed to occupy the highest stage in any comparative ranking of civilizations. As Jane Rendall has pointed out, however, many Scottish writers in the late eighteenth and early nineteenth centuries sought to pre-empt such a construction of their work.[9] In *An Historical Disquisition concerning the Knowledge which the Ancients had of India* (1791), William Robertson, like Mill, referred to "the permanence of [India's] institutions, and the immutability in the manners of its inhabitants," stating that "what now is in India, always was there, and is likely still to continue."[10] Unlike Mill, though, Robertson did not gloss the "permanence" of Indian institutions and manners in a denigratory way, but pointed instead to the early achievements of Indian civilization, in a bid to temper European ethnocentrism. "[T]o the disgrace of ancient philosophy," Robertson stated, the Greeks asserted "a right of dominion" over the other peoples they encountered by giving them "the degrading appellation of Barbarians"; for the Hindus of modern India to be treated with the respect they deserved, it needed to be more widely recognized that they constituted "a knowing and ingenious race of men," "descended from ancestors who had attained to a very high degree of improvement, many ages before the least step towards civilization had been taken in any part of Europe."[11]

Robertson claimed at different times both that India had *once* enjoyed a high level of civilization, and that it *remained* at a relatively advanced stage of development. If Robertson asserted that "the commercial genius of Europe" had given it "a visible ascendant over the three other divisions of the earth," he also claimed that certain features of modern Indian society – such as the distinction of ranks or the separation of professions – could only be found "among men in the most improved state of society, and under the best forms of government."[12] Rather than consider the role of the British as rulers of India, Robertson's work looked to the benefits of a more extensive commercial traffic with India, that would further "familiariz[e] and reconcil[e] men of hostile principles and discordant manners to one another."[13] This account of a past and future partnership with India needs to be approached with skepticism, not least since such an idealized commercial reciprocity has historically served as "capitalism's ideology of itself."[14] Robertson's matter-of-fact emphasis on the long history of interaction between Europe and Asia strikingly foregrounds, nonetheless, the possibilities of peaceful and mutually beneficial contact.

Many Scottish writers on India after Robertson took British political control as a given, in the short to medium term at least, and asserted Western or European superiority in a less equivocal manner. The version of "improvement" favored by influential provincial governors such as Thomas Munro, Mountstuart Elphinstone, and Sir John Malcolm, however, was clearly distinct from the kind of development that was envisaged by both utilitarians and evangelicals, which involved the emancipation of India from itself. Munro, Elphinstone, and Malcolm all defended customary property arrangements, and opposed the extension of the Permanent Settlement instituted by Cornwallis in 1793. Members of this "paternalist school," as it has been dubbed by Eric Stokes, saw themselves less as agents of transformative modernization, consequently, than as overseers of gradual change.[15] In his *Sketch of the Political History of India* (1811), for example, Malcolm underlined the responsibility of the British to their Indian subjects, "whose condition it must be our continual study to improve."[16] "Empire is held solely by opinion," Malcolm claimed, and "though we must continue to govern as conquerors, it is our duty to make our rule a benefit to mankind; and to carry among those whom we have subdued, the blessings of peace, knowledge, and improvement."[17] This emphasis on "duty" can easily be read, of course, as a bid to sanitize an exploitative interventionist agenda. As Martha McLaren has argued, however, many Scots were optimistic about the potential benefits of British rule to India and its people, partly at least as a result of their assessment of the benefits that accrued to Scotland from the Union of 1707. If Sir John Malcolm "thought in terms of a more permanent British imperium," according to McLaren, writers such as Munro and Elphinstone fashioned themselves as "mentors," seeking to guide India to "a 'stage of improvement' that would allow them to govern their own country – presumably as independent but friendly allies of Britain."[18]

In his works of history and ethnography dealing with India and Persia, Sir John Malcolm stressed both that "Human nature is always the same, in whatever garb it is clothed," and that the "dispensation of happiness and misery" over the globe was more or less equal.[19] For Malcolm, as for many other contemporary Scottish writers, any focus on Eastern peoples or societies was also necessarily an exploration of "the general history of mankind."[20] As Norbert Peabody has argued, a work such as James Tod's *Annals and Antiquities of Rajast'han* (1829–32), for example, often deployed analogies with feudalism in its survey of Rajput society, instead of simply resorting to the familiar mythology of oriental despotism. "Indological discourse," according to Peabody, was not simply "premised on the attribution of discrete, oppositional essences, that ontologically separated East from West," but was also "based on the idea that there was a fundamental unity, or single essence, underlying all mankind."[21] Most commonly, perhaps, analogies were drawn in this period between a variety of mountain-dwelling "Eastern" peoples and the inhabitants of the Scottish Highlands. In the notes to the second canto of *Childe Harold's Pilgrimage* (1813), for example, Lord Byron famously claimed to have been struck by the "resemblance . . . in dress, figure, and manner of living" between the "Arnaouts, or Albanese" and "the Highlanders of Scotland."[22] John Leyden similarly bestowed a "mountaineer's approbation" upon the "frank, open and bold demeanour" of the Tamils of southern India, while

Mountstuart Elphinstone, in much more detail, noted the resemblance of "the Afghaun country" to the situation of Scotland "in ancient times."[23] Such analogies, drawn by different observers of Eastern peoples, were seen to bear out abstract intellectual (or "philosophical") claims about the universal applicability of stadial history. Afghan society "has so many features in common with the ancient state of the Teutonic nations of Europe," James Mackintosh claimed in a review of Elphinstone's work, "that the picture might be suspected of being at least insensibly colored by the fancy of a theorist, if closer examination did not discover numerous peculiarities which characterize all real objects."[24]

Elphinstone's later work clearly testifies to the declining authority of the "philosophical" position that underpinned such comparative ethnography, so that where his *Account of the Kingdom of Caubul* had compared different peoples with reference to the universally applicable stages of civil society, his *History of India* (1841) at times asserted instead that "some races are certainly less vigorous than others."[25] Eighteenth-century Scottish writers such as Lord Kames and John Pinkerton had already speculated about the essential characteristics of different peoples or races,[26] but the shift of emphasis in the work of Elphinstone was continuous with a much larger-scale reaction against the language of stadial development. Drawing attention to the permanent and unchanging "defects of character" in the Hindu population of India, Elphinstone now privileged the explanatory power of "moral causes" and "physical constitution" ahead of environmental determinants such as "soil and climate."[27] In a hostile 1827 review of the *Memoirs of Baber, Emperor of Hindustan*, a work translated by John Leyden and William Erskine, Francis Jeffrey similarly claimed that it was impossible to explain the apparently "stationary and degenerate condition" of modern India on "what are called philosophical principles," and therefore concluded that there was "a natural and inherent difference in the character and temperament of the European and Asiatic races." Europeans, according to Jeffrey, possessed "a superior capacity of patient and persevering thought," along with "a more sober and robust understanding, and a more reasonable, principled, and inflexible morality"; "the Eastern races," by contrast, were not only lacking in such qualities, but also incapable of acquiring them, and therefore eternally condemned to their "vices and sufferings," and a state of "palpable inferiority."[28]

Jeffrey's essay went with the tide of an increasingly censorious commentary on Eastern cultures, represented most famously by the writing of James Mill and T. B. Macaulay. In the work of Scott, however, the conceptual frame provided by philosophical history continued to override the authority of the position taken by figures such as Jeffrey. In his 1816 essay "The Culloden Papers," for example, Scott appealed to Elphinstone's analogy between Afghans and Highlanders so as to stress the universality of human nature: eighteenth-century Highland manners revealed far more about the stage of society which was their primary determinant than about any essential characteristics of the Highlanders themselves.[29] Scott's later works, too, clearly testify to the impact of his intellectual inheritance, as well as to his affiliation with some of the writers already discussed. Novels dealing with the East such as *The Surgeon's Daughter* and *The Talisman* to some extent construct India and Palestine as fantastic romance settings, it is true, and in comparison with his earlier and more famous works set in Scotland, pay little attention to the detail of customs and manners. The denigratory tone that characterizes so much of the writing on the East by Scott's contemporaries is nonetheless almost entirely absent from *The Surgeon's Daughter* or *The Talisman*. Like the works of Scottish Enlightenment cultural comparison referred to above, these novels eschew speculation about the innate character of Eastern peoples, and playfully contest the mythology of oriental despotism that was so widely and uncritically invoked to characterize Eastern societies. But these novels do not simply underwrite a pre-ordained, homogenizing trajectory of societal development. Whereas the Scottish orientalists discussed above generally took for granted the necessity and inevitability of "modernization" along Western lines (certainly in the case of India), *The Surgeon's Daughter* and *The Talisman* make little resort to the rhetoric of temporalization in their treatment of India and Palestine; if a novel such as *Waverley* defines the contrast between cultures as a contrast between primitive and advanced epochs or stages of society,[30] this framing of "contrast" is far less prominent in *The Surgeon's Daughter*, and entirely absent from *The Talisman*.

Scott's interest in the juxtaposition of European and Asian peoples is clearly illustrated by his second novel, *Guy Mannering* (1815), published a year before "The Culloden Papers." *Guy Mannering* established the conjunction of domestic and imperial themes that was to characterize many of the later Waverley novels, drawing a suggestive comparison between the eviction of a gypsy community from the estate of Ellangowan and the dispossession of Indian labourers from their land by the Permanent Settlement.[31] Like *Guy Mannering*, *St. Ronan's Well* (1823) deals with the impact of a returning "nabob," employing the caricatured figure of "Peregrine Touchwood" – a far more ambivalent character than Guy Mannering – in order to bring about the resolution of its plot. To a greater extent than either of these works, though, *The Surgeon's Daughter* addresses the interconnection of Scotland and the East, and pays tribute to the famed Scottish affinity for India in particular. Since India is "the true place for a Scot to thrive in," Andrew Fairscribe advises his friend Chrystal Croftangry in the novel's preface, it must also be the right place for any aspiring author to send the "Muse of Fiction."[32] Croftangry invokes "the various religious costumes, habits, and manners of the people of Hindustan" as potentially "glorious and unbounded subjects" (155), only to add that he lacks the credentials to write about them, since he has never been to India; in response to this objection, Fairscribe replies that "You will tell us about them all the better that you know nothing of what you are saying" (155). Scott's letters and journal entries of the mid 1820s reveal a similar awareness of the need for literary diversification, as well as comparable anxieties about finding the appropriate "seasoning of curry powder," the right balance between the familiar and the exotic, that would help to make a work such as *The Surgeon's Daughter* attractive to its audience.[33] Even if Scott always kept in mind the imperatives of the marketplace, however, his novel clearly sought to disrupt the expectations that readers brought to a work of fiction dealing with the East.

Recalling the way that he was "induced to face a tea-party" (286) with the manuscript of his novel, Scott's narratorial persona Chrystal Croftangry states that his audience only began to seem interested over halfway through his performance – "when we got to the East Indies" (287). The novel's early scenes, set in Britain, nonetheless crucially establish the contrasting characters of Richard Middlemas and Adam Hartley, apprentices to the Scottish village doctor, Gideon Gray. The relationship between the two is defined in the schematic terms of an opposition between "adventure" and "duty," concepts which are mapped in turn upon an opposition between England and Scotland. Middlemas's status is complicated by the fact that he is implicitly orientalized even before he gets to India, since he is the dark-eyed, illegitimate son of the "Jewess" Zilia de Moncada. But Middlemas significantly claims to be a "free-born Englishman" (182), and repudiates the land of his birth, whereas Hartley, despite being born "on the English side of the Border" (187), personifies the prudence and respectability that Middlemas disdainfully identifies with the Scots. The gulf between the two apprentices continues to widen as a result of their competition over the surgeon's daughter of the title, Menie Gray. Hartley's response to the news of his rival's secret engagement to Menie is to leave the scene of his disappointment, and to travel to India as surgeon's mate on a ship in the Company's service. Already signaling his desire to join the army, and hinting at "the supposed rank and importance of his parents" (186),

Middlemas for his part finds that the pull of India overrides any attachment to his fiancée. Middlemas rebels against the fate mapped out for him in the "infernal wilderness" of Scotland, and dreams instead of the "lacs and crores of rupees" (199) to be gained in India, a land "where gold is won by steel," and "where a brave man cannot pitch his desire of fame so high, but that he may realize it" (198).

Shortly after this exchange with Hartley, Middlemas's ambition is further stoked by the English recruiting agent, Tom Hillary, who seduces him with "lavish oratory" about "the exploits of a Lawrence and a Clive" (203):

Palaces rose like mushrooms in his descriptions; groves of lofty trees, and aromatic shrubs unknown to the chilly soils of Europe, were tenanted by every object of the chase, from the royal tiger down to the jackall. The luxuries of a natch, and the peculiar Oriental beauty of the enchantresses who perfumed their voluptuous Eastern domes for the pleasure of their haughty English conquerors, were no less attractive than the battles and sieges on which the captain at other times expatiated. (203)

The Surgeon's Daughter makes the most of a formulaic exoticism in a passage such as this, accentuating the "gaudy splendour" of the East in a manner reminiscent perhaps of Thomas Moore's best-selling poem *Lalla Rookh* (1817).[34] Even if Scott's India remains to some extent a romance space, however, his work also contextualizes such "lavish oratory," since the "scenes of ... Indian adventures" (212) invoked by Hillary are shown to serve the purpose of enticing more recruits into the Company's service. This recruitment process is represented in some detail, indeed, as the distance between myth and reality is starkly delineated. Middlemas is drugged and robbed by Hillary, before he finds himself in a military hospital on the Isle of Wight, where he dreams in De Quinceyan terms of "parched deserts, and of serpents whose bite inflicted the most intolerable thirst" (212), rather than of oriental beauties and limitless riches. Scott's novel makes it clear that the methods of Tom Hillary belonged to an earlier, superseded phase of Company rule, of course, and offers little to any reader looking for direct comment on more contemporary policy debates. The influence of Hillary over Middlemas is clearly labelled as a "despotic" (206) one, nonetheless, and Scott therefore confronts the reader with the spectacle of Company despotism *before* introducing those familiar figures from the rogue's gallery of oriental despots, Hyder Ali and Tipu Sultan.

The initial opposition between Middlemas and Hartley is maintained as the focus of the novel moves to India. Having eventually gained a commission via the secret intervention of his father, Middlemas rapidly becomes an outcast from European society, after killing his commanding officer in a dispute about his birth and his real family name. Middlemas subsequently becomes a double agent, but his motives are the subject of speculation, and he is widely suspected of being in the service of Hyder Ali. According to the captivity narrative of James Scurry, published in 1824, Hyder Ali and Tipu Sultan were "distinguished, and not less detested, throughout every part of the civilized world, for the cruelties which they practised on their prisoners of war."[35] Regardless of this popular reputation, however, Scott's work still says little about Hyder and his son at this stage, underlining instead that it is Middlemas whose character is stained with dishonor. (Having encouraged Menie Gray to follow him to India, Middlemas plans to use his fiancée as the bait in a trap to capture Tipu Sultan, and thereby regain his reputation.) Hartley, by contrast, is depicted throughout as a selfless figure who sublimates his love for Menie Gray, and is motivated by ideals of duty and service to the extent that he "attended the poor of all nations gratis, whenever he was called upon" (245). Furthermore, Hartley establishes a significant relationship with one of Hyder Ali's agents, Barak El Hadgi, at a time when there is still said to be a "good understanding" (248) between their respective governments. This friendship is described in relatively sober and unsentimental terms, but it briefly establishes the possibility of peaceful cross-cultural dialogue and exchange. On his first visit to Barak, for example, at the tomb of Cara Razi, Hartley "laid aside his shoes at the gates of the holy precincts," in compliance with "the Mahomedan custom," and offered "the usual salutation of Salam Alaikum" (247). After declining payment for the consultation, Hartley goes on to state his belief that "the wise of every country are brethren," a sentiment endorsed by the shocked Barak: "A Feringi then can refuse gold!" (247).

When Hartley first encounters Menie Gray again, she is in the service of the Amazonian Madame de Montreville, "the Queen of Sheba" (249), a shadowy figure who acts on her own account; like Middlemas, Madame de Montreville is suspected of apostasy, living "in the black town" (253) of Madras. Hartley uses his friendship with Barak as a means of making a direct appeal to Hyder Ali, so as to save his childhood friend from the "deceit about to be practised towards [her]" (260). The threat faced by Menie Gray has to be presented as a genuine one, and Scott describes the way that Menie was "destined by a profligate and treacherous lover to the fate of slavery to a heathen tyrant" (277). If Tipu Sultan is presented here in conventional terms as a licentious oriental despot, however, Hyder Ali subsequently intervenes to rebuke his upstart son, and is popularly acclaimed in the process as a deus ex machina: "the good, the wise, the discoverer of hidden things, who cometh into the Divan like the sun bursting from the clouds" (282). Hyder interrupts the ceremony of Middlemas's investiture as the "Bukshee," or commander-in-chief, of Tipu's armies, and orders his son to renounce his claim on Menie Gray: "cursed is the prince who barters justice for lust" (282). Not only does Hyder free Menie Gray, though, but he also passes judgment on Middlemas as a plotter against the government of Mysore. In a remarkable scene a few pages before the close of the novel, Middlemas is told to accept "the fruit of the justice of Hyder," and subsequently crushed to death by an elephant: "Curling his long trunk around the neck of the ill-fated European, the monster suddenly threw the wretch prostrate before him, and stamping his huge shapeless foot upon his breast, put an end at once to his life and crimes" (284). Hyder's bypassing of legal process clearly conforms to stereotypes of oriental despotism, and Scott can perhaps be seen here to contribute towards the evangelically inspired "Gothicization" of India.[36] At the same time, though, Hyder is clearly presented as a potent and legitimate ruler, and Scott's work offers no comment on the ethical dimensions of Hyder's conduct; the scene of the execution, the reader is told, is one of "just punishment . . . faithfully exhibited" (285).

"Hitherto I have been in the Carnatic as a mild Prince," Hyder Ali exclaims after the execution of Richard Middlemas, "in future I will be a destroying tempest!" (284). Although *The Surgeon's Daughter* takes the British presence in India as a given, it is significant not only that Hyder is left undefeated at the close of the novel, but that he is even in effect provided with a justification – in the form of Middlemas's treachery – for the resumption of hostilities. (The editor of the recent Edinburgh edition convincingly dates the action of the work in the period preceding the second Mysore War of 1780–4.)[37] The military defeat of Tipu Sultan in 1799 is often represented as a pivotal moment in the establishment of the British ascendancy in India, yet despite Scott's well-documented fascination with military history, and with the Battle of Seringapatam in particular,[38] his work only minimally alludes to the eventual fall of the Kingdom of Mysore and the subsequent consolidation of British rule. Though *The Surgeon's Daughter* valorizes Adam Hartley's ethic of service, and implicitly underwrites the concept of imperial duty outlined by Sir John Malcolm, the novel does little to locate the British role in India within any larger framework of either military domination or administrative and economic "improvement." *The Surgeon's Daughter* seems so non-affirmative, furthermore, since it also rejects what Scott's narratorial persona claimed ought to be its "natural conclusion." Rather than depict the marriage of Hartley and Menie Gray, Scott concluded instead by describing how "the gallant and disinterested Hartley fell a victim to his professional courage," and died from "a contagious distemper" (285). The character of Hartley was apparently modeled on Scott's protégé, the polymath John Leyden, who travelled to India as a Company surgeon in 1803, and died of malaria in Java in 1811; Leyden, Scott wrote in a memoir of his life, was "perhaps the first British traveller that ever sought India, moved neither by the love of wealth nor of power."[39] As Iain Gordon Brown has emphasized, Scott wrote *The Surgeon's Daughter* at a time when his own son Walter was faced with the prospect of being posted to India with his regiment.[40] Far from appealing to any grand narrative of empire, therefore, Scott tempered sensation with pathos, focusing on the everyday toil of individuals devoted to the service of British interests in India.

The sombre conclusion of *The Surgeon's Daughter* has few parallels in British fiction of empire before the last decades of the nineteenth century. Scott's novel is all the more remarkable since by the time it was written the dominant prose works dealing with the East were picaresque novels such as Thomas Hope's *Anastasius, or, Memoirs of a Greek* (1819), James Morier's *The Adventures of Hajji Baba of Ispahan* (1824), and William Browne Hockley's *Pandurang Hari, or Memoirs of a Hindoo* (1826). Whereas eighteenth-century writers such as Smollett had resorted to the picaresque as a means of fostering cultural comparison and mutual understanding, the works referred to above accentuated the denigratory tone of Mill's *History of British India*, presenting their fictitious narrators as sources of inside information as well as amusement. In the introduction to *Pandurang Hari*, for example, Hockley characterized "the Hindoo," "from the rajah to the ryot," as "ungrateful, insidious, cowardly, unfaithful, and revengeful"; Morier's *Hajji Baba*, similarly, presented itself as a survey-type focus on the innate character of "the Persian," and was widely acclaimed for the perspective that it appeared to offer on the comical corruption and despotism of Persian society.[41] Conscious as ever of the literary marketplace, Scott claimed in his Magnum introduction to *The Talisman* that he adopted the topic of the Crusades so as to avoid "entering into competition" with novelists such as Hope and Morier, and poets such as Byron, Moore, and Southey, who had "already so successfully" dealt with Eastern material.[42] Not only did Scott lay claim to a degree of fictional novelty, though, but he also clearly distanced his work from the example set by picaresque narratives such as *Anastasius* or *Hajji Baba*. Even more than *The Surgeon's Daughter*, *The Talisman* disrupts the expectations of its readers, and complicates its account of the encounter between East and West.

The Talisman is clearly informed both by the eighteenth-century revisionist polemic against the folly and insanity of the crusading enterprise, and by the focus of historians such as William Robertson on the beneficial consequences, to the West, of this encounter with "a more polished people."[43] In the Magnum introduction to *The Talisman*, Scott playfully recasts the opposition between Richard, "the Christian and English monarch" who "showed all the cruelty and violence of an Eastern sultan," and Saladin, who "displayed the deep policy and prudence of a European sovereign" (2). Although "cruelty and violence" remain somehow essentially "Eastern" properties in this equation, Scott nonetheless foregrounds the issue of contact or exchange as the subject of his work.[44] As is well known, *The Talisman* begins with a long description of the contest of arms between the Scottish "knight of the Red-cross" (13) Sir Kenneth and the "Saracen cavalier" (16) Sheerkohf – Saladin in disguise. This resonant episode, seemingly establishing an irreducible antagonism between Christianity and Islam, was excerpted in numerous reviews of the novel, and commended for its picturesque qualities. Yet many readers also complained that Scott's work failed to depict any further, larger-scale conflict: "here we are altogether among the Crusaders," the *Monthly Magazine* stated, "in the very heart of the camp, and yet without a battle."[45] Sir Kenneth and Sheerkohf terminate their combat with a truce, and thereafter develop a friendship founded on "mutual respect" (26) and curiosity, in a similar manner to Adam Hartley and Barak El Hadgi in *The Surgeon's Daughter*. The erstwhile adversaries communicate in an established "lingua franca" (18), and Scott's work further acknowledges the consequences of the contact that has already taken place by referring to the way that the Saracens "gradually caught" chivalric manners from the invading "Western Christians" (20). *The Talisman* supplied an insight into "the glorious, gorgeous East," as one reviewer claimed, but nonetheless offered "too little Orientalism" in relation to other contemporary works such as Moore's *Lalla Rookh*.[46] Rather than resort to a familiar register of exoticism, Scott's work insistently returns to the issue of the apparently inevitable interaction between East and West, all the while eschewing those metaphors of contagion, disease, or infection that characterize so many other Romantic accounts of actual or imagined "contact."[47] Halfway through the novel, for example, Saladin defends his claim on the hand of Lady Edith of Plantagenet by pointing to the precedents afforded by Muslim Spain: "Seest thou not how the Mahommedan princes daily intermarry with the noble Nazarene maidens in Spain, without scandal either to Moor or Christian?" (160). Shortly afterwards, Scott describes how "the luxury and indulgence of the Christian leaders had occasioned a motley concourse in their tents," comprising "Jewish merchants, Copts, Turks," and so on: "the caftan and the turban, though to drive them from the Holy Land was the professed object of the expedition, were nevertheless neither an uncommon nor an alarming sight in the camp of the Crusaders" (219).

The intimacy of the contact between the forces of the Cross and the Crescent is most clearly figured in the implicitly homoerotic relationship between the warrior-kings Richard and Saladin (perhaps the closest that Scott comes in these novels to the depiction of transcultural desire). Even though he usually refers to him as an "infidel" or "paynim," Richard – like Sir Kenneth – proclaims his admiration of Saladin throughout the work, stating that Saladin "loves me as I love him – as noble adversaries ever love each other" (94). Sheerkohf advertises his descent from the Muslim Satan, Eblis, early in the novel, and Edward Said has plausibly suggested that Scott got much of his information about Islam from writers such as William Beckford and Lord Byron.[48] If Scott's Saladin is a composite romance figure, though, his conduct throughout the novel is still so impressive as to make him, as one reviewer stated, "almost the hero of the tale."[49] Saladin is a rational critic of the crusading zeal personified by the Hermit of Engaddi, and he remains a tolerant protector of "the good men who, without stirring up nation against nation, worship sincerely in the faith of Issa Ben Mariam" (30). (Sir Kenneth shows himself to be the bigoted one, meanwhile, by referring to the prophet Mohammed as "the camel-driver of Mecca" [31].) In the guise of the physician El Hakim, Saladin later refuses money for his treatment of Richard, just as Adam Hartley refuses payment for treating Barak El Hadgi in *The Surgeon's Daughter*; "this Moor, in his independence," according to Richard, "might set an example to them who account themselves the flower of knighthood" (130).

Praise of Saladin as an individual was a feature of work by contemporaries of Scott, such as Charles Mills, as well as of histories by Hume and Gibbon.[50] In addition to disrupting the opposition between the Cross and the Crescent, however, *The Talisman* also undermines the united front pledged by the supporters of the Cross. As in *Ivanhoe*, the Templars are shown to pursue their own agenda, and their Grand Master is said to be a "worse pagan" (77) than Saladin. The Christian princes nominally allied with Richard, the reader is told, "would have sacrificed all hope of victory over the Saracens, to the pleasure of ruining, or at least of humbling, Richard of England" (102). Richard, in turn, claims that if Saladin would but "abjure his false law," he would help him "drive this scum of French and Austrians from his dominions" (108). After his initial refusal to countenance the proposed marriage between Saladin and his "kinswoman"

Edith, Richard asks why he should not after all "seek for brotherhood and alliance with a Saracen" (200) at a time when "the princes of Christendom shrink from the side of their allies" (201). An aggressively expansionist Christendom is superseded by a more securely grounded British Unionism as the virtues – and the nobility – of the Scot Sir Kenneth become clear to all. If the rhetorical movement of *The Talisman* can be characterized by such a shift in allegiances, then this process reaches its climax when Saladin summarily executes the Grand Master of the Templars, guilty of having finished off his partner in crime, the wounded Conrade of Montserrat. Having opened with such a resonant contest of arms, apparently symbolizing the irreducible enmity between rival religions or rival power blocs, *The Talisman* closes with the slaughter of an offender against the joint Christian enterprise by its main adversary. Like Hyder Ali's despatching of Middlemas in *The Surgeon's Daughter*, Saladin's execution of Giles Amaury is recognized, by Richard, as a "great act of justice" (311).

According to the *New Monthly Magazine*, Scott deflated the aura that surrounded the Crusades, "divesting the magnificent fiction of half its wonders."[51] One of the things that makes *The Talisman* such a fascinating novel is that it was written at a time when the counter-revisionist reaction against Enlightenment historians was in full swing. Kenelm Digby's conduct book *The Broad Stone of Honour* (1823), for example, repudiated the work of, among others, Hume and Gibbon, and presented the Crusades as an idealistic enterprise, in which "all Europe was united in a band of brothers to worship the Saviour of mankind."[52] Numerous writers in this period also positioned the Crusades in the context of a series of violent conflicts between apparently eternal enemies. For Chateaubriand, in his *Travels in Greece, Palestine, Egypt, and Barbary* (1811), for example, the Crusades represented an early phase in the ongoing antagonism between Islam, "a religion hostile to civilization, systematically favourable to ignorance, despotism, and slavery," and Christianity, "a religion which has revived among the moderns the spirit of learned antiquity and abolished servitude."[53] Robert Southey similarly claimed to "love and vindicate the crusades," and he elevated the Peninsular war against Napoleonic France to the status of "a crusade on the part of us and the Spaniards."[54] Southey's references to an earlier "holy war" against the Moors in eighth-century Spain were especially bloodthirsty, and one reviewer commented on "the peculiar gusto with which the Saracens are slaughtered" throughout Southey's epic poem *Roderick, the Last of the Goths* (1814).[55] In *The Talisman*, by contrast, Scott frustrated any demand for scenes of battle or combat, as he did almost throughout the Waverley novels. Works such as *Ivanhoe* and

The Betrothed, like *The Talisman*, complicate any sense of the crusades as a national endeavor, and have far more to say about the lack of common purpose among the disunited (and ethnically heterogeneous) English than about the inevitability of the opposition between Christians and Muslims; given that the Jews Isaac and Rebecca flee to Grenada at the end of the novel, indeed, *Ivanhoe* suggests that Muslim Spain in the late twelfth century is a more tolerant place than Christian England. Scott's often playful treatment of the antagonism between Christianity and Islam, Crusader and Saracen, is just as evident in his penultimate novel, *Count Robert of Paris* (1831). Set in late eleventh-century Byzantium, on the eve of the First Crusade, *Count Robert*, like *The Talisman*, focuses on the feuding and rivalry among the gathered Christian forces; their Muslim adversaries are all but absent from the novel, and the mythology of oriental despotism is invoked only in order to describe the *Grecian* Emperor, Alexius Comnena.

This account of Scott's critical distance from the example of his contemporaries needs to be qualified, not least since so many readers have found it possible to assimilate the Waverley novels into a genealogy of imperialist adventure-fiction, and since so many later writers went on to use Scott's work as a model for more clearly celebratory accounts of the networks and circuits of empire.[56] For all the playfulness and the rhetorical complexity of the Waverley novels, indeed, Scott never questioned the morality of the British presence overseas, and – judging by the evidence of his correspondence or his Journal – seemed most exercised by his role as a patron of East India Company recruits.[57] As I have argued, though, novels such as *The Surgeon's Daughter* and *The Talisman* offer striking accounts of peaceful contact and exchange, which are all the more remarkable when considered in the context of other writing about the East in the early nineteenth century. These novels also offer an important perspective on the afterlife of the Scottish Orientalism discussed at the beginning of this chapter. "The history of [the] Scottish contribution to orientalist writing" from Robertson to James Mill, as Jane Rendall has argued, "is also . . . the history of the decline of this distinctive approach."[58] By the 1820s the University of Edinburgh was renowned far less for the philosophical history of writers such as Robertson than for nascent theories of race grounded in biology and comparative anatomy. In an increasingly uncongenial intellectual climate, nonetheless, Scott upheld the idea of human uniformity and eschewed the language of type and essence; in novels such as *The Surgeon's Daughter* and *The Talisman*, furthermore, Scott disrupted the assimilatory trajectory of stadial progression and improvement, and examined the often unpredictable consequences of cultural contact and encounter.

NOTES

Many thanks to Harriet Guest and Jane Rendall for reading the first draft of this chapter.

1. Sir Walter Scott, "The Culloden Papers," first published in the *Quarterly Review* 1816, rpt. in *The Miscellaneous Prose Works of Sir Walter Scott*, 28 vols. (Edinburgh: Robert Cadell, 1835, 1836), xx: 1–93 (p. 10).

2. Jane Rendall, "Scottish Orientalism: from Robertson to James Mill," *The Historical Journal* 25, 1 (1982): 43–69.

3. See Francis Jeffrey's review of the translation of the *Memoirs of Baber, Emperor of Hindustan, The Edinburgh Review* 46 (June 1827): 39–75.

4. See, for example, John M. Mackenzie, "On Scotland and the Empire," *International History Review* 15 (November 1993): 714–39.

5. James Mill, *The History of British India* (Chicago: University of Chicago Press, 1975), 228.

6. *Ibid.*, 248.

7. *Ibid.*, 212. Note, however, Javed Majeed's persuasive argument that the *History* was a "self-reflexive" work, which was "first and foremost an attack on the ruling British ideology of the time," *Ungoverned Imaginings: James Mill's "The History of British India"* (Oxford: Clarendon Press, 1992), 195.

8. James Mill, *The History of British India*, 234 and 248.

9. Jane Rendall, "Scottish Orientalism", 44.

10. William Robertson, *An Historical Disquisition concerning the Knowledge which the Ancients had of India; and the Progress of Trade with that Country prior to the Discovery of the Passage to it by the Cape of Good Hope. With an Appendix, containing Observations on the Civil Policy – the Laws and Judicial Proceedings – the Arts – the Sciences – and Religious Institutions of the Indians* (London, 1791), 261.

11. *Ibid.*, 336.

12. *Ibid.*, 167 and 270.

13. *Ibid.*, 103.

14. Mary Louise Pratt, *Imperial Eyes: Travel Writing and Transculturation* (London: Routledge, 1992), 84.

15. Eric Stokes, *The English Utilitarians and India* (Oxford: Clarendon Press, 1959), 18.

16. Sir John Malcolm, *Sketch of the Political History of India, from the introduction of Mr Pitt's Bill, A.D. 1784, to the Present Date* (London, 1811), 9.

17. *Ibid.*, 169.

18. Martha McLaren, "From Analysis to Prescription: Scottish Concepts of Asian Despotism in Early Nineteenth-Century British India," *International History Review* 15 (August 1993): 469–501 (500).

19. Sir John Malcolm, *The History of Persia, from the most early Period to the present Time*, 2 vols. (London: William Miller, 1815), 1: 620 and 619.

20. Sir John Malcolm, *Sketch of the Sikhs; a singular Nation, who inhabit the Provinces of the Punjab situated between the Rivers Jumna and Indus* (London, 1812), 5.

21. Norbert Peabody, "Tod's *Rajast'han* and the Boundaries of Imperial Rule in Nineteenth-Century India," *Modern Asian Studies* 30, 1 (1996): 185–220 (188).
22. Lord Byron, *Selected Poems*, eds. Susan J. Wolfson and Peter J. Manning (Harmondsworth: Penguin, 1996), 131.
23. John Leyden, quoted in Nigel Leask, "Towards an Anglo-Indian Poetry? The Colonial Muse in the Writings of John Leyden, Thomas Medwin and Charles D'Oyly," in Bart Moore-Gilbert (ed.), *Writing India 1757–1990: The Literature of British India* (Manchester: Manchester University Press, 1996), 52–85 (59); Mountstuart Elphinstone, *An Account of the Kingdom of Caubul, and its Dependencies in Persia, Tartary, and India* (London, 1815), 173.
24. James Mackintosh, "Western Asia," *The Edinburgh Review* 25 (October 1815): 398–442 (424).
25. Mountstuart Elphinstone, *The History of India. The Hindu and Mahometan Periods*, 4th edn (London, 1857), 194.
26. See, for example, Henry Homes, Lord Kames, *Sketches of the History of Man* (1st edn, Edinburgh: printed for W. Creech, Edinburgh; London: printed for W. Strahan and T. Cadell, London, 1774) and John Pinkerton, *A Dissertation on the Origin and Progress of the Scythians or Goths* (London: printed by John Nichols, for George Nicol, 1787).
27. Elphinstone, *The History of India*, 194.
28. Francis Jeffrey, review of *Memoirs of Baber*, *The Edinburgh Review* (1827): 42–4.
29. Scott, "The Culloden Papers," *Quarterly Review* (1816); see also Colin Kidd, *Subverting Scotland's Past: Scottish Whig Historians and the Creation of an Anglo-British identity, 1689–c.1830* (Cambridge: Cambridge University Press, 1993), 259–60.
30. For an account of the pastness of the Highlands in *Waverley*, see Saree Makdisi, *Romantic Imperialism: Universal Empire and the Culture of Modernity* (Cambridge: Cambridge University Press, 1998), 70–99.
31. See Peter Garside's essay, "Meg Merrilies in India," in J. H. Alexander and David Hewitt (eds.), *Scott in Carnival: Selected Papers from the Fourth International Scott Conference, 1991*, (Aberdeen: Association for Scottish Literary Studies, 1993), 154–71 (164).
32. Sir Walter Scott, *Chronicles of the Canongate*, ed. Claire Lamont (Edinburgh: Edinburgh University Press, 2000), 155. Future references to this edition will be given in the text.
33. Quoted in Iain Gordon Brown, "Griffins, Nabobs and a Seasoning of Curry Powder: Walter Scott and the Indian Theme in Life and Literature," in Anne Buddle, with Pauline Rohtagi and Iain Gordon Brown (eds.), *The Tiger and the Thistle: Tipu Sultan and the Scots in India 1760–1800* (Edinburgh: National Gallery of Scotland, 1999), 71–9 (73).
34. The phrase "gaudy splendour" comes from the *Critical*'s review of *Lalla Rookh* (June 1817): 561–81 (562).
35. *The Captivity, Sufferings, and Escape, of James Scurry, who was detained a Prisoner during ten years, in the Dominions of Hyder Ali and Tippoo Saib* (London: Henry Fisher, 1824), 49. For a recent discussion of captivity narratives, see Linda

Colley, *Captives: Britain, Empire and the World 1600–1850* (London: Jonathan Cape, 2002), ch. 9.

36. For the "Gothicization of India" in the period, see for example Marilyn Butler, "Orientalism," in David B. Pirie (ed.), *The Romantic Period* (Harmondsworth: Penguin, 1994), 395–447 (415).
37. Scott, *Chronicles of the Canongate*, ed. Lamont, 448–9.
38. See Brown, "Griffins, Nabobs and a Seasoning of Curry Powder," 74.
39. John Leyden, *Poems and Ballads: with a Memoir of the Author by Sir Walter Scott, Bart* (Kelso: J. and J. H. Rutherford, 1858), 42.
40. Brown, "Griffins, Nabobs and a Seasoning of Curry Powder," 74.
41. William Browne Hockley, *Pandurang Hari, or Memoirs of a Hindoo*, 3 vols. (London, 1826), 1: xiv.
42. Sir Walter Scott, *The Talisman* (London: J. M. Dent, 1991), 2. Future references to this edition will appear in the text.
43. William Robertson, *The History of the Reign of the Emperor Charles V. With a View of the Progress of Society in Europe. From the Subversion of the Roman Empire, to the Beginning of the Sixteenth Century*, 3 vols. (London, 1769), 1: 26.
44. Ian Duncan discusses "the chiasmus or crossover of properties of 'East' and 'West' personified in the rival princes," in "Scott's Romance of Empire: The Tales of the Crusaders," in Alexander and Hewitt (eds.), *Scott in Carnival*, 371–9 (377).
45. Review of *Tales of the Crusaders*, *Monthly Magazine* 59 (July 1825): 551–2 (552).
46. Review of *Tales of the Crusaders*, *The Edinburgh Magazine* 16 (June 1825): 641–6 (645 and 646).
47. See, most recently, Alan Bewell, *Romanticism and Colonial Disease* (Baltimore: Johns Hopkins University Press, 1999).
48. Edward Said, *Orientalism* (Harmondsworth: Penguin, 1991), 101.
49. Review of *Tales of the Crusaders*, *The Literary Gazette* 440 (1825): 401–5 (401).
50. See, for example, Charles Mills, *The History of the Crusades for the Recovery and Possession of the Holy Land*, 4th edn, 2 vols. (London, 1828), II: 143.
51. Review of *Tales of the Crusaders*, *New Monthly Magazine* 14 (July 1825): 27–32 (28).
52. Kenelm Digby, *The Broad Stone of Honour: or, Rules for the Gentlemen of England* (London: C. and J. Rivington, 1823), 49.
53. F. A. de Chateaubriand, *Travels in Greece, Palestine, Egypt, and Barbary, during the Years 1806 and 1807*, trans. Frederic Shoberl, 2 vols. (London: Henry Colburn, 1811), II: 62.
54. Robert Southey, letter to G. C. Bedford, November 17, 1808, in *The Life and Correspondence of the late Robert Southey*, ed. Charles Cuthbert Southey, 6 vols. (London: Longmans, 1850), III: 187.
55. Herman Merivale, review of Southey's *Poetical Works*, *The Edinburgh Review* (1839), rpt. in Lionel Madden (ed.), *Robert Southey: The Critical Heritage* (London: Routledge & Kegan Paul, 1972), 408.
56. See Martin Green's *Dreams of Adventure, Deeds of Empire* (London: Routledge & Kegan Paul, 1979); in works published by *Blackwood's Edinburgh Magazine*

especially, Katie Trumpener has claimed, "Scott's often ambivalent exploration of the nexus of nation and empire hardens into a celebratory . . . line," *Bardic Nationalism: The Romantic Novel and the British Empire* (Princeton: Princeton University Press, 1997), 270.

57. See Iain Gordon Brown, "Griffins, Nabobs and a Seasoning of Curry Powder," 77.

58. Rendall, "Scottish Orientalism," 69.

CHAPTER 6

Walter Scott's Romantic postmodernity

Jerome McGann

In 1884 "The Art of Fiction" was not what it was in 1819, or what it would become in the late twentieth-century aftermath of Henry James's celebrated Modernist manifesto. For James the art of fiction is *unam, sanctam, catholicam*, as is clear in his dismissal of the distinction, authoritative since Scott, between novel and romance.[1] "I can think of no obligation," James writes, "to which the romancer would not be held equally with the novelist." And why? Because the issue is a craft issue: "the standard of execution is equally high for each [and] it is of execution we are talking" ("The Art of Fiction," 56). Fair enough, one thinks. But when we recall what James says about Trollope in the same essay, we realize there are many rooms in the house of fiction, not all of them to James's fastidious taste:

Certain accomplished novelists have a habit of giving themselves away which must often bring tears to the eyes of people who take their fiction seriously. I was lately struck, in reading over many pages of Anthony Trollope, with his want of discretion in this particular. In a digression, a parenthesis or an aside, he concedes to the reader that he and his trusting friend are only "making believe." He admits that the events he narrates have not really happened, and that he can give his narrative any turn the reader may like best. Such a betrayal of a sacred office seems to me, I confess, a terrible crime [and] it shocks me every whit as much in Trollope as it would have shocked me in Gibbon or Macaulay. It implies that the novelist is less occupied in looking for the truth . . . than the historian, and in doing so it deprives him at a stroke of all his standing room. To represent and illustrate the past, the actions of men, is the task of either writer, and the only difference that I can see is, in proportion as he succeeds, to the honour of the novelist, consisting as it does in his having more difficulty in collecting his evidence . . . (46–7)

Although James calls Trollope to account, his real target is a far greater one, Walter Scott. Is it part of James's case for an art of discretion that he withholds the master's name at this crucial point? It is difficult not to think so. Scott's name seems written in invisible ink, that favored Jamesian medium, across this passage.

James's argument for a realist fiction, a Flaubertian argument, focuses on the artist's craft – on his ability to create verisimilar worlds that appear to stand on their own – looking, like Browning's duchess, as if they were alive. So far as James is concerned, Scott's work must be at best charming, at worst crude, rarely rigorous. How could one possibly install an integral imaginative world with all those Jedidiah Cleishbothams and Peter Pattiesons, Drs Rochecliffe and Dryasdust, who come to tell us in no uncertain terms that "the Author of Waverley" is only making believe?

An equally authoritative proponent of the great realist tradition appeared a half-century after James to explain how Scott brought off this feat of art. Consciously anti-Jamesian and anti-Flaubertian, Lukács argues that Scott's greatness "is not the product of a 'search for form' or some ingeniously contrived 'skill'."[2] It derives from his insight into the precise and complex dynamisms of society and history. This repudiation of Aestheticism comes with a critique of traditional, uncritical views of Scott. "What in Scott has been called very superficially 'authenticity of local colour' is in actual fact [the] artistic demonstration of historical reality. It is the portrayal of the broad living basis of historical events in their intricacy and complexity, in their manifold interaction with acting individuals" (*The Historical Novel*, 43).

In developing his case for Scott, Lukács makes two crucial moves. First, he insists that Scott has been mistakenly seen as a Romantic writer. On the contrary, Scott's work is "a renunciation of Romanticism, a conquest of Romanticism," and a repudiation of the "lyrical-subjectivist absolute" (33–4) that defines the essence of a Romantic art. The latter is epitomized in the heroes of the Gothic and Byronic tradition, and Scott's heroes, Lukács correctly observes, do not get measured in such terms. The second move involves a kind of deliberate amnesia: Lukács says nothing about the elaborate comic apparatus that Scott created to support and transmit his novels to the public. This material seems to have struck Lukács as inconsequential to Scott's great project: the epic portrayal of human beings struggling within an "Historical necessity . . . of the most severe, implacable kind" (58).

And yet Lukács might have fitted his argument to the Shandean material scattered about the Prefaces, Postscripts, Appendices, and Notes of Scott's novels. Lukács, that is to say, might have pursued the implications of one of his most acute insights about Scott: that the books feed off a deliberate and "necessary anachronism." Unlike "post-1848" writers, Scott "*never modernizes* the psychology of his characters" (60), and Lukács shrewdly connects this commitment of the writing to Hegel's view that a true historical insight is only possible "if the past . . . is clearly recognized and experienced by contemporary writers as the *necessary pre-history* of the present" (61). In this view of the matter one would have wanted Lukács to treat Jedidiah Cleishbotham, Peter Pattieson, *et al.* as fictional materials that define more precisely the historical divisions joining and separating the past from the present.

Why does Lukács not elaborate that argument? To answer the question I would return to James's critique of Trollope, and through Trollope to the whole line of fiction writers who "bare the device" of their artistic presence. In Scott, "the Author of Waverley" is a character of conscious make-believe; as such he is the determining focus of the fiction's recurrent patterns of comic spell-castings and spell-breakings. For his part Jedidiah Cleishbotham is a similar fantastic creature, like his many framing and prefatory cronies. All are characters drawn from the contemporary historical setting that is as crucial to the historicality of these fictions as are the scenes and events called from the past. For James, of course, all are equally characters drawn from a primitive stage of the art of fiction.

For Lukács, however, these figures locate a serious problem. They implicitly undermine his key argument about the anti-Romanticism of Scott's work. Romanticism for Lukács is a phenomenon of localities and individuals and its model is Byronism: on one hand the self-involved tumult of Giaours and Corsairs spinning to issueless exhaustion; on the other an airy or airless vortex, whether comical as in *Don Juan*, or brooding as in *Childe Harold*, Keats's *Hyperion*, Wordsworth's *Prelude*. Scott's work is perceived as different – a representation of "processes of historical change" whose accuracy stems from Scott's own conservative class and historical position. The "necessary anachronism" that Lukács sees there underpins an Hegelian/Marxist argument about history as a system of dynamic and progressive transformations. The historical dialectic traced out in the work casts what Shelley would call "the shadow of futurity" across a revolutionary history stretching from 1830 to 1930. That coming time is for Lukács both modeled and forecast in Scott's work. The novels comprise an Hegelian act of summation, a pivotal moment in the great historical shift from mercantile capitalism to international socialism.

And the novels might well have been precisely that – in a sense, they are precisely that – had Lukács's historiography proved true. In truth, however, his reconstruction of history must now seem to us in certain respects as quaint and idiosyncratic as Scott's history has often seemed to others. The quaintness is just inflected differently: in Scott it is antiquarian, in Lukács, theoretical.

Let me say here that these remarks make no pretense to a Higher Criticism of Scott, or for that matter of readers of Scott as eminent as James and Lukács. Scott's work is immense – like Shakespeare's, like James's own – and the history with which it is involved has not, of course, taken any final turn. Lukács's view may once again prove a great resource. But I find it helpful now to recover that early, originary view of Scott-as-Romantic, the view that Lukács was committed to oppose.

In a European perspective he and Byron were predominant cultural presences for almost two generations. They achieved this authority in large part because both constructed world-historical matrices for themselves and their work. They did this Romantically, however, that is to say, by keying their work to the idea of the individual – the cultural quanta named Byron and Scott. On one hand we have a romance focused in contradiction, on the other a romance focused in reconciliation.

If both James and Lukács were out of sympathy with those romances of Romanticism – each for good reasons – James seems to have had a clearer view of the functional presence of Scott's Romanticism in the art of fiction. Scott is not simply a kind of fantastical historian – the "Ariosto of the North," as Byron named him: he makes a parade of his imaginary moves.[3] If, for James, this will never do, Scott nonetheless does it all the time, starting with the game he makes of his books' authorship. The famous act of self-concealment begun with *Waverley* leads directly to the games of the Introductions, chapters Preliminary, Dedicatory Epistles, and all their associated paratextual maneuvers. The introduction to the 1816 *Tales of My Landlord* is typical: elaborate, preposterous, and – so far as a Jamesian art of fiction would be concerned – wholly irrelevant to the two "tales" it prefaces. "TALES OF MY LANDLORD," it is headed, "*Collected and Reported by*/ JEDIDIAH CLEISHBOTHAM/ *Schoolmaster and Parish-Clerk of Gandercleugh.*"

As I may, without vanity, presume that the name and official description prefixed to this Proem will secure it, from the sedate and reflecting part of mankind, to whom only I would be understood to address myself, such attention as is due to the sedulous instructor of youth, and the careful performer of my Sabbath duties, I will forebear to hold up a candle to the daylight, or to point out to the judicious those recommendations of my labours which they must necessarily anticipate from the perusal of the title-page.[4]

The comic absurdity of this should not obscure its fundamentally Romantic character. We are entering NeverNeverLand in a self-conscious passage of style. More importantly, by choosing to begin this way Scott ensures that we shall only come to this place with full awareness that we are entering a house of fictions. This is romance at a second order, as it were: not the Romanticism of *The Prelude* or of Coleridge's conversation poems, but of *The Monk, Don Juan,* and "The Eve of St. Agnes." Readers join in this work through a conscious undertaking. That is the contract Scott insists upon.

Or consider the following passage. The voice this time is that of Peter Pattieson himself, rather than his editor and posthumous factotum. It is the opening passage of chapter 1 of *The Bride of Lammermoor.*

Few have been in my secret while I was engaged in compiling these narratives, nor is it probable that they will ever become public during the life of their author. Even were that event to happen, I am not ambitious of the honoured distinction, *monstrari digito.* I confess, that, were it safe to cherish such dreams at all, I should more enjoy the thought of remaining behind the curtain unseen, like the ingenious manager of Punch and his wife Joan, and enjoying the astonishment and conjectures of my audience. Then might I, perchance, hear the productions of the obscure Peter Pattieson praised by the judicious, and admired by the feeling, engrossing the young, and attracting even the old; while the critic traced their style and sentiments up to some name of literary celebrity, and the question when, and by whom, these were written, filled up the pause of conversation in a hundred circles and coteries.[5]

The wit of that kind of thing – Edward Bostetter called it "romantic ventriloquism"[6] – seems to me beyond praise. The whole game of Scott's art is being put on display – indeed, is being drawn into the fictional space of the text. More wonderfully still, readers everywhere, readers of every kind, are already here as well, imagined into this fiction before they ever knew they were, and awaiting their inevitable encounter with themselves when they undertake this passage. Not every reader of the book in 1819 would have seen and heard Walter Scott within these words of Peter Pattieson – the fiction of Scott's anonymity was still officially intact. But every 1819 reader *was* already involved with "the question when, and by whom" the Waverley novels were written. Besides, after five years of intense curiosity the truth was spreading that Scott was "The Author of *Waverley.*" He wrote this passage explicitly to play with, and upon, the rumors, and thus to engage different readers at different levels of awareness. In 1819 Byron was one reader who read that ventriloquized passage knowing its author was Scott – a knowledge he did not have in 1816. Whatever the reader's case in 1819, it would not be long before all would have complete access to the pleasure of such texts.

This kind of writing – so replete in Scott – installs neither a truth of fact nor a truth of fiction but the truth of the game of art. It is more than make-believe, it is conscious make-believe. Scott wants to draw his audience into his fictional world by assuming and playing upon his reader's distance and disbelief. His Romantic reconciliations therefore begin in an imaginative deployment of a non-fictional idea of truth and reality. There can be no Romantic escape to imaginary worlds unless there is first of all a real world, or rather the idea of a real world, from which to escape. Scott's game of authorship forms a crucial part of his elaborate method for imagining the audience's idea of the real world and integrating it into his fiction. More than that, the game largely organizes his general method for directly involving his audience in a social, a cooperative venture of fictional making. Ultimately this encompasses more than the epical creation of past history; it necessitates the invention of the present as well. Scott does not create that history by himself, however. His fictions become the means by which individuals, isolated readers, are led to become willing participants in this large cultural enterprise.

A full apparatus of complex narrative framing did not appear until 1816 when "The Author of *Waverley*," with three novels out, initiated the "Tales of my Landlord" series. Nevertheless, the rhetoric of this Author's fiction is operating from the start. *Waverley* begins with an "Introductory" chapter in which the (unnamed) Author discusses his fictional procedures with the reader. It is important to the book that this chapter is not separated from the main body of the tale as prefatory or paratextual matter. So here we discover as a first order of fictional business that the book's title, subtitle, and narrative genre are part of the fiction called *Waverley; or 'Tis Sixty Years Since*. We also discover that the Author and his reader have been incorporated into the fiction as assumed presences, quasi-characters. The complete continuity of these materials is clear from the first sentence of the imbedded tale that the Author has set out to tell – the first sentence, that is to say, of chapter II. Having informed us about his book, what it is and how it got made, he ends "Chapter I. Introductory" and begins "Chapter II. Waverley-Honour. A Retrospect" thus: "It is *then* [my emphasis] sixty years since Edward Waverley, the hero of the following pages, took leave of his family to join the regiment of dragoons in which he had lately obtained a commission."[7] "Then" signals the time of the Author's book whose clock was set going in the previous chapter. But this Author is no mere rhetorical device, he is – according to his own text – a historical personage. We see this from another shrewd deployment of the word "then." It comes earlier, in chapter I: "By fixing then the date of my story Sixty Years before this present 1st November 1805, I would have my readers understand," etc. etc. (*Waverley*, 4).

1st November 1805! But, gentle reader, here and now it is 1814, 'tis nine years since what you are reading was written.

The telling of this tale and its reading, the writing of it, the publishing of it, the printing of it (think of its famous and crucial title-page): all have been incorporated into the work, which emerges as a complex textual condition. Sixty or so years later James will deplore a fictional imagination that could so bare its own artifice as to produce such regular, casual demystifications as the Author's reference to "the hero of the following pages."

Some of the most distinguished Scott scholars have urged readers to forego these paratexts and begin further along, where the text picks up the actions of the core characters – for instance, with *Old Mortality*, in chapter II, "The Wappenshaw."[8] Disagreeing with scholars like Angus Calder, Jane Stevenson, and Peter Davidson is not easy to do, but on this matter I must disagree. To enter this great book at chapter II means you will not read Jedidiah Cleishbotham's "Dedicatory Epistle" to the first of the *Tales of My Landlord* series or Peter Pattieson's Introduction to *Old Mortality* and the oral narratives and anecdotes comprising the archive of his materials.

Why are these matters and materials important? Simply, they establish the basic narrative terms of Scott's fiction. These are not Jamesian terms. They are terms that have far more in common with works like *At Swim-Two-Birds, If on a Winter's Night a Traveler, Gravity's Rainbow,* and *Lanark* – that is to say, they make the subject of tale-telling an explicit and governing preoccupation of the fiction. The first series of *Tales of My Landlord* comes in four volumes headed with Jedidiah Cleishbotham's "Introduction" where we are introduced to Scott's complex scene of tale-telling. The key figures here – others will be invented later – are Cleishbotham and his "young friend" Pattieson, the "now deceased" recensor of the tales. Then come the first two stories, *The Black Dwarf,* in the first volume, and *Old Mortality,* which makes up the next three volumes. Each of the stories has a chapter "Preliminary" where Pattieson gives "a short introduction," as Cleishbotham explains, "mentioning the persons by whom, and the circumstances under which, the materials thereof were collected" (*The Black Dwarf,* 9).

All this is simply – simply? – to put the reader in the most self-conscious relation to the whole fictional enterprise that the books are unfolding. *The Black Dwarf*'s "Preliminary" chapter literally italicizes its purpose here with a series of passages that are set off from the main body of roman print. The first of these comes at the point where the subject of the Black Dwarf gets raised in an adventitious way, as a mere rhetorical flourish in the speech of a character whose name we never learn and who figures not at all in the tale his casual remark will provoke. Cleishbotham's interest is piqued, and Pattieson's narrative records the moment: "'The Black Dwarf!' said *my learned friend and patron*,* Mr Jedidiah Cleishbotham, 'and what sort of personage may he be?'" The phrase in italics, *my learned friend and patron*, is asterisked to the following "Note by the publisher":

We have in this, and other instances, printed in italics some few words which the worthy editor, Mr. Jedidiah Cleishbotham, seems to have interpolated upon the text of his deceased friend, Mr. Pattieson. We must observe, once for all, that such liberties appear only to have been taken by the learned gentleman when his own character and conduct are concerned; and surely he must be the best judge of the style in which his own character and conduct should be treated. (*The Black Dwarf*, 12)

So we are dealing with a text, with a tale, where the boundaries between fiction and fact have been made as porous as possible. Characters in the tale revise the text and its publisher turns out to be himself a minor character of its fiction.

   Scott's framing personages pass from our ken throughout the core narrative treating the Black Dwarf, but they return in a new and even more remarkable way when the tale of *Old Mortality* begins in volume II. Here the "Preliminary" chapter comes with another witty typographical signal. Printed entirely in inverted commas, the chapter explicitly mediates Pattieson's narrative through the editorial devices of Cleishbotham, Pattieson's "worthy and learned friend and patron." This is how the chapter begins:

"Most readers," says the Manuscript of Mr. Pattieson, "must have witnessed with delight the joyous burst which attends the dismissing of a village-school on a fine summer evening. The buoyant spirit of childhood, repressed with so much difficulty during the tedious hours of discipline, may then be seen to explode, as it were, in shout, and song, and frolic, as the little urchins join in groups on their play-ground, and arrange their matches of sport for the evening. But there is one individual who partakes of the relief afforded by the moment of dismission, whose feelings are not so obvious to the eye of the spectator, or so apt to receive his sympathy. I mean the teacher himself, who, stunned with the hum, and suffocated with the closeness of his school-room, has spent the whole day (himself against a host) in controlling petulance, exciting indifference to action, striving to enlighten stupidity, and labouring to soften obstinacy.["]⁹

The narrative now comes with a series of footnotes authorized by the publisher and signed by Cleishbotham, who annotates a text he seems to have scripted from Pattieson's original manuscript. But if the inverted commas tell us this text is a verbatim report of Pattieson's original, they also, by that very move, raise a question about their textual status. Why put all this material in quotation marks at all, why not simply give Pattieson's "pre-liminary" exposition as it was given to us in *The Black Dwarf*? That text's series of minor scriptural interpolations "may [here] be seen to explode, as it were, like restive schoolchildren, into a condition of indeterminate free-dom." Just how faithful is Cleishbotham's recension to Pattieson's original? Scott works to provoke that question here for the same reason that he plays on the public mystery of his authorship at the beginning of *The Bride of Lammermoor*. He is urging his readers to attend to the artifice of the work before them.

From such attention comes awareness of the reflexive character of this chapter's own small narrative. Quasi-allegorical in form, it draws an explicit set of parallels between Old Mortality, on one hand, and Peter Pattieson on the other. Both cultivate a knowledge of the past and work to preserve it from effacement. The education of society being the purpose of what they do, the running references to schoolmasters and schoolchildren are much to the point. Both are, moreover, irregular kinds of instructors, op-erating with their tales outside the schoolroom. If all of these relations are easy enough to register, they prepare us to see others of equal, perhaps even greater, note. Putting the entirety of the chapter in quotation marks underscores the further parallel, never far from our attention in any case, between the recensor Pattieson and his literary agent Cleishbotham. And that equation entirely "explodes" the Chinese-box structure of the narrative as a whole. The legendary figure of Old Mortality dissolves and mutates into the invisible Author of *Old Mortality*, "renewing . . . the half-defaced inscriptions of the past" with his fragile fictions.

Framed as they are in this way, Scott's narratives regularly, if also ran-domly, break out of their narrative enclosures into the freedom of self-conscious romance. Often the moments are brief – for instance, in chapter 23 of *Quentin Durward*. Having been fitted out in disguises by the Syndic Pavillon and his family, Quentin and Lady Isabelle set off from Liège. Two brief paragraphs intervene at that point before the narrative returns us to the central characters.

The instant her guests had departed, Mother Mabel took the opportunity to read a long practical lecture to Trudchen [her daughter] upon the folly of reading romances, whereby the flaunting ladies of the Court were grown so bold and venturous, that, instead of applying to learn some honest housewifery, they must ride, forsooth, a damsel-erranting through the country, with no better attendant than an idle squire, debauched page, or rake-helly archer from foreign parts, to the great danger of their health, the impoverishing of their substance, and the irreparable prejudice of their reputation.

All this Gertrude heard in silence, and without reply; but, considering her character, it might be doubted whether she derived from it the practical inference which it was her mother's purpose to enforce.[10]

The passage inevitably turns our attention to Scott's own novel, whose core situation Mother Mabel has simply summarized. The text all but demands that readers be prepared to formulate the response that Gertrude did not give. What *is* the point of romance fiction, of reading *this very book*? For Scott that is precisely a historical question and problem. There are fifteenth-century answers to the question and there are nineteenth-century answers, as this very text reminds us to remember.

Scott's books are all conscious efforts to reflect upon that question, if not to answer it directly and definitively. The problem is vigorously brought forward in *Kenilworth*. Lounging in her barge on the Thames, Elizabeth starts a conversation among her courtiers about the relative merits of bear-baiting and play-going as civil entertainments. When Shakespeare's plays come to focus the issue, the scene immediately turns reflexive. To an 1821 reader the debate initially seems comical, a moment for the reader to stand back from the tensions of the romance narrative and observe for a brief space from a cool and amused distance. The Author of *Waverley* is at his ventriloquist games once again, most plainly, I suppose, when he uses Elizabeth as his mouthpiece in the following text: "And touching this Shakespeare, we think there is that in his plays that is worth twenty Bear-gardens; and that this new undertaking of his Chronicles, as he calls them, may entertain, with honest mirth, mingled with useful instruction, not only our subjects, but even the generation which may succeed to us."[11] The text says "this Shakespeare" but it (also) means "The Author of *Waverley*."

But the scene involves far more than a diverting moment of reflexive comic relief. When the Queen asks for some serious judgments on the question, Sussex begins by debunking the "nonsensical bombast and irreality of the theatre," arguing that blood-sports are a more effective means for training a vigorous citizenry. Leicester responds "in behalf of the players" by arguing that the "rants" and "jests" of the theatre are useful means of social control. The plays "keep the minds of the commons from busying themselves with state affairs, and listening to traitorous speeches, idle rumours, and disloyal insinuations. When men are agape to see how Marlow, Shakespeare, and others, work out their fanciful plots ... the mind of the spectators is withdrawn from the conduct of their rulers" (*Kenilworth*, 175). Cutting as it does into the fanciful plots of Scott's own fictions – of *this* fiction even now being transacted by the reader – Leicester's argument seems highly equivocal, and not least because Leicester is himself at this point deeply involved with a fanciful and labyrinthine plot of his own. So when the Queen quickly responds, "We would not have the minds of our subjects withdrawn from consideration of our own conduct" (175) the remark applies as much to the immediate technical management of Scott's fiction as it does to his work's social and educational aims.

The stakes are raised further when the Dean of St. Asaph's weighs in against the theatres in a puritan diatribe that carries, for later readers, the substance of historical prophecy – that is to say, the coming closing of the theatres. Shakespeare and his fellows promote lewdness, profanity, social discontent – "blaspheming heaven . . . slandering . . . earthly rulers [and] set[ting] at defiance the laws both of God and man" (175). The Queen answers by drawing a distinction between moral and immoral artists, and she closes her response with the passage, quoted earlier, about how artists like Shakespeare bring "useful instruction [to] the generation which may succeed to us." In this highly reflexive moment, that remark comes as much to comment on the work of Scott and Byron as on Elizabethan theatre. Unlike Byron, Scott is not like those artists denounced by the Dean of St. Asaph's: he is the contemporary avatar of Shakespeare. This passage is the fictional equivalent of Scott's view of Byron's ideas about "religion and politics." Nor is it the first time he would use his fiction to mount a critique of his famous contemporary and close acquaintance. The judgment on King Richard that comprises the final paragraph of *Ivanhoe* involves a concealed reference to Byron. When Scott ends by (mis)quoting Johnson's "Vanity of Human Wishes" –

> He left the name at which the world grew pale,
> To point a moral, or adorn a TALE[12]

– one can scarcely *not* recall Byron, as "rash and romantic" – these are Scott's words – as the crusading king the words describe. For it was Byron who reclaimed those lines for his age when he reworked them at the end of *The Corsair*:

> He left a Corsair's name to other times,
> Linked with one virtue, and a thousand crimes.[13]

It is important to remember that these reflexive interludes in Scott's work are rarely disengaged from the central plot action. This scene, for example, takes place when Leicester's duplicity towards the Queen has thrown him into a dangerous position. Caught in his own web of deceit and the complicating intrigues of the court, he almost decides not to join the river party. "Go, say I am taken suddenly ill," he tells Varney, "for, by heaven, my brain can sustain this no longer" (*Kenilworth*, 171). But politics forces him on, and throughout the scene we are kept as much aware of the extreme tension and anxiety in his mind as of the external events transpiring before us. As is almost always the case, Scott explicitly gives us the formula governing the fictional events: "Leicester . . . endeavoured to divert his thoughts from all internal reflection, by fixing them on what was passing around . . . abstract[ing] his thoughts and feelings by a strong effort from every thing but the necessity of maintaining himself in the favour of his patroness" (173). This formula explains why "what was passing around" – the eventualities of the action – here serves primarily to index Leicester's mental state and "internal reflection." And by giving the formula so explicitly Scott ensures that his readers will not lose themselves in the psychology of the characters and forget what is passing around – forget, in other words, that we are transacting the passages of this text. Leicester's behavior is a textual signal indexing Walter Scott in 1821 – as involved in the current issues raised by his tale-telling as his characters are in the events of the plot.

This reflexive inertia persists in his work to the very end – I mean, to late works like *Count Robert of Paris*, a preposterous undertaking that yet involves a remarkable feat of style. The book opens with a series of reflections on the decadent world of the Byzantine Empire, which will be the scene of the action, and in particular on the euphuistic style practiced at the court. In attempting to recreate that world for his tale, Scott moves to become what he beholds, as it were. And so we get the remarkable chapter IV where Scott lays out a pastiche of the decadent and all but unreadable prose of the Byzantine historian Anna Comnena.

The event is comic both at the textual and at the narrative level. It is also boldly reflexive given the way Scott has put the issue of Byzantine style at the foreground of his tale. For Scott's own style has over the years grown increasingly elaborate and formulaic. To pastiche Comnena's prose at this point is to fashion a critical measure of his own.

That second-order awareness is written large in the reception history, though perhaps not exactly as Scott himself would have liked. For readers have closed the book on Scott's book as a stylistic disaster. That judgment, plainly correct, also seems to me not correct enough. *Count Robert of Paris* is not a good book, a "neglected work." It *is* all but unreadable. But the book, and in particular its opening chapters, involves an important and characteristic feat of style: the pastiche of Comnena's notoriously decadent prose. The move turns reflexively on Scott's own tale, suggesting that we might register certain equations between Comnena and Scott.

Of course many great writers – Wordsworth, for instance – have no ability or even interest in that kind of self-conscious art. It is as essential to Scott as it is to Byron, however, which is why the last book I want to discuss, *Ivanhoe*, is such a key work. In the perspective I am taking here, it is clearly Scott's masterpiece.

Consider again, briefly, the Johnson quotation that ends the book. The witty contemporary reference to Byron is grounded on another, more immediate turn of wit. For the name of King Richard is not simply, in the context of *Ivanhoe*, a proverbial figure. He points a moral in *this* work and he is *this* tale's adornment. It is as if the ultimate point of Richard's spectacular career would only be reached when he was turned into a character in Scott's novel.

That way of conceiving his book, as if it were the measure of history's meanings and events (and not vice versa), is written into every line of Scott's text. And Scott is explicit about this matter, though his forthrightness comes in his usual comic ways. Laurence Templeton in his Dedicatory Epistle tells Dr. Dryasdust that he makes no pretense to "historical accuracy in his details," whether large or small, for his interest in the past is driven by his concern for the present and the future. Part of his present concerns, of course, involves a desire to make contact with Great Britain's historical inheritance. But for Scott this always means renegotiating our relations with the past. Simply, Scott's histories – the eventualities of the past as well as the textualities of the present – are all living inventions.

So one of *Ivanhoe*'s chief concerns is that we never lose sight of its inventiveness. To measure its success in this regard, think of the main line of attack the book drew out. None of Scott's fictions treat their historical details so cavalierly or break so far from the conventions of novelistic realism. The following sequence of passages typify Scott's manner of proceeding:

Our history must needs retrograde for the space of a few pages, to inform the reader of certain passages material to his understanding the rest of this important narrative. (*Ivanhoe*, 230)

Our scene now returns to the exterior of the castle, or preceptory, of Templestowe, about the hour when the bloody die was to be cast for the life or death of Rebecca. (382)

A flight of steps . . . leads up to a low portal in the south side of the tower, by which the adventurous antiquary may still, or at least could a few years since, gain access to a small stair within the thickness of the main wall . . . (370)

This is the sort of thing that provoked James's dismay. To read texts of this kind, he says in his condescending 1864 review of Scott's work, we have to become like children at sunset listening to bedtime fairy tales.[14]

And perhaps we do, though not in the sense that James intended. For what *Ivanhoe* requires is a reader with the understanding and conscious intelligence that Scott calls for in these very passages. The first passage (from chapter 28) continues, for instance, like this: "[The reader's] own intelligence may indeed have easily anticipated that, when Ivanhoe sunk down, and seemed abandoned by all the world," etc. (*Ivanhoe*, 230). Or when, in chapter 40, Scott tells us that it "becomes necessary to resume the train of [the Black Knight's] adventures," he addresses us directly: "You are then to imagine this Knight, such as we have already described him ... mounted on his mighty black charger" (352).

Such a reader is summoned, as usual in Scott's works, at the outset of the book, in Laurence Templeton's fictitious Dedicatory Epistle. One of the most artful of Scott's imaginary introductions, it comes to present the case for *Ivanhoe* as a work different from the "idle novels and romances of the day." Templeton's fussy prose wanders in and around that issue until he finally admits that he has only written a "romance," or fictitious narrative and that its admittedly "slight" character "might not suit the severer genius of our friend Mr. Oldbuck." So instead of contradicting the charge of idleness, Templeton craves the reader's, and Dryasdust's, indulgence:

If, therefore, my dear friend, you have generosity enough to pardon the presumptuous attempt, to frame for myself a minstrel coronet, partly out of the pearls of pure antiquity, and partly from Bristol stones and paste with which I have endeavoured to imitate them, I am convinced your opinion of the difficulty of the task will reconcile you to the imperfect manner of its execution. (12)

Representing himself as a pasteboard minstrel, Templeton develops a dialectical figure composed of a modest and unassuming author on one hand, and a perspicacious yet indulgent reader on the other. But that rhetorical figure, like the character Templeton, flaunts its own pasteboard condition, as we see in the very next passage where Templeton closes his introduction with a discussion of his tale's principal archival source, the "Wardour MS." At this point the structure of Scott's textual masquerade comes into full view, for Sir Arthur Wardour, the owner of the precious MS, is none other than a character we have already met, not in ordinary factive history, but three years earlier, in 1816, in the fictitious realms of *The Antiquary*.

All this is amusing and artful enough, but when we enter the history proper called *Ivanhoe*, we find Scott driving us to negotiate the text as a consciously imaginary realm. The texts already cited underscore this urgency of the tale, but its self-conscious fictionality is coded far more deeply and thoroughly. Several times in the book, for example, all at strategic and widely separated points, the Author of *Ivanhoe* recalls us to his archival sources. The first comes to authenticate the decorative details of the tournament at Ashby, in chapter 7. A second, halfway through the book, supports the representation of De Bracy's barbarous treatment of Rowena. In this case the Wardour MS is a second-order authority attesting the truth of another text, the legitimate *Saxon Chronicle*. What is especially interesting here is the way Scott's text calls attention to the imaginary status of its own principal source text: "Such and so licentious were the times . . . recorded by Eadmer; and we need add nothing to vindicate the probability of the scenes which we have detailed, and are about to detail, upon the more apocryphal authority of the Wardour MS" (193). In Scott's fictional world, vindicating probabilities is not the function of spurious texts like the Wardour MS. It is rather an authenticating sign – a true index – of Scott's powers of historical invention. So it is that details "given at length" in the Wardour MS become the authority for winding up various narrative threads in the last chapter of the book.

As the romantic history of Ivanhoe, Rowena, Rebecca, and Bois Guilbert develops, the book puts more and more of its fictionality on display. The narrator's outspoken interventions, noted earlier, are relatively muted in the first half of the book, but with that famous "blast of a horn" before the gates of Torquilstone at the end of chapter 21, Scott explodes his fictional spaces and makes the making of the book one of his least disguised central subjects. From the horn blast to Ulrica's ominous chant of death at the end of chapter 31, the entirety of the book's central action moves through a series of reflexive turns that emphasize the constructed character of the narrative. The horn blast and its narrative consequences signal how involved Scott means to be in the fortunes of his tale and how attentive to that involvement his readers are expected to be. Scott, it seems, takes his fictional art every bit as seriously as James. Only the touch is lighter, perhaps less pretentious.

Consider just a few of his most wonderful acts of creation. His two chief comic characters, Gurth and Wamba, compose and deliver a formal "letter of defiance" to Front-de Boeuf and his allies that tranforms a central chivalric ceremony to low comedy (chapter 25). The Magician of the North then manages a parodic resurrection from the dead (in three days, no less!); and at the climax of the action, when Ivanhoe rides against Bois Guilbert to decide Rebecca's fate, Scott brings off his most brazen conjuring trick. The Templar unhorses the wounded hero with his "well-aimed lance," an "issue of the combat all had foreseen" since it is clear Ivanhoe has no possible chance of defeating Bois Guilbert. But if the Templar's shield is barely grazed by Ivanhoe's lance, Bois Guilbert nonetheless "reeled in his saddle . . . and fell in the lists, dead. 'This is indeed the judgment of God,' said the Grand Master, looking upward – *Fiat voluntas tua!*'" (391–2). Scott's will indeed be done. This belated trial by combat doubles and completes the work begun in the lists of Ashby – that "passage of arms" whose meaning is here fulfilled to the law of the letter: "In the beginning was the deed."

Which is to say – after Goethe, after Scott, after Derrida – "the pen is mightier than the sword." In the death of Bois Guilbert – at once a Regency and a Romantic event – we see precisely how it is that God takes a hand in every stroke.

Like *Don Juan*, so admired by Scott, the world of *Ivanhoe* aspires to Brechtian transparency. Behind both lie other favorite texts: *Tristram Shandy*, of course, but *Don Quixote* even more. All are the works of gods whom we may learn to look upon and live. But generous and good-natured as they are, these greatly illusionistic works suffer few illusions. The two chief parts of *Ivanhoe*, we want to recall, each end in scenes that cast premonitory shadows across the triumphs they bring. The climax of the victory at Torquilstone comes at the same time as Ulrica's song of death, whose dark formula hurls this prophecy at the histories of the aspirants of power: "All must perish" (270). And the marriage of Ivanhoe and Rowena, the book's finale celebration, is turned into a literal anti-climax when Scott decides to end his tale with Rebecca's visit to the newly married Rowena. The scene reminds us that if Rowena and Ivanhoe inherit their world, it is Rebecca who represents whatever moral authority that world might hope, however vainly, to possess. This is why, when Rebecca refuses Rowena's well-meaning but absurd invitation to become a citizen of that world, we realize how nicely Scott measures out his sympathetic judgments. Rebecca turns away from Rowena, "leaving [her] surprised as if a vision had passed before her." History, Scott is telling us, will pursue that vision for ever – as it will for ever move in fear and trembling of the vision of Ulrica, Rebecca's darker double.

Scott's book also tells us where those two visionary forms, dream and nightmare, may be most helpfully engaged: in the imaginary fields of books like *Ivanhoe*. Pagan and Jew will not truly find a place in English culture until James Joyce and John Cowper Powys have imagined ones for them. The expectation of such a future defines the Romanticism of Scott's work. Cutting across such a Romanticism, however, is what I have labeled Scott's "postmodernity": the ironic awareness with which he constructs and pursues his Romantic quest, the awareness that forbids him from turning his poetic tale into a form of worship. Is that complex vision the reason that Victor Hugo, speaking for many, declared *Ivanhoe* "the true epic work of our age"? I am not sure. But I do know that when Lukács, quoting Hugo (*The Historical Novel*, 77), defined the epic character of Scott's work, he saw it in a very different way. And I suspect, as we all work to recover and reunderstand this remarkable writer, that we might begin all over again further back, with Hugo and the other pre-Jamesian intelligences whose readings we might now once again find useful.

NOTES

1. Henry James, "The Art of Fiction," in *Henry James: Literary Criticism, Volume I*, eds. Leon Edel and Mark Wilson (New York: Library of America, 1984). Page citations are given in the text.
2. Georg Lukács, *The Historical Novel* (1937) (Boston: Beacon Press, 1962), 37. Further page citations are in the text.
3. Byron, *Childe Harold's Pilgrimage*, Canto iv. Stanza 40.
4. Sir Walter Scott, *The Black Dwarf*, ed. P. D. Garside (Edinburgh: Edinburgh University Press, 1993), 5.
5. Scott, *The Bride of Lammermoor*, ed. J. H. Alexander (Edinburgh: Edinburgh University Press, 1995), 3.
6. Edward E. Bostetter, *The Romantic Ventriloquists* (Seattle: University of Washington Press, 1963).
7. Scott, *Waverley*, ed. Claire Lamont (Oxford: Oxford University Press, 1986), 5–6.
8. Scott, *Old Mortality*, ed. Angus Calder (Harmondsworth: Penguin, 1975), "Introduction," 9; Scott, *Old Mortality*, ed. Peter Davidson and Jane Stevenson (Oxford: Oxford University Press, 1993), "Introduction," xxxix.
9. Scott, *The Tale of Old Mortality*, ed. Douglas Mack (Edinburgh: Edinburgh University Press, 1993), 5.
10. Scott, *Quentin Durward*, ed. J. H. Alexander and G. A. M. Wood (Edinburgh: Edinburgh University Press, 2001), 251–2.
11. Scott, *Kenilworth*, ed. J. H. Alexander (Edinburgh: Edinburgh University Press, 1993), 175.
12. Scott, *Ivanhoe*, ed. Graham Tulloch (Edinburgh: Edinburgh University Press, 1998), 401.
13. Byron, *The Complete Poetical Works*, ed. Jerome McGann, 5 vols. (Oxford: Clarendon Press, 1981), III:214.
14. James's remarks come in his review of Nassau Senior's *Essays on Fiction*; see James, *Literary Criticism*, 1199–204.

CHAPTER 7

Putting down the Rising

John Barrell

Early nineteenth-century Edinburgh had a lot less time for James Hogg than for "the Ettrick Shepherd," the literary persona created partly by Hogg himself, partly by the tight circle that ran *Blackwood's Edinburgh Magazine*. Comic, bibulous, full of naïve folk-wisdom, easy to patronize, the Ettrick Shepherd was invented as a souvenir of the pastoral lowlands, a survival whose presence among one of the Edinburgh literary élites could represent both the continuity of modern Scots culture and the impolite past it had left behind. The Ettrick Shepherd, though perhaps more pliable, certainly more reassuringly conservative than Burns had been, could not always be relied upon to play this part, and had occasionally to be reminded of his place by editors, reviewers, even by himself. But he was much more comfortable to be with than James Hogg, the author of obsessive, experimental fictions which either satirized or ignored the decencies of polite letters. To some degree even these could be bowdlerized and domesticated, as many of them were in the Victorian collections of Hogg's fiction published after his death, and passed off as written "by the Ettrick Shepherd."[1] But one in particular, and for my money the best of them – *The Three Perils of Woman* – was immediately recognized as irredeemable by its first reviewers, and until 1995 had never been reprinted.[2]

The Three Perils of Woman was published in 1823, a year before *The Private Memoirs and Confessions of a Justified Sinner*. It pretends to consist of three novellas, each devoted to a separate moral failing by which the happiness of women is undermined: love (or loving too young and too thoughtlessly), leasing (or lying), and jealousy. In fact, however, the last two novellas form one connected story, which has been divided to make the book look like a sequel to Hogg's earlier extraordinary romance, *The Three Perils of Man* (1822). The narrator, whose attitudes and motives become increasingly sinister towards the end of the book, may be as unreliable a guide to what happens in these stories as he usually is in Hogg's fiction. He has a hard time making the stories fit the title: each story is a compendium of all three perils, and in the second, two-part story his sententious insistence on the dangers of lying and jealousy align him with the character he most satirizes, a minister of religion in love with his maidservant and given to lecturing her on her moral failings.

Both stories are generically diverse, self-consciously impure. Hogg described them as "domestic tales," apparently soliciting a female readership whose delicacy he then assaults with speculations about promiscuity and prostitution, and with prayers so chattily informal that reviewers found them blasphemous.[3] Both stories modulate suddenly from comedy to tragedy, though one – but which? – struggles through to what may be a happy ending. Both seem to be imagined as critical versions of the genres they most nearly inhabit: the first is – or at least begins as – a comic and delightfully impolite version of the novel of polite sentiment, the second is a historical tale in the manner of Scott but arguably without the consolations of romance or the safety of historical distance. But among all these other things they are both versions of the early nineteenth-century genre, the "national tale," a genre that imagines the coming-together of opposed communities, usually in Ireland or Scotland, and thus the constitution of a new national unity.[4]

The national tale usually imagines this rapprochement through the figure of a mixed marriage whose offspring will represent the future unity of a now divided nation. Agatha ("Gatty") Bell in the first story, Sally Niven in the second, are lowland women who marry highland men, though in circumstances which involve the rejection, with fatal consequences, of a third lover, a rejection which risks the success of the union, both marital and national. Both women bear children, but though Gatty's son is alive and thriving at the end of her tale, apparently the vigorous embodiment of the future of modern Scotland, Sally's daughter dies at birth or shortly after. The order in which the stories appear is important here. Gatty's tale is set in Hogg's own time; Sally's story is about a few months either side of the Battle of Culloden. In terms of historical time, therefore, the happy ending of Gatty's tale – the survival of the child, the recovery of Gatty after her apparent death and years of mental illness – seems to repair the tragedy of Sally, who dies along with her daughter, as if the divisions of North and South, Tory and Whig, Catholic and Protestant, which had been reopened in 1745, could be healed in the early nineteenth century. In the order of reading, however, Sally's tragedy seems to reopen the wounds which Gatty's tale had closed, as if questioning the tidy optimism of the national tale, or suggesting that the history of Scotland is a history of divisions which can never finally be repaired.

The move by which Gatty's tale is transmuted from comedy to tragedy culminates in a moment of grotesque horror which, though versions of it occur throughout Hogg's fiction, is nowhere else so terrifyingly elaborated. For years the highlander McIon has been in love with Gatty, but she, out of a mistaken delicacy, has given him no clear indication that his love is returned. When he becomes engaged to her cousin Cherubina the true state of Gatty's feelings is revealed, and Cherubina, a dependant, is persuaded to allow the engagement to be broken so that McIon and Gatty can marry. But the cost of this sacrifice is more than Cherubina can bear; she dies of a broken heart, and, Gatty, apparently overcome with guilt, becomes convinced that she too will die, though she seems to be suffering from no physical illness. On the very day she has named, she appears to breathe her last, and is laid out in her shroud; then, suddenly, the corpse jerks up into a sitting position, so violently that it collides with her father, sitting on the bed beside her, and nearly knocks him out.

McIon uncovers her face and immediately wishes he had not: instead of the calm composure of death he discovers the wild, rolling eyes, "the dead countenance of an idiot ... in the very lowest state of debasement" (*Three Perils of Woman*, 200, 202), "a degradation of our nature" (203) – as if the soul had left the still animated, now uncontrollable body. Soon, however, the body becomes dormant again, but the terrible expression remains. Gatty is consigned to an asylum, where, still dormant, she gives birth to a son; after three years she wakes, with no memory of her convulsion, and no sense of the time she has lost. She is now more beautiful than ever, her face that of an angel. The narrator predicts long life and happiness for Gatty, her husband and son.

The image of Gatty's horrifying resurrection and relapse is so powerful that it has inevitably come to dominate critical accounts of the novella. It has been read as an instance of the danger of imposing, as the national tale does, the task of national reconstruction on the female body which, in the sentimental novel, is so often represented as frail in proportion to the virtue of the soul that inhabits it. The resurrection has been explained by invoking contemporary interest in galvanism, in animal magnetism; it has equally been suggested that to explain it is to miss the point, which is, precisely, that it is an instance of the uncanny, or of Hogg's canny determination to resist the rationality of the Scottish Enlightenment with images which, like the popular superstitions he refuses to renounce, resist explanation.[5] All this seems to make sense, even in its contradictions; but the multiple implications of the image look still more complicated when we attempt to read them in comparison with the host of other such apparent resurrections which occur elsewhere in Hogg's writings, as Ian Duncan has recently begun to do in an essay, "The Upright Corpse," from which I partly borrow, partly depart.[6]

Throughout Hogg's fiction, bodies that are dormant or apparently dead or, according to the narrator, really are dead, have the unnerving habit of sitting up, or at least of refusing to lie down. As Duncan has pointed out, one such upright corpse appears in his early novella "The Renowned Adventures of Basil Lee," where the narrator, returning from the War of American Independence, makes landfall on Lewis, and half-skeptical of, half-fascinated by the popular superstitions of the Hebrides, spends a night in the cottage of an old woman reputed to be visited by spirits. During the course of a hideous night, the corpse of her dead son materializes in a corner chair, and shortly after the mother dies too, and promptly sits up in bed, shaking her head, stretching out her withered arms.[7]

But there are upright corpses, too, in a number of Hogg's other novels and stories, including the most famous of all. The first victim of Robert Wringhim the justified sinner, and his diabolical shadow Gil-Martin, is a minister who sits up when shot; and when Wringhim's own body comes to be buried, it has stiffened into a sitting posture, so that one of the burial party, in a passage expunged in Victorian editions of the novel, has to trample it into a recumbent position, driving its nose into its skull. When Wringhim's body is first exhumed, it jerks back up into a sitting posture.[8]

Corpses sit up everywhere in the second story of *The Three Perils of Woman*. They appear first as actors in a comedy, as if in grotesque parody of Gatty's apparent resurrection. A mysterious lowlander, perched on the edge of a grave being dug to receive the body of a murdered highland woman, is shot in the mistaken belief that he is a stag. He starts upward before collapsing on top of Davey Duff, the excitable and superstitious parish sexton who is digging within the grave. When the lowlander's friends come to retrieve his body, they think Duff is dead as well, until he sits bolt upright among them. The obsession with upright corpses is shared even by the Minister's horse, who is terrified of bodies that lie dormant, not because they might be dead, but because they might not be, and so might suddenly spring upward.

The first half of this story, by treating these upright corpses as comic, seems to exhaust any inclination in us to find them funny. When they start turning up in the second half – more unobtrusively than my summary can suggest – they are much more sinister, and much more evidently charged with meaning: it is as if Hogg is tracing the figure to its imagined source, as if he believes the figure conceals the origin of his imaginative power. Sally, searching the Highlands in the months after Culloden for her husband and second lover, arrives at a cottage and attempts to sleep in a bed on the first floor. She thinks she hears her husband's name "breathed from female lips" (*Three Perils of Woman*, 368); she feels dizzy, gasps for breath, and sits up in bed; through a gap in the floorboards she discovers her husband in the arms of another woman, who, much too late for the peace of all concerned, is revealed to be his sister. When she dreams that she has found the corpse of her first love, Peter Gow, on the battlefield, it suddenly starts up at her. She dreams that she too has been killed, and, waking, finds Gow himself, alive, beside her bed; she springs up into a sitting posture, nearly colliding with him (373–4). They spend the night together without, the narrator assures us, any impropriety, for she slept in the bed and he beside her on the floor. But we have long learned to be wary of the narrator's account of things, especially where Sally's virtue is concerned. The other inmates of the cottage are less certain: "some asserted that the two slept together, some that they did not; some said that they stripped off their clothes, for anything that they knew; others, that neither of the two threw off a stitch, except their brogues" (379).

Uncertain intimations of sexual congress, bodies that bump into each other, heavy breathings, overhearings, spyings upon – the contexts in which these dormant bodies suddenly jerk upwards seem now to be composing the *mise-en-scène* of primal fantasy. This is still more the case when Sally is apparently found dead, though in fact she has a page and a month or two still to live. The passage repeats, detail for detail, the apparent death and resurrection of Gatty. Both of course are beautiful lowland women in love with highlanders; believed to be dead, in fact alive; and, unknown to everyone, pregnant with the nation's future. As Gatty lies stretched on her bed, her husband puts his hand on her breast in the desperate hope that she is still breathing; as Sally lies stretched on the ground, Davey Duff fumbles at her breast in search of the money tucked into her stays. Both women suddenly jerk up; both collide into the men who hover above them; both wear a mad expression, or a look of demonic possession. And in the narration of both scenes there are secrets not disclosed, either too harrowing or, in the context of tragedy, "too ludicrous to be described" (406).

In the careful symmetry by which Sally's apparent death repeats Gatty's, there is a sense that the obsessive figure at the heart of each narrative has at last discovered its final form. And yet at exactly this moment, when the figure seems to have been shrunk by the very process of its elaboration, and to have become the vehicle of meanings specific to a personal rather than a national history, it becomes something much more as well. Can the identity of Scotland, as at once its own nation and united with England, be based on the disavowal, the concealment of its past wounds, or must they be acknowledged? By what right, and with what motives, does the historian presume to force the nation to confront what it might be better to forget? The figure of the upright corpse, of the resurrection of what we think – even wish – safely consigned to the past, becomes the main means by which the novella conducts its ambiguous meditations on how modern Scotland should regard its violent history.

The novella has been read by some of Hogg's critics as a deliberate attempt to undo the decencies of *Waverley* (1814), as a story intended to restore to the history of Scotland what Scott had chosen to delete, the terrible aftermath of Culloden.[9] To some degree it does this, in its description of Sally's journey through the scorched and desolate landscape of the Highlands, in its account of how Duff's prosperity increases with increased oppression, and of how jocularly familiar he becomes with death and dismemberment. It needs also to be read, however, in the light of Peter Pattieson's anxieties, in the opening chapter of Scott's *Old Mortality*, about the wisdom of dragging the injuries of the past from oblivion into the light of day: the solace he finds in walking among graves, so long as the traces of death are "softened and deprived of their horror by . . . distance"; his implicit relief at the death of the old stone-cutter, which has ensured that the monuments he tended are now hastening to decay; above all his admonition, borrowed from Home's tragedy of *Douglas*: "Oh, rake not up the ashes of our fathers!"[10]

In the second, tragic half of Sally Niven's tale, Davey Duff has been promoted: from an impoverished, part-time parish sexton he has become a relatively prosperous, full-time, itinerant grave-digger, employed by the Duke of Cumberland to bury the corpses of those killed at Culloden and in the bloody months of repression that followed. He has become a kind of anti-type of Old Mortality; instead of repairing, as Old Mortality does, the graves of slaughtered covenanters and thus ensuring the survival of their memory, Davey's job is to conceal, in unmarked graves, the evidence of Cumberland's butchery of the Catholic highlanders, as if to wipe it from the record of history. In a story in which corpses continually rise up, Duff's task is to make sure they stay down – to put down, once and for all, the Rising of the Clans. At the end of the novella one of Sally's wounded, prostrate, Jacobite lovers tries, the other manages, to – well, you know what. Davy buries them both.

A story that figures the concealment of the past as the burial of the dead is committed to figuring its disclosure as their exhumation. If we read Sally Niven's story as a critique of *Waverley*, the task of the narrator appears to be to trudge round in the wake of Duff, digging up what Duff conceals. The narrator, however, is much more undecided about whether or not to take on this job, and even about what it would mean to do so. At one point he tells us that he is passing over the worst of the atrocities (*Three Perils of Woman*, 357), at another he complains that those atrocities have been deliberately hushed up (332). His indecision might be imagined to proceed from his sense of the responsibilities of the historian or from plain squeamishness, but in fact he has a developed taste for the ghoulish, and it is this which sometimes leads him to prefer revelation to concealment. Some think the events of 1746 are best forgotten, he writes: "But there is no reason why these should die. For my part, I like to rake them up" (332).

There is even a suggestion that he might mean this quite literally; that he has been involved in, at least complicit with, the literal exhumation of Sally's corpse. For an act of special heroism, the Young Chevalier had rewarded Sally with a sum of gold in a purse "richly and curiously wrought with silver" (325). It was this purse, presumably, that Davey had fumbled for but failed to retrieve from Sally's bosom; she was presumably buried with it; but the narrator tells us that this very purse had later come into his possession, that he had secured it "altogether for a very small sum" (325). Sally and her baby died on the grave of her two lovers and were apparently buried in it. The narrator, visiting it years later, records that "it appeared a little hollowed, as though some one had been digging in it" (406).

It is a moment that recalls the macabre delight of the narrator in *Memoirs and Confessions* at managing to get possession of Wringhim's blue bonnet, one of the souvenirs taken from his grave by the three waves of resurrectionists who exhume his body, each time dismembering and destroying it a little more. But the comparison with the *Memoirs and Confessions* also suggests another way of understanding the narrator's glib talk of "raking things up," as not so much ghoulish as self-protective. The final exhumation of Wringhim is conducted, it seems, not so much to see if he would start up again, as to confirm that he would not. The souvenirs extracted from his grave seem to function as talismans that offer protection against the returning dead, or as picturesque relics which, by standing for, substituting for, the uncomfortable past they call to mind, seem to promise, however deceitfully, that it is truly dead. Seen in this light, a tale like Sally Niven's, that rakes up the uncomfortable past, may do so in the hope not of making it live and breathe, but of converting it into a harmless keepsake; to exhume the past may be just a better way of making sure that it is properly dead.

One of Hogg's late fictions describes the cholera epidemic of 1831–2 in three letters supposed to have been written by victims and observers.[11] The writer of the first tells us that he died of the epidemic, but once wrapped in his shroud and placed in his coffin, he of course sits up and recovers. When his sweetheart catches the disease, he prays earnestly for her death, in the belief (or so he tells us) that she too will only recover if first she dies. But when she does die, he is as much terrified at the prospect of her starting back to life as he is eager (or so he tells us) for her recovery.

His ambivalence points back to the chief problem in *The Three Perils of Woman*, that its upright corpses are inextricably entangled in two different histories, national and personal. It may be, as recent readers of the novel seem to suggest, that the story of Sally Niven insists that the identity of the nation must be based on a confrontation with, an avowal of, what it would rather forget. But if the wounds of history become entangled, as they appear to have done in this figure, with a personal psychic trauma, it is hardly surprising that Hogg's best fictions, and Sally Niven's story in particular, should be ambivalent, as I take them to be, about the desirability of confronting those wounds, however often they force themselves into notice. From this point of view, the death and burial of Sally and her daughter may be at least as happy an ending as Gatty's recovery.

In the end, however, there is no possibility of interrupting the narrator's dialogue with himself at one point or another, and announcing that here, rather than there, is to be found the true meaning of the novella. What matters about *The Three Perils of Woman* is not the conclusions it may or may not reach about the issues it raises, but the painful urgency with which it addresses them. These issues have recently become urgent once again, and will continue to be so; and if the book provides an especially useful way of thinking about them, it is because it offers an "unflinching" account of a violent national past while acknowledging the temptation, the impulse, even the need, to flinch.

NOTES

1. *Tales and Sketches by the Ettrick Shepherd*, 6 vols. (Glasgow: Blackie and Son, 1837); reprinted throughout the nineteenth century.
2. James Hogg, *The Three Perils of Woman; or, Love, Leasing, and Jealousy. A Series of Domestic Scottish Tales*, ed. David Groves, Antony Hasler and Douglas S. Mack (Edinburgh: Edinburgh University Press, 1995). References to this edition will be given in the text.
3. David Groves describes the reception of *The Three Perils of Woman* in an "Afterword" to the 1995 edition, 409–20.

4. On the typology and history of the "national tale" see Katie Trumpener, *Bardic Nationalism: The Romantic Novel and the British Empire* (Princeton: Princeton University Press, 1997), 128–57.

5. See Douglas S. Mack, "Gatty's Illness in *The Three Perils of Woman*," *Studies in Hogg and his World* 1 (1990): 133–5; Valentina Bold, "Traditional Narrative Elements in *The Three Perils of Woman*," *Studies in Hogg and his World* 3 (1992): 42–56; Ian Duncan, "The Upright Corpse: Hogg, National Literature and the Uncanny," *Studies in Hogg and his World* 5 (1994): 41–5; David Groves, "Afterword," *The Three Perils of Woman*, 425–7.

6. Duncan, "The Upright Corpse," 29–54.

7. Hogg, *Winter Evening Tales, Collected among the Cottagers in the South of Scotland*, 2 vols. (Edinburgh: Oliver & Boyd, 1820), 1: 74–6.

8. Hogg, *The Private Memoirs and Confessions of a Justified Sinner* (London: Oxford University Press, 1969), 244, 248.

9. See Antony Hasler's "Introduction" to *The Three Perils of Woman*, pp. xxv–xliii.

10. Walter Scott, *The Tale of Old Mortality*, ed. Douglas S. Mack (Edinburgh: Edinburgh University Press, 1993), 7, 14.

11. Hogg, "Some Terrible Letters from Scotland. Communicated by the Ettrick Shepherd," *Metropolitan Magazine* 3 (April 1832): 422–31. See also Joan McCausland, "James Hogg and the 1831–32 Cholera Epidemic," *Studies in Hogg and his World* 10 (1999): 40–7.

CHAPTER 8

Joanna Baillie stages the nation

Alyson Bardsley

In 1824 *Blackwood's Edinburgh Magazine* summarized Joanna Baillie's achievement: "the deep tones of Joanna Baillie's genius struck upon the ear with a thrilling sublimity ... [She] sought to direct the taste of the nation and the exertions of its authors, to the legitimate objects of poetry; she brought to the task her counsel and her example."[1] Such praise almost measures up to Baillie's own ambition – although she would have preferred to see "drama" in the place of "poetry." Baillie's theoretical writing specifically figures theatre as an ideal means to "direct the taste of the nation."[2] The question of what nation that is, is complicated for Baillie, an expatriate Scot,[3] by the status of Scotland within Great Britain, and Baillie's status within both. If we recognize that for Baillie Great Britain is truly "forged" (to borrow, as others have done, Linda Colley's phrase)[4] we only begin to assess the complexity of her position. Rather than finding Great Britain to be an organic or homogeneous entity, Baillie's historical fictions acknowledge the degree and kind of labor it takes to make England and Scotland into Britain; together with her theatre theory, they assume the task of keeping up that process of making.[5] Tracing the historical and territorial representation of Britain in plays written across her career – *Ethwald* (1803; her single English historical tragedy), *The Family Legend* (1810), and *The Phantom* (1836) – makes plain the degree and kind of work involved.[6]

A suggestive though loose analogy can be drawn between "the nation" and "the theatre" in Baillie's work. "Theatre," and individual plays, are only ever partially instantiated by particular productions, or readings; similarly, if Colley is right, the idea of Great Britain succeeds by not belonging to, or supplanting, any particular locality in England or Scotland, but by being an entity that any locality within either historic nation could invoke or lay claim to without seeing itself intrinsically changed. Baillie's theoretical "landscape" of the human mind, indicated in her famous "Introductory Discourse" to volume 1 of the *Series of Plays*, depends on a similar logic as it posits the national moral usefulness of drama. Baillie imagines the theatre as

139

an environment where players and audience together constitute "a public" whose morals and opinions are then formed for good or ill. Interestingly, current criticism often figures this space as a borderland, with all that that implies of contestation and fluidity, between the domains of the personal and the political, masculine and feminine.[7]

The now-familiar trope of a contested territory clearly felt fresh and urgent to Baillie. At one revealing point in the "Introductory Discourse," she describes the drama as a collection of interior landscapes, and the theatre as a shared site for their observation and comparison. This forms the basis of drama's moral effect:

> To hold up for our example those peculiarities in disposition, and modes of thinking which nature has fixed upon us, or which long and early habit has incorporated with our original selves, is almost desiring us to remove the everlasting mountains, to take away the native land-marks of the soul; but representing the passions brings before us the operation of a tempest that rages out its time and passes away. We cannot, it is true, amidst its wild uproar listen to the voice of reason, and save ourselves from destruction; but we can foresee its coming, we can mark its rising signs, we can know the situation that will most expose us to its rage, and we can shelter our heads from the oncoming blast. ("Introductory Discourse," *Series of Plays*, 1: 42–3)

Baillie's metaphor provides an important insight into her theories of identification and of the theatre. Not only does the storm image capture the dynamism Baillie attributes to the passions, and the sense of their independent existence apart from the subject or sufferer;[8] it also conveys her sense of the futility of expecting a rational response from someone – person or character – under passion's influence. The self's underlying landscape is concrete, and resistant to a wholesale transformation, whatever intellectual or emotional stimulus might be applied.[9] Thus for Baillie didactic or morally improving works do not change the basic tenor of a mind. Audience members can learn to prevent the worst effects of passionate storms in themselves, yet no one can change his or her own mental landscape.

Baillie's phrase "native landmarks of the soul" raises, without answering, the question of what is intrinsic to and unchangeable in the mind, and what learned. It is still more striking to see a Scotswoman living permanently in Hampstead relying upon a metaphorical association between the self and a "native" place to express the limits of her own artistic and moral project. The difficult and imperfect mapping of internal onto external landscapes, and the crossing and aligning of imaginary and real boundaries, function as tropes for personal and collective identity in Baillie's plays. It may be useful at this point to borrow geographers' terms for discussing categories of landscape and territory: specifically, the distinction between space and place.[10] In this discourse, space designates an abstract dimension – measurable, even mappable, but essentially homogeneous – whereas place designates environments that have been moved through and used by particular human beings: not necessarily owned, but made familiar and personal.[11] Thus Baillie's underlying self, which direct moral education cannot change, is analogous to a *place*. Yet her theatre theory and these particular plays not only depend upon but evoke the *space* of "the theatre," dwelling precisely on its being able poignantly to evoke placedness while remaining transposeable and widely, if not universally, instantiable. It is here that the analogy emerges between the theatre and "Great Britain" as an idea that does not correlate to a place. In the context of particular plays the tension between place and space, particular and abstract, reflects ambivalent critiques both of the naturalization of the nation as place and of any complete erasure of the sentiments associated with placedness. The result is a theatre that simultaneously mobilizes and questions such sentiments, and a national fiction that at once requires constant maintenance and invites skeptical scrutiny – in an acknowledgment of the nation's fictionality that values it the more, not less, for that knowledge. Thus in three plays, set in the ninth-century British kingdom of Mercia, fifteenth-century Mull, and western Scotland in the eighteenth century, Britain's landscape takes on peculiar forms, involving genuine localities and imagined borders imaginatively contested. *The Family Legend* may be the work in which Baillie most successfully combines Scottish patriotism and British nationalism.[12] *Ethwald* represents a purely territorial, non-political attempt at the "making of Britain" that turns out to be catastrophic, whereas *The Phantom* evokes its Scotland less as a place or set of places than a topos for thinking through the problems of cultural heterogeneity within a supposed collective entity.

With *The Family Legend*, her "Highland Play,"[13] Baillie positions herself for the first time as a dramatist in relation to specifically Scottish themes. In doing so, she reinforces rather than undermines her evident commitment to Union.[14] The play, based on an oral history source,[15] involves the marriage of Helen, daughter of the chief of the Campbells (who live on the mainland), to the chief of the Macleans (based on Mull), a union designed to create civil bonds between the two warring families with the alliance between their leaders. After a son is born, the Macleans reject Helen, her child, and the prospect of peace. Rather than murder her outright, however, they leave her stranded on a rock between the two chiefdoms, to be drowned by the rising tide.[16] An English lover (an invention of Baillie's), whom Helen renounced to undertake her political role, rescues her and restores her to her family. The Macleans, denying their crime, pay a funeral visit to the Campbells, and are punished. Rejecting the violence associated with a stereotypical Highlands for a pacific model of Union, the play celebrates Britishness while painting a heroic picture of Scottish history – and it was received accordingly, Baillie consequently claiming kin with English and Scottish audiences alike.[17]

A closer look at the play's representation of territory reveals the strain of its triumphalism. After all, the central drama consists of Helen's stranding, a literalization of her political and social position. Evidently to be in neither her husband's nor her father's place is to be in no place. When the tide shifts, the place is gone, leaving only an in-between-ness, a space – at once uninhabitable and unstable. The last speech in the play reinflects Helen's predicament by looking forward from its historical setting to the present: the demand for a harmonious relation between Britishness and Scottishness warps space and time. The Campbell chief declaims,

> O that the day were come when gazing southron,
> Whilst thee our mountain warriors, marshaled forth
> To meet in foreign climes their country's foes
> Along the crowded cities slowly march
>   . . .
> Shall say, with eager fingers pointing thus
> "Behold those men! – their sunn'd but thoughtful brows:
> Their sinewy limbs; their broad and portly chests
> Lapp'd in their native vestments rude but graceful! –
> Those be our hard brothers of the north
> The bold and generous race, who have, beneath
> The frozen circle and the burning line,
> The rights and freedom of our native land
> Undauntedly maintain'd . . . " (v.iv [148–9])

Earlier the chief has mentioned the warriors' "noble service" to "the public weal," i.e., interests far broader and more impersonal than any clan's, as they serve the British state abroad in foreign wars. They represent a Highlands whose "primitive" energies continue into the present, but are usefully channeled elsewhere. The operations of the British military abstract the globe into geometric figures and geographical and climatic extremes: the frozen circle and burning line, the pole and the equator, oddly distant settings for the protection of Britons' "native land." The human figures moving through this abstract space are by contrast emphatically bounded and material. British colonial expansion – the diffusion and displacement of locality, theirs and others' – seems both to demand these fantastic Highlanders and to be the precondition of their existence in the present. A broad, abstract spatial system, imagined as empty territory, is the only safe place for so sharply delineated and vigorous a local character – which has nevertheless just appeared onstage.[18]

Much later in Baillie's career, after the *succès fou* of the Waverley Novels had made all of Scotland into Scott country, *The Phantom* develops the emerging stereotype of Scotland as a place internally divided but destined to be united.[19] Set sometime in the eighteenth century in the western Highlands, six hours' ride from a Glasgow growing prosperous with trade,[20] the play involves a wealthy Provost's daughter sent to marry an impoverished Highland chief's son; he, however, is in love with Ellen Graham, another Glasgow girl. In the play's only two acts, one of which is set in the Highlands and the other in Glasgow, the cultural differences between the two locales are emphasized, but only insofar as they balance each other perfectly. Ecstatic landscape description characterizes the Highlands: the mountains manage to be both picturesque and sublime in Baillie's terms. In a similar stereotyping, crowds and business paint a picture of Glasgow: the first scene is set at "the cross," the city's main crossroads and marketplace. The chief's old-fashioned hospitality corresponds to the busy magistracy of the Provost.

Having established these conventional views of a divided Scotland, Baillie undoes the divide through a kind of bait and switch. Ellen, beloved of the Highland chief's son, is also sought by the son of the Provost; she dies of a fever, becoming the Phantom of the title. She appears in the Highlands (home of second sight) to the (Lowland) Provost's daughter, before anyone knows of her death. The vision seems to have been real,[21] since its message proves accurate: a paper in her room discovers that before her death Ellen had secretly become engaged to a Roman Catholic Scot, a Gordon, said to have served in foreign wars. Thus the cultural differences between Highland and Lowland, conventionalized through loco-description, shrink to nothing when figured as romantic rivalry and then set against religious difference – even though Baillie insists on the Scottishness of her "papist" Gordon and makes her characters sincerely mourn him when he joins his beloved in death. The treatment of Scotland as a site of cultural differences and uneven development, divisions at once obvious and destined to be overcome, has become startlingly routine.

Despite the general ideological conscription of territorial issues, these still provide sites of conflict that echo Baillie's earlier concerns. Ellen, dead, easily bridges Highlands and Lowlands in spectral form. Yet before they know of her engagement the two men, Highlander and Lowlander, actually fight on her grave over the right to mourn there: a *reductio ad absurdum* of territorial disputes. In the scene that closes the play, one lover says to the other (referring to Ellen),"We've tacked our shallow bark for the same course! / And the fair mimic isle, like Paradise / Which seem'd to beckon us, was but a bank / Of ocean's fog, now into air dissolved" (*The Phantom* II.vi [590]). Both think of their desire in terms of possessing territory, and that is their shared mistake. Baillie seems to insist: see the bank of clouds for what it is; your desire is both a phantom and real, most real in your sharing it.

A much earlier moment in Baillie's career, on English rather than Scottish soil, yields a less sanguine view of the nation as potentially useful fiction.[22] *Ethwald* is a tragedy of territorial ambition. Having killed one king and imprisoned and executed his heir so as to become king himself, the eponymous Ethwald dreams of uniting all of Britain.[23] Ethwald's almost boundless desire for power leads to his downfall and death.[24] Baillie's characters reinflect her metaphor for the passions – a storm passing across a landscape – in the play's exploration of the relationship between interior and exterior, metaphorical and literal landscapes. Three main points of view emerge: one purely local, one purely metaphorical, and one dynamically combining the two.

A peace-loving thane, Ethelbert, opens the play, expressing his thoroughgoing horror of war through landscape: he describes morning vapor lifting from the land, cottage chimneys smoking, a lark singing, the breeze playing on the woodman's brow, the smell of flowers, and the winding of a hunting horn. These airy images reflect ephemeral pleasures; as imagery they eschew grandeur, and as geography they avoid all issues of mastery or property. War soon disturbs Ethelbert's living lightly on the land. He announces, "the land is full of blood": peaceful cultivation and curling smoke have disappeared (Part I, III.v [174]). Throughout the play Ethelbert idealizes human cultivation. He imagines a "land of peace," of "yellow fields unspoiled and pasture green / Mottled with herds and flocks," which harbors its inhabitants in picturesque harmony: "See through its tufted alleys to heaven's roof / The curling smoke of quiet dwelling rise" (Part II, I.ii [252]).[25] In contrast, for Ethwald himself there is no actual landscape, only a metaphorical terrain providing scope for his ambition. Thus he insistently uses sublime metaphors – storms, mountains, huge waves – but as he strives to take over more and more kingdoms, the approximation of his internal landscapes wreaks havoc on Britain's literal terrain. As he sees upward paths and mountains to climb before him, images of sublime landscape drive him onward: from every mental view there is a further one to reach for. Throughout, Ethwald fails to notice that the sites of his conquests are inhabited and cultivated, domestic and agricultural; the disjunction between them and the sublime landscapes of his mind constitutes part of his insatiability, and part of its dreadful cost.

Ethwald's continued push for expanded dominion, according to his opponents, renders him "hostile" to "the public good" (Part I, v.i [218]). Like Ethelbert, they generally forgo sublime abstractions and rely on landscape description. If for Ethwald the land is pure idea, and for Ethelbert pure place, Hereulf (another thane promoting peace) opens a middle ground. He offers a variation on Ethelbert's theme by describing the wilderness of war that has replaced the scenes of peaceful cultivation: "Worn with our rude and long continued wars / Our native land now wears the alter'd face / Of an uncultur'd wild" (Part II, 1.iii [263]). After noting the land's "alter'd face" Hereulf, like Ethelbert, goes on to count the human cost of conquest in a description of a war-torn family: old men, young boys and women, all working too hard and too sadly in the absence of the men gone to war. The result? Cultivation's end, and barrenness: "The youth and manhood of our land are laid / In the cold earth" (Part II, 1.iii [263]). Whereas in the play's opening Ethelbert had given a simple description of rural pleasures, Hereulf, explicitly using the land as a rhetorical topos, moves landscape imagery in the direction of abstract principles, although he still grounds them in the literal and material, even affirming the naturalness of peacetime cultivation by so easily moving back and forth from natural to social description. This speech precedes the only philosophical statement about war in the play, which is unsurprisingly localist in tenor: "War is honorable / In those who do their native rights maintain" (Part II, 1.iii [263).

Ethwald replies by transforming the literal, if exemplary, family that Hereulf describes into the metaphorical family/landscape of the nation:

> I much commend
> The love you bear unto your native land.
> Shame to that son nurs'd on her generous breast
> Who loves her not! and be assur'd that I,
> Her reared child, her soldier and her king,
> In true and warm affection yield to none
> Of all who have upon her turfy lap
> Gambol'd in infant sport. (Part II, 1.iii [264])

Ethwald's abstract rhetoric of patriotism, love of a "mother land" that has little to do with the crushed and bleeding villages around him, involves no real mothers: only a symbolic mother with a turfy lap who soon disappears in a stream of concepts – weal, gain, pleasure, misery, loss, and sorrow – which are in turn compared to the still more abstract glory, disgrace, and shame. Ethwald's is the rhetoric of nationalism that obliterates its local referent.

Storm imagery, recalling the landscape metaphor in the "Introductory Discourse," characterizes Ethwald's impact. Ethelbert describes his ascent to the throne through an extended analogy with an earthquake.[26] Ethwald thinks of himself as a terrible storm too: "Like those grand visitations of the earth / That on its altered face for ages leave / The traces of their might" (Part I, v.iii [231]). Anticipating Ethwald's death, Ethelbert describes him as an iceberg, a stormy northern swell stopped short by freezing (Part I,v.iii [237]). After Ethwald's death, Hereulf closes the play with a speech that brings together the two threads of pastoral settlement and sublime storm. In Hereulf's words the volcano that is Ethwald implodes; eventually the "hollow vale" it leaves behind will be recolonized. Future people will settle on the site of past disturbances, and the eruption that was Ethwald's life be covered over with the "sunned cots" of peaceful settlement where once there was only "deep and fearful shade" (Part II, v.v [360]). Hereulf's prophetic solution to the play's conflicts, like the close of *The Family Legend*, requires a warping of time. The vision of a cataclysmic rift filled up by pastoral settlement naturalizes historical violence even as it relegates it to a superseded past.

In *Ethwald* as in the other two plays, Baillie stages contested territory at her most melodramatic moments: melodramatic, in the sense of using hyperbolic theatrical gestures which acknowledge themselves as such, seeking and exceeding moral and political limits.[27] The gravesite profaned by a lovers' fight and Helen's soon-to-disappear rock are complementary emblems of the poverty of territorial thinking put on stage by Baillie. In *Ethwald*, the consequences of imagining territory as abstract scope for imperial ambition rather than specific sites of habitation are similarly literalized in scenes of refugees who have fled to caves – their former homes no longer habitable – as well as graphic scenes of dead and dying soldiers, and executions carried out on stage.[28] Feelings of place and ideas of space are amply *described* by the characters, but what Baillie *stages* is the disaster when those feelings and ideas compete.

The stage is the safest and most efficacious site for this competition to take place, according to the large claims Baillie and her admirers make for the theatre. Are these claims substantiable? And can the borderland of the theatre really substitute for disputed territory? After all, the storm sweeping through a landscape in the "Introductory Discourse" is a mental one, and the place in question metaphorical; on closer inspection, the analogy between self and place begins to appear weak. Indeed Baillie seems to insist on the analogy through, rather than despite, its weakness. She seems to be cultivating an increasingly remote relationship between selves and locations – to be wearing away the literalness of the connection with her weak figures for it. If "the theatre" is where the mental landscapes of an audience and of characters, landscape imagery, and literal bodies in space all come together to forge a link between abstract and concrete, universal and particular; and if the successful combination of a more localized identity with the idea of Britishness is predicated on a similarly weak analogy, then Baillie's self-appointed task is at once to work on that combination and to keep it incomplete.[29]

NOTES

1. "Celebrated Female Writers," *Blackwood's Edinburgh Magazine* 16 (August 1824): 163ff.

2. One reason for Baillie's preference for theatre, according to the "Introductory Discourse," is the social and demographic breadth of the theatre audience, including the illiterate and "uncultivated" as well as the higher classes among her "countrymen" ("Introductory Discourse," *A Series of Plays in which it is Attempted to Delineate the Stronger Passions of the Mind, Each Passion being the Subject of a Tragedy and a Comedy*, 3 vols. [London: Longman, Hurst, Rees, and Orme, 1798, 1803, 1812], reprinted, ed. Donald Reiman [London and New York: Garland Press, 1977], 1: 66). Francis Jeffrey, in *The Edinburgh Review*, expressed deep skepticism towards Baillie's claims for the moral effects of the drama, dismissing plays as entertainment: *The Edinburgh Review* 2, 4 (July 1803): 271 ff. The reviewer in *Blackwood's* adduces the historical existence of theatre censors policing public access to the drama as evidence of its social importance ("Celebrated Female Writers," 169).

3. For the life see Margaret Sprague Carhart, *The Life and Work of Joanna Baillie* (New Haven: Yale University Press, 1923).

4. Linda Colley, *Britons: Forging the Nation 1707–1837* (New Haven: Yale University Press, 1992). Leith Davis, whose own project is to "consider how the work of Scottish and English writers over the eighteenth century attempted to articulate an identity by sometimes denying but more often acknowledging the contradictions within that identity'" critiques Colley: "Colley sews Britain together into a seamless fabric of Protestant and then imperial interests after the Union." Davis, *Acts of Union: Scotland and the Literary Negotiation of the British Nation 1707–1830* (Stanford: Stanford University Press, 1998), 12, 6.

5. While he does not discuss Baillie, William Jewett offers a high estimate of the moral and psychological ambitions of Romantic drama:

   The romantic poets wrote and read dramas to understand how we come to take others, and ourselves, as moral and political agents and why we sometimes refuse to do so.

For drama, by countering the ironic dispersion of voices with the solidity of bodies on stage, is able to demonstrate, as neither narrative nor lyric can, the possibility of turning our passive consumption of literature into a means of recovering a sense of ourselves as practical agents. (*Fatal Autonomy: Romantic Drama and the Rhetoric of Agency* [(Ithaca, NY: Cornell University Press, 1997], 16).

6. *Ethwald* appears in vol. ii of *A Series of Plays; The Family Legend: A Tragedy* (1821), reprinted, with *Metrical Legends of Exalted Characters*, ed. Donald Reiman (London and New York: Garland, 1976); *The Phantom* (1836), reprinted in *The Dramatic and Poetical Works of Joanna Raillie* (London: Longman, Reese, Brown and Orme, 1851). Further references to these editions will be given parenthetically by act, scene, and page number, in the absence of line numbers. *Witchcraft* (1836) is equally worthy of discussion in this context but I omit it for reasons of space.

7. Anne K. Mellor writes, "The leading women playwrights of the Romantic era [Baillie among others] . . . consciously used the theatre to restage and thereby revise both the social construction of gender and the nature of good government. They were writing at a time when . . . the theatre was an intensely political place and its influence on the cultural and political life of the nation widely recognized": *Mothers of the Nation: Women's Political Writing in England, 1780–1830* (Bloomington: Indiana University Press, 2000), 39–68(39). In an earlier essay, "Joanna Baillie and the Counter-Public Sphere," Mellor, drawing on Habermas's *Structural Transformation of the Public Sphere*, locates in Baillie's work the notion of a "'counter' public sphere to that constructed by a masculine bourgeois Enlightenment ideology, a public sphere in which the values and concerns of women predominate": *Studies in Romanticism* 33 (Winter 1994): 559–67 (560). One basis for Mellor's claim is Baillie's focus on sympathy, understood as the opposite of masculine reason. Since for Baillie sympathy, as formulated by Adam Smith in *The Theory of Moral Sentiments*, is not gender-coded, the opposition does not hold. More tenable perhaps is Catherine Burroughs's argument (in Mellor's summary) that Baillie's theatre theory "subtly erased the division between the public and the private, formulating the ways in which domestic 'closet drama' could be staged in public arenas": Mellor, "Theatre as the School of Virtue," *Mothers of the Nation*, 40; Catherine Burroughs, *Closet Stages: Joanna Baillie and the Theatre Theory of British Romantic Writers* (Philadelphia: University of Pennsylvania Press, 1997).

8. Adela Pinch argues that in the Romantic period feelings take on the character of "transpersonal . . . autonomous entities that do not always belong to individuals but rather wander extravagantly from one person to another." *Strange Fits of Passion: Epistemologies of Emotion, Hume to Austen* (Stanford: Stanford University Press, 1996), 3; cited in Andrea Henderson, "Passion and Fashion in Joanna Baillie's 'Introductory Discourse'," *PMLA* 112.2 (March 1997): 198–214 (198–9).

9. Baillie's theory has led to a series of seemingly incompatible interpretations. According to Marlon B. Ross, Baillie "encourag[es] the reader to consider not

only the apparent effects of the most obvious emotional outbursts on individual behavior but also how the more hidden, subterranean mental states function within the larger realm of social conduct": *The Contours of Masculine Desire: Romanticism and the Rise of Women's Poetry* (New York: Oxford University Press, 1989), 286. Ross places Baillie among the Romantic theorists of depth psychology, of the modern developmental subject complete with proto-unconscious; see Clifford Siskin's critique, *The Historicity of Romantic Discourse* (New York: Oxford University Press, 1988). In contrast Andrea Henderson emphasizes Baillie's categorization and inventory of human emotions and character based on the observations of surface behavior, claiming that for Baillie the passions, rather than revealing deep truths about individuals, are independent phenomena, reified and verging on the status of commodities. Through physiognomy and landscape aesthetics, Henderson traces the growing value of a kind of staged naturalness, a fashion for anti-fashion, as she puts it: "Passion and Fashion," 200. Somewhere between Ross and Henderson, Catherine Burroughs sees in Baillie a "performative" theory of identity in general and gender in particular: "The English Romantic Closet: Women Theatre Artists, Joanna Baillie, and *Basil*," *Nineteenth Century Contexts*, 19 (1995): 125–49. What these different critical constructions of personal identity share is their engagement with discourses of the borders of public and private personality and activity.

10. See Gillian Rose, who cites Yi Fu Tuan as the exemplar of "humanistic geography" that emphasizes the emotional and sensuous aspects of the experience: *Feminism and Geography: the Limits of Geographical Knowledge* (Minneapolis: University of Minnesota Press, 1993), esp. chapter 3.

11. This use of "space" differs significantly from the Bakhtin-influenced use of the term in, e.g., Saree Makdisi, *Romantic Imperialism: Universal Empire and the Culture of Modernity* (Cambridge: Cambridge University Press, 1998), especially chapter 4: "*Waverley's* Highland space is . . . a *fluid* spot of time, one that can extend itself like an amoeba to enwrap and claim other areas; and one that can, conversely, be beaten back so that it can lose its hold over areas that it once held firmly in its grip" (85).

12. Beth Friedman-Rommell (who provides a wonderful performance history of the play) claims that *The Family Legend* "promotes a specific political message – that peace, liberty and empire will be the fruits of the resolution of internecine conflict": "Dueling Citizenships: Scottish Patriotism versus British Nationalism in Joanna Baillie's *The Family Legend*," *Nineteenth-Century Theatre* 26, 1 (Summer 1998): 25–49 (29).

13. *The Family Legend*, "Preface," xxi.

14. Peter Womack remarks on Scott's "Prologue" to *The Family Legend*:

The inflection of nationality is insistently elegiac, as if "romantic Caledon" is a country from which all Scots are exiled, whether they live in India or Edinburgh . . . The poetical Highlands function as the lost spirit of Scotland; spiritual because lost . . . By 1810 . . . Scotland ceased to be a victim of "British" imperial and commercial expansion and became instead a partner in it ... In this situation, the attitude of the indigenous ruling class towards its own Scottish-ness was inevitably a contradictory one. It needed to assert national identity if this junior partnership was not to collapse in a simple English take-over of its intra Scottish functions. But such assertions could not afford to have any serious economic or political content which might threaten the smooth and increasingly profitable running of the partnership itself. The solution was a de-politicized nationalism ... (Peter Womack, *Improvement and Romance: Constructing the Myth of the Highlands* [London: Macmillan, 1989], 147)

15. A few years earlier, Thomas Holcroft published a three-act melodrama, *The Lady of The Rock*, purportedly based on the same source as Baillie's play, in which he has the heroine and her cross-clan husband reconcile, bringing peace to their two peoples; Baillie's version of historicism seemingly precludes such a resolution. *The Lady of the Rock: a Melo-drame, in two acts; as it is performed at the Theatre Royal, Drury-Lane* (London: Longman, Hurst, Rees, and Orme, 1805). Friedman-Romell details other versions of the story that were in circulation at the time ("Dueling Citizenships," 32).

16. Where Holcroft's stage directions include a woman on a rock waving a handkerchief, Baillie leaves it offstage, allowing one character to glimpse it from a distance, and another to provide a full retrospective narration. Holcroft, *Lady of the Rock* ii.iv (23–4); Baillie, *Family Legend* iii.ii (78–9), ii.iii (85–6).

17. "Preface," xii-xii; see also Friedman-Romell ("Dueling Citizenships," 41).

18. Friedman-Romell informs us that actual soldiers were used in the play's battle scenes ("Dueling Citizenships," 29).

19. Recently intellectual historians have re-emphasized that Scottish Enlightenment thinkers and their followers conceived of the notion that different cultures could exist in different socio-economic stages at the same time. This stadial model of history gave rise to the notion of "uneven development," new in the period when Baillie was writing. According to James Chandler, "The crucial element in this new Scottish-Enlightenment sense of history ... is a dialectical sense of periodization in which particular 'societies' or 'nations,' newly theorized as such by just these writers, are recognized as existing in 'states' that belong at once to two different, and to some extent competing, orders of temporality." *England in 1819: The Politics of Literary Culture and the Case of Romantic Historicism* (Chicago and London: University of Chicago Press, 1998), 128.

20. Scott's *Rob Roy* (1817) perhaps set the precedent for this Highlands/Glasgow juxtaposition.

21. Michael Gamer notes that *Ethwald* and *The Phantom* are "the only plays containing 'real' supernatural scenes in the Baillie dramatic corpus" and asserts that in the latter she "exploit[s] the Scottish Highlands as both an exotic yet safely national locus" whereas in the former she "posited a ... British supernatural by locating [the play] in Britains' druidical ancestry." "National Supernaturalism: Joanna Baillie, Germany, and the Gothic Drama," *Theatre Survey* 38, 2 (November 1997): 59–88 (81).

22. *Ethwald* is based on Robert Henry, *History of Great Britain from the first invasion of it by the Romans under Julius Caesar; written on a new plan* (1771). Baillie writes:

> The scene of these plays is laid in Britain, in the kingdom of Mercia, and the time towards the end of the Heptarchy. This was a period full of internal discord, usurpation, and change; the history of which is too perplexed, and too little connected with any very important or striking event in the affairs of men, to be familiarly known . . . even to the more learned in history. I have therefore thought, that I might here, without offence, fix my story . . . In so doing, I run no risk of disturbing or deranging the recollection of any important truth or of anything that deserves to be remembered. However though I have not adhered to history, the incidents and events of the plays will be found I hope consistent with the character of the times with which I have also endeavoured to make the presentation I have given of manners, opinions, and persons, uniformly correspond. . . . (*A Series of Plays,* II: xi)

    Though appearing in the middle of Baillie's series of plays on the passions, *Ethwald* was not necessarily conceived of as central; see the "Preface" to volume III for Baillie's reasons for curtailing her series.

23. Ethwald declares:

> I, in my march to this attained height,
> Have moved still with an advancing step
>
> . . .
>
> What might not be achiev'd? Ay, by this arm!
> All that the mind suggests, even England's crown
> United and entire. . . . (Part II, II.iii [276–7])

24. There are several parallels with *Macbeth* (Ethwald is also told of his future by witches, for example). Ethwald's imperial ambition is also probably a topical reflection on Napoleon. On how Romantic dramas in general reflect and refract the history both of their setting and of their composition see Terence Hoagwood, "Romantic Drama and Historical Hermeneutics," in Terence Allan Hoagwood and Daniel P. Watkins (eds.), *British Romantic Drama: Historical and Critical Essays* (Madison, WI: Fairleigh Dickinson University Press, 1998), especially 46–7. See also Colley, *Britons*, for how the Napoleonic conflict cemented Scotland's role in Britain through Scots' inclusion in the military (100–45).

25. The immediate referent for Ethelbert's pastoral may be Virgil's first Eclogue; thanks to Ian Duncan for this observation.

26. Compare Hoagwood:

> In the Romantic dramas . . . hierarchical organization of society, under conditions of a revolutionary or reactionary change . . . is often represented as earthquake, deluge, or conflagration. That hierarchical organization, however, is also treated in terms of representational illusion. The problem of the fictive and the false escapes the relatively safe condition of a human dilemma in the abstract and it escapes the even safer condition of playful introversion on the part of the dramatic medium itself. ("Romantic Drama and Historical Hermeneutics," 48)

27. See Peter Brooks, *The Melodramatic Imagination: Balzac, Henry James, Melodrama, and the Mode of Excess* (New Haven: Yale University Press, 1995), 11–13, 54–5, and 106. See also Maureen A. Dowd, " 'By the Delicate Hand of a Female': Melodramatic Mania and Joanna Baillie's Spectacular Tragedies," *European Romantic Review* 9, 4 (Fall 1998): 469–500.
28. Francis Jeffrey was horrified by the violence Joanna Baillie contemplated staging in *Ethwald* (*The Edinburgh Review* 2, 4 [July 1803]: 280). Dowd cites the violence as an instance of Baillie's use of melodrama and spectacle, rather than seeing it in thematic terms: "'By the Delicate Hand of a Female'," 476–7.
29. This may resonate with the idea of surrogation proposed by Joseph Roach, "Echoes in the Bone," *Cities of the Dead: Circumatlantic Performance* (New York: Columbia University Press, 1996), 33–71.

CHAPTER 9

William Wordsworth and William Cobbett: Scotch travel and British reform

Peter J. Manning

I bring together the roughly contemporary tours of Scotland of William Cobbett and William Wordsworth in part to enable distinctions between two figures often associated as nostalgic relics of the agricultural order of their childhoods – Cobbett the farmer, Wordsworth the eulogist of Lake District smallholders – and in part to suggest a more general point about the relation between geographical place and the rhetorical places of argument by laying out the differences in what by title alone would appear to be accounts of common materials – differences in style, format, price, audience, and authorial stance.

Responding in April 1831 to a request for a poem, Wordsworth lamented that "the Muse has forsaken me – being scared away by the villainous aspect of the Times."[1] The Reform Bill, introduced in the House of Commons the previous month, had deranged his equilibrium: "Poor Father," Dora wrote in June, "is quite overpowered by the horrors and sorrows which seem to him hanging over his hitherto favored spot of earth. He can neither think nor talk on any other subject."[2] In part to escape his fears that "if this Bill passes in any thing like its present shape a subversion of the Constitution and a correspondent shock to all institutions . . . is in my judgement inevitable," Wordsworth and Dora set off in September to Scotland (*LY*, II: 504–5).

Wordsworth also wished to see Sir Walter Scott, and the tour began with the meeting commemorated in the poem "Yarrow Revisited," which Wordsworth placed at the head of his new collection, to which it gave its title, in 1835. A prominent dedication, "To Samuel Rogers, Esq. as a Testimony of Friendship, and an Acknowledgment of Intellectual Obligations, this volume is affectionately inscribed," places *Yarrow Revisited* within the circuit of social exchange among three established and by now elderly authors. By the 1830s Rogers, the wealthy Whig banker-poet (born 1763), Scott (born 1771), and Wordsworth (born 1770) were all fixed at the conservative, polite end of the literary-political spectrum. Rogers's

sumptuous reissue and revision of his poem *Italy*, with illustrations by
J. M. W. Turner and Thomas Stothard, had appeared in 1830, and readers
"who have learnt to live in Past Times as well as Present" might have interpreted Wordsworth's dedication as signaling a comparably reflective venture in national characterization.[3] The first section of the volume, "Poems
Composed During a Tour in Scotland, and on the English Border, in the
Autumn of 1831," consists of "Yarrow Revisited" and twenty-two sonnets,
plus two other poems. The Muse had returned, or, as Dora plainly put it,
Wordsworth had "betaken himself to writing verses to drive, if possible, all
that relates to Reform out of his head" (Moorman, *Biography*, p. 465). At his
return he rejoiced that "for more than a month I scarcely saw a newspaper,
or heard of their contents. During this time we almost forgot, my daughter
and I, the deplorable state of the country" (*LY*, II: 448). The month had been
tumultuous; after the dissolution of Parliament in the spring, the Reform
Bill had been introduced for the second time and passed in Commons in
late September, just as William and Dora set out; in October, just before
they returned, the House of Lords rejected it, igniting a nationwide explo-
sion. The poems are not wholly free of the "rash change, ominous for the
public weal" ("Apology," lines 28–9) that impelled their creation.[4] By and
large, however, they reflect the willed suspension of everyday concerns that
in summarizing the trip Wordsworth implicitly defined as "the poetic":

The foliage was in its most beautiful state; and the weather, though we had five
or six days of heavy rain, was upon the whole very favourable; for we had most
beautiful appearances of floating vapours, rainbows and fragments of rainbows,
weather-gales, and sunbeams innumerable, so that I never saw Scotland under a
more poetic aspect. Then there was in addition the pleasure of recollection, and
the novelty of showing to my daughter places and objects which had been so long
in my remembrance. (*LY*, II: 447)

Despite this emphasis on remembrance, once past the tribute to Scott
in "Yarrow Revisited" the poems lack the weight of personal history that
one might have expected from Wordsworth as he returned to ground he
had gone over with Dorothy in 1803 and Mary in 1814. The poems are
surprisingly impersonal, many of them devoted to the expected tourist
sights: Roslin Chapel, the Trossachs. And as they lack a defined narrative
consciousness, so are they empty of other actors. "The Cave of Staffa," a
sonnet in the second series of sonnets that Wordsworth added on returning
to Scotland in 1833, is almost unique in being inhabited, and it is so only
to register Wordsworth's annoyance at his fellow tourists: "Each the other's
blight, / Hurried and hurrying, volatile and loud" (lines 3–4).

In representing Scotland less as an actual place than as a space for solitary contemplation, Wordsworth forgoes a staple of the Scots tour genre. Its heart, for an English traveler, was the occasion to encounter ancient traditions and manners, to stage a contrast between what was seen as a romantic, because vestigial, survival of primitive ways and the commercial society from which the traveler came, and to which he would return. Wordsworth's Scotland is inflected by British political events, but suspends them – a month without newspapers, a month of enchantment.[5] "The time fled away delightfully," he wrote on reaching home, "and when we came back into the world again, it seemed as if I had waked from a dream that was never to return" (*LY*, II: 449).

Wordsworth begins the removal of his sequence from an urgent present with his initial poem. The headnote connects the poem to Scott's imminent departure for Italy, the withdrawal of the figure who had shaped the international image of Scotland, and to Wordsworth's earlier publications: "[The following Stanzas are a memorial of a day passed with Sir Walter Scott, and other Friends visiting the Banks of the Yarrow under his guidance, immediately before his departure from Abbotsford, for Naples. The title *Yarrow Revisited* will stand in no need of explanation, for Readers acquainted with the Author's previous poems suggested by that celebrated Stream.]" The declaration that no explanation is necessary, like the brackets which enclose the note, suggests a self-canceling superfluity, but the rhetorical effect is important. Wordsworth places his collection in the registers of personal friendship and literary history, and defines the present as an absence: Scott's departure. The next poem, the first sonnet, titled "On the Departure of Sir Walter Scott from Abbotsford, for Naples," sets the elegiac tone: "Spirits of Power, assembled there, complain / For kindred Power departing from their sight" (lines 4–5); as power retires, the spirits of Scotland can only be "Mourners" (line 8). The last stanza of "Yarrow Revisited" evacuates the present except as it is the repository of an attenuated past:

> Flow on for ever, Yarrow Stream!
> Fulfil thy pensive duty,
> Well pleased that future Bards should chant
> For simple hearts thy beauty,
> To dream-light dear while yet unseen,
> Dear to the common sunshine,
> And dearer still, as now I feel,
> To memory's shadowy moonshine! (lines 105–12)

Attenuated but tenacious. The dynamic is clear in the closing movement
of the sixteenth sonnet, "Bothwell Castle":

> But, by occasion tempted, now I crave
> Needless renewal of an old delight,
> Better to thank a dear and long-past day
> For joy its sunny hours were free to give
> Than blame the present, that our wish hath crost.
> Memory, like Sleep, hath powers which dreams obey,
> Dreams, vivid dreams, that are not fugitive:
> How little that she cherishes is lost! (lines 7–14)

Memory supplants the present and renders it needless, but it is a memory
devoid of specific contents, and sealed in the past. Though the sonnet
looks back to a previous visit and the occasion provokes Wordsworth to
remember that "Once on these steeps *I* roamed at large, and have / In mind
the landscape, as if still in sight" (lines 4–5), the comparison of past and
present goes no further.[6]

"Poems Composed During a Tour in Scotland, and on the English Border, in the Autumn of 1831" deliberately eschews the fluid exploration and
interpenetration of times that had characterized Wordsworth's earlier poetry. The difference stems in part from the difference in form: the sonnet
invites distilled reflection rather than the nuanced fluxes and refluxes of
the mind, in the words of the Preface to *Lyrical Ballads*, fostered by blank
verse. But verse form alone does not account for the distinction, because
it is also true that the sonnets do not form a narrative sequence: there is
no change in self-perception or gain in knowledge across the twenty-two
poems. As Alan Liu has remarked of the Memorial Tour that looms large in
Wordsworth's successive collections, "the later poet, we may say, is the ide-
ologue of the post-self-conscious and post-imaginative": he is intentionally
"*dis*imaginati[ve]."[7] The sonnets of the tour display a poet who stands un-
ruffled outside, above, or beyond disturbance. Even when life and death are
startlingly juxtaposed, as in the ruins of the Earl of Breadalbane's mansion
and "*new*" mausoleum, the subject of the eleventh sonnet, and the poet
acknowledges "No style / Of fond sepulchral flattery can beguile / Grief of
her sting" (lines 2–4), he remains composed:

> Yet here they stand
> Together, –'mid trim walks and artful bowers,
> To be looked down upon by ancient hills,
> That, for the living and the dead, demand
> And prompt a harmony of genuine powers;
> Concord that elevates the mind, and stills[.] (lines 9–14)

Cobbett's Tour in Scotland; and in the Four Northern Counties of England: in the Autumn of 1832 powerfully contrasts with this detachment. Published in January 1833, the book was made up mainly of accounts already printed in *Cobbett's Weekly Political Register*, and there publicized in advance: "The volume shall be compact and cheap, well printed and on good paper; and it will live long after the whole of the '*feelosofers*' and all their stupid and tyrannical supporters shall be rotten and forgotten."[8] Cobbett's antagonism to the *feelosofers*, the political economists of *The Edinburgh Review* – Brougham and Malthus – was longstanding, and his tour enabled him, in his phrase, to confront his enemies on their own dunghills.

Cobbett occasionally notices a famous site, and occasionally provides the picturesque that readers of a tour would expect:

No man living has ever beheld, in my opinion, a river, the banks of which presented a greater number and a greater variety of views, or more beautiful views than those which are presented to the eye on the banks of the CLYDE. Some persons delight most in level pastures on the banks of rivers, some in woods of trees of various hues; some in hills rising up here and there nearer to, or more distant from, the banks, some of the hills clothed with woods and others with verdure; others (delighting more in utility than in show) seek on the sides of rivers for an intermixture of corn-fields, pastures, and orchards; others, (having a taste for the wilder works of nature) want to see deep banks, some of them three or four hundred feet high, with woods clinging to their sides down to the water's edge; while there are others (caring nothing about sterility so that they have the romantic) that are not satisfied unless they see the waters come foaming and tumbling down rocks thirty or forty feet high, with perpendicular sides, as if cleft by a convulsion of nature... Such are some of the various tastes of various persons: let them all come to the banks of the CLYDE, and each will find that which will gratify, as far as this matter goes, every wish of his heart. (*Register* 78,7 [November 17, 1832], 386)

But Cobbett was not in search of the picturesque. A farmer, he looked at landscape to gauge its productivity, and throughout his life his standard of judgment was the condition of the working men upon it. In this his precursor is the agriculturalist Arthur Young, author of a monumental *Tour in Ireland* (1780) and of *Travels in France* (1792), that by their detailed observation of French conditions shaped British response to the Revolution. Cobbett could tolerate no comparisons; Young, he remarked, "was very weak-sighted all his life, and blind several years before he died" (*Tour*, 260). Before Young came Defoe, who concluded his *Tour Through the Whole Island of Great Britain* with a description of the commerce of Scotland at a similarly momentous period, not long after the 1707 Act of Union

(1724–7). Closest of all was Samuel Johnson, whose *Journey to the Western Islands of Scotland* (1775), and its companion volume, Boswell's *The Journal of a Tour to the Hebrides* (1785), the celebrity of the traveler and popular perception of his antipathy to the Scots had made notorious.[9] For Cobbett, whose *Tour* was published from Bolt Court, once Johnson's residence, the Tory Johnson was a figure to combat. After several passing swipes at "Dr. DREAD-DEVIL" he concludes his book by recurring to Johnson:

> And, now, I, for the present, take my leave of Scotland with expressing a hope, that, going from, and returning to, that very identical room, in *Bolt Court*, from which Dr. Johnson went, and to which he returned to spread over England the belief, that there was not a tree in Scotland, and that all was sterility and worthlessness, I have done something, at any rate to remove the errors which he so largely contributed to plant in the minds of Englishmen, relative to Scotland. (*Tour*, 264)

Cobbett went to Scotland

> to assist in doing justice to the character . . . of our brethren in that very much misrepresented part of the kingdom. This is a duty particularly incumbent upon me, for though I have never carried my notions of the sterility and worthlessness of Scotland, and of the niggardly character of its inhabitants, to the extent which many others have; though I have, in reprobating the conduct of the "*booing*" *pro-consular feelosofers*, always made them an exception in favour of the *people* of Scotland . . . still, I could not prevent myself from imbibing, in some degree, the prejudices, which a long train of causes . . . have implanted in the minds of Englishmen . . . In any other man it would have been of some importance that these erroneous notions should be corrected; but, in me, whose writings, I might fairly presume, extended to every part of the civilized world, it became of very great importance . . . to make, by a true statement of facts, derived from ocular proof, that atonement for past errors, which I have in these pages endeavoured to make. (*Tour*, viii–ix)

Setting himself against "the *prejudices* . . . which have been sedulously propagated and perpetuated by those who found their own interest in the oppressing of us" (*Tour*, iv), Cobbett advances the political agenda signaled by that "us." Rather than seeking difference between Scotland and England, he wrote to establish a consensus for reform cutting across the boundaries of class and nation, to persuade his readers of a common interest sufficient to refute the "crafty and malignant," "old and sound maxim . . . 'Divide and oppress'" (*Tour*, iii).

Cobbett's description of Scotland was inseparable from his political goals. The *Tour* is dedicated to the people of Oldham, who before the book appeared had elected Cobbett to Parliament: "I beg you to accept of it as containing a record of the patriotic sentiments of the people of Scotland, and of the approbation which they, beforehand, gave to that choice which you have made" (*Tour*, iii). The tour had taken place in the time between the signing into law of the Reform Bill in June 1832 and the elections for the first reform Parliament in December. Invited to stand as a Member for Manchester in January 1831, Cobbett was later invited to stand also for the much smaller borough of Oldham, six or seven miles to the north.[10] To embark on a tour of eighty-seven days, a month of which was passed in Scotland, would seem a curious mode of solidifying a candidacy for a Manchester constituency. What made it possible was the immense circulation of the *Register*, which, wherever Cobbett was, continued to appear weekly from London, and from London to reach all of Britain. Hence the curious and potent ambiguity of *place* in the *Tour*; its rhetorical place lies in Cobbett's "incandescent" relationship to his readers, to use the term of E. P. Thompson.[11] Cobbett understood that journalism on his scale effectively dissolved the borders between the nations; thanks to the *Register*, he could campaign in Oldham while touring in Scotland. The rhetoric of the tour is always somewhere other than where Cobbett actually is.

As his title indicates, Cobbett's *Tour* was not *of* Scotland, but *in* Scotland. His destination was the cities, where the people were concentrated, and new parliamentary seats allocated; the focus was not the territory through which the narrator passed, but the narrator himself. "Hundreds of thousands of persons that have not seen me want to see me," he vaunted in announcing his itinerary, "and. . . . as I shall, I dare say, soon be a *law-giver*, I hold it to be necessary that I should see all the people whom I am to assist in making laws" (*Register* 77,8 [August 25, 1832], 459; 457). Cobbett's faith rested on decades of ceaseless political activity, as ceaselessly portrayed in the *Register*:

> I am satisfied in my own mind that the regeneration of the political state of the country would not take place; and that instead of regeneration, anarchy and confusion would come, were I not to be in the first reformed Parliament; there being no man in whom the people have that confidence in his judgment that they have in mine, in the proportion of a thousand to one in my favour . . . [H]ere is this singular thing belonging to me, that I am *known*, more or less, to every rational creature in the kingdom; my enemies are the trumpeters of my talents . . . (*Register* 77,3 [July 21, 1832], 141–2)

Cobbett's nearest audience is the "chopsticks," his usual term for the agricultural laborers whose worsening condition led to riots and burnings all across southern England in the 1830s. His tour carried special urgency because of the use being made in English political debate of the circumstance that Scotland lay outside the operation of the English poor law. Discontent with the functioning of the poor law in England was soon to produce the first major piece of legislation of the reformed Parliament, the New Poor Law of 1834, whose punitive provisions demonstrated that Whig-dominated Reform would never deliver the benefits for the working classes for which Cobbett fought. His split with middle-class reformers such as Brougham, Burdett, and Hobhouse sharpened as he came to fear that the Scots example might be taken as grounds for altogether abolishing poor relief in England. Accordingly, embedded in the *Tour* are two addresses titled "Cobbett's Advice to the Chopsticks" of southern England (*Register* 78, 3 [October 20, 1832], 146).[12] Cobbett begins by praising Scotland, so different from the stereotype of poverty and barrenness. "This is the finest city that I ever saw in my life," he declares of Edinburgh; a page later he adds of the countryside: "the land is the finest that I ever saw in my life." And then comes a dramatic reversal. Cobbett imagines that he has so inspired the workers of the depressed English counties that they will flock to Scotland: "Oh! How you will wish to be here! 'Lord,' you will say to yourselves, 'what pretty villages there must be there . . . Come, Jack, let us set off for Scotland!'" Cobbett interrupts this fantasy of magically effective writing by turning on the speakers that he has just conjured up: "Stop! Stop! I have not come to listen to you, but to make you listen to me!" (148). Perhaps no traveler has ever been so frank about his relationship to those whom he has come to visit, but what makes the outburst extraordinary is that it is not aimed at the Scots among whom he was: "come" does not function deictically as a pointer to Scotland, Cobbett's destination, but to the moment in the argument in which Cobbett confronts his projected audience, the phantasms of his imagination, his English readers. "The government and the parsons tell you the same thing; and they tell you, that if you were as well-behaved as the Scotch, and as quiet, you would be as well off as they are" (147). Against this tendentious use of the Scots to beat down the English laborer, Cobbett deploys a summary of the misery that he has witnessed. A combination of large-scale agriculture – "the farm-yards are, in fact, *factories* for making corn and meat, carried on principally by the means of horses and machinery" (152) – absentee landlords, and a legal system that rendered the worker dependent on the "character" his employer would give him, robbed the laborer of his freedom: "The rent of the land is enormous . . . [but] almost the whole of the produce of these fine lands goes into the pockets of the lords; the labourers are their slaves, and the farmers their slave-drivers" (152). The laborer and his family were reduced to living in a "boothie," a small room in the farmyard shed in which the hands were housed.

On this evidence Cobbett denounced those who preached "*the happy state of Scotland arising from the absence of poor laws*" (*Register* 78, 6 [November 10, 1832], 335). "I have been into the accursed '*boothies,*'" he raged, "I have sent my account of them over the world; I have brought it back to be read in Scotland, while I am here and publicly exhibiting myself with that description having been read by the people of Scotland. I have shown; I have proved, the doctrines of MALTHUS and the EDINBURGH crew to be damnable doctrines: I have proved to the chopsticks of England, that they ought to perish to the last man to maintain the poor-law of *Elizabeth* unimpaired" (335).

Through the *Register* what Cobbett the man sees travels to London to become print, to sway English laborers and to return to Scotland, where his writing both validates Cobbett and is validated by his presence: "while I am here and exhibiting myself." Nor is this all, for the "Advice to the Chopsticks" is prefaced by instructions to the printers

to put it in a half sheet or quarter sheet of demy paper, with a title to it, just as I shall here give. I hereby direct them to print ten thousand copies of this address; to put at the bottom of it, price O N E   P E N N Y; and I hereby direct the person keeping my shop at *Bolt-court*, to sell these addresses at *five shillings a hundred*; or at *three shillings for fifty.* (146)

Writing could scarcely seem more immediate and ubiquitous. Cobbett, dating his account from Edinburgh on October 14, publishing the *Register* from London on October 20, even as we read promulgates a broadside to be disseminated yet more widely and cheaply, and whose effect, in England or Scotland, he could report in subsequent issues of the *Register*.

As this process of observation, publication, distribution, and feedback witnesses, Cobbett's audience was neither exclusively the chopsticks for whom he had organized a huge festival just before starting on his tour, nor the Scots. Starting from Coventry, Birmingham, and Manchester at the end of August, Cobbett descended on the cities along his way, giving one, two, or sometimes three lectures in each. The payment for entrance was one shilling, though he also lectured free to those who could not afford the fee. The price ensured a middle-class, respectable audience at the fashionable theatres and halls at which he chose to perform: "I have found it impossible to lecture in quietness and with order *without taking money*" (*Register* 77, 8 [October 25, 1832], 458). At its conclusion Cobbett summarized his "speechifying tour":

> Speeches out of doors to great assemblages of people   25
> Lectures to persons in-doors   50
> Speeches at dinners   3
>   ——
>   78

In this eighty-seven day period, the sixty-seven-year-old Cobbett, eight years older than Wordsworth, boasted,

I have written . . . thirteen *Registers*, each containing more matter written by myself, than is usually contained in a two-shilling pamphlet. During the same time, I have travelled one thousand four hundred and sixty-four miles, and have slept in five different cities and twenty-four different towns; and, if that be not a pretty good eighty-seven days' work, let the gin-drinking "*feelosofers*" look out for better. (*Register* 78,8 [November 24, 1832], 469)

The price of admission to the lectures, like the immense public dinners offered to Cobbett, was integral to his strategy. At each stop the ritual was the same. As the *Register* described in detail, an "address of congratulations" was delivered to Cobbett at each stop – at Newcastle it was printed on white satin (*Register* 77, 13 [September 29, 1832], 782) – hailing him as the champion of reform. Cobbett thanked the presenters, and then delivered his harangue (his term). Address and speech of thanks were then both printed in the *Register*. Almost more important was the roster of signers of the address, page after double-columned page of names, hundreds of signatures, which demonstrated that Cobbett could not be dismissed as the spokesman of the unenfranchised only. In an abrupt shift typical of his work, Cobbett trained the publicity on the Prime Minister:

[I]f my Lord GREY could have seen the deputation that came twenty miles to bring me the following paper, and could have heard what they said, in addition to what they say in the paper itself, he would have said to himself: "If any considerable portion of such men as these, think as these men think, and have formed the resolution that these men appear to have formed, I must adopt the propositions of COBBETT, or, after a vain struggle, sink in the attempt to resist them." (*Register* 78,4 [October 27, 1832], 220)

The mobility of Cobbett's rhetoric, ventriloquizing speakers from the bottom of the social scale to the top, discloses both the disintegration of the eighteenth-century public sphere into competing class interests and Cobbett's determination to speak across the rifts between them. Again and again Cobbett appeals to his reception in Scotland to persuade Lord Grey of his stature with the actual electorate:

I beseech him to think of this matter seriously; and not to imagine that this unequivocal popularity of mine is a thing confined to the breasts of the *working people*. It was not of these that the audiences at the theatre of EDINBURGH were composed. It was not with these that I was invited to dine in that city of science of all sorts. (*Register* 78,4 [October 27, 1832], 195)

Cobbett might physically have been at the margins of the kingdom, but his rhetorical location was the center of power. Scotland, as a real place, recedes before the narrated presence of Cobbett and the intense political drama that he stages around himself. Though Cobbett controlled every aspect of the *Register*, the paper never lapses into monologue. He dominates, but he composes his character from an array of voices. When the London *Globe* ran an abusive account of his reception at Edinburgh, which the *Caledonian Mercury* reprinted together with a refuting eyewitness account of "the repeated rounds of applause" that had greeted Cobbett, he reprinted both the story in the *Mercury* and the false one of the *Globe*, in order to expose its "filth and . . . beastly ignorance," while at the same time revealing that while editing the paper in London the writer for the *Globe* was receiving pay as a colonel ostensibly stationed at Chatham (*Register* 78,4 [October 27, 1832], 193–4). Taken on a jaunt round Glasgow, Cobbett bypassed his own impressions and instead printed the report of his sightseeing from the *Glasgow Chronicle*, building the vision of his own importance through the words of others. An extract from the *Fife Herald* appears, to confirm the response to Cobbett's lectures in Edinburgh (*Register* 78,6 [November 10, 1832], 345–8). The *Register* is the weapon with which Cobbett turns "[his] enemies" into the "trumpeters of [his] talents."

Published as a separate volume in 1833, Cobbett's *Tour in Scotland* retains much of this vital inner dialogism. But read as it first emerged in the pages of the *Register*, the *Tour* is merely one thread in a texture of reports on the London markets, gazettes of bankruptcies, debates in Birmingham, the reprinting of Cobbett's *Paper Against Gold* (1815), funds, politics in Lancashire, advertisements for Cobbett's publications, and letters from the *Morning Chronicle*, edited by the Benthamite John Black, one of Cobbett's pet hates, originally sent to *The Times*. Cobbett makes the Scots tour part of the ongoing, violently contested, historical evolution of the nation.

And so does Wordsworth, if less obviously. The most obvious convergence between Cobbett and Wordsworth comes in the twenty-seven page Postscript to *Yarrow Revisited*. Wordsworth begins by acknowledging that in the previous poems "the reader will have found occasionally opinions expressed upon the course of public affairs," declaring his wish "to add a few words in plain prose" about those "affecting the lower orders of society" (323). The first section of the three-part essay that follows is devoted to a critique of the Poor-Law Amendment Act that in its insistence that the poor "are entitled to maintenance by the law" (324) parallels Cobbett's stand. Wordsworth argues passionately, but his "plain prose" is not Cobbett's. He explicitly rejects "the periodical press" as a vehicle, choosing instead the "less fugitive shape" of book publication, but the choice is governed not only by considerations of transience. It is the anonymity of periodical publication that Wordsworth rejects: like Cobbett, he expects that his thoughts will "derive some advantage . . . from his name." The signification and the rhetorical effectiveness of the name depends upon the stance of withdrawal cultivated in the verse: "It is also not impossible that the state of mind which some of the foregoing poems may have produced in the reader will dispose him to receive more readily the impression the author desires to make, and to admit the conclusions he would establish" (323). Nominally a mere afterthought, the Postscript thus reconfigures the entire volume as preparation for its emphatic concluding position. Cobbett as onrushing traveler and political candidate illustrates one mode of celebrity and of influencing opinion; Wordsworth as domestic, contemplative Sage of Rydal Mount an antipodal. On the one hand the immediacy of journalism, on the other the deliberations of "a reflective mind" (327), the considered judgments of a "philosophic mind" (336). From their common concern with the condition of the poor the two looked to different remedies: in the brief second part of his essay Wordsworth adverts to the "workmen congregated in manufactories" and urges the "repeal of such laws as prevent the formation of joint-stock companies." In phrases that hark back to Edmund Burke's *Reflections on the Revolution in France* (1790) he argues that the workman cautious for his "little capital" would "more clearly perceive the necessity of capital for carrying on great works [and] better learn to respect the larger portion of it in the hands of others."[13] Just as Wordsworth – unexpectedly – would make the laborer into a bourgeois, so he condemns the man "who, enrolled in a union, must be left without a will of his own" (347). The contrast with Cobbett's recognition that social amelioration could come only with collective action could scarcely be clearer. Rather than Parliament or the unions, the corporate body Wordsworth advocates is the church, to whose organization he devotes the last, long section of the Postscript. Defending the employment of curates, the Scots model he would repudiate is not the exemption from the Poor Law that alarmed Cobbett but the "equality of income, and station" that prevails in the Church of Scotland (342). Cobbett's contrasting contempt for the established Church had culminated not long before in his "blow at the church-parsons," his *History of the Protestant "Reformation"* (part-publication from 1824; book form 1829).

The consonance of their attacks on the hegemony of "systems of political economy" (Postscript, 328) in the 1830s and the vast differences in their counter-measures underlie Wordsworth's mixture of respect for and detestation of Cobbett. He is "a most able and sagacious Man," Wordsworth wrote Henry Crabb Robinson in 1833, though the praise turned as he continued:

Cobbett was asked how he liked the Reform Bill – he replied I am more than satisfied – but I would say to the Minister – 'Father forgive them for they know not what they do.' But replied the Interrogator – I thought you were for the triennial and perhaps annual parliament, and universal suffrage. All that will follow and more if desirable, it is a Revolution, a bloody one would it have been if the Bill had not passed but a Revolution it is, to all intents and purposes. (*LY* II: 610)

Wordsworth's inability to see the Reform Bill as Cobbett and others saw it, as heading off worse violence, arose from the kind of sealed-off memory that operates affirmatively in the poems of *Yarrow Revisited*: "[T]he scenes that I witnessed during the earlier years of the French Revolution, when I was resident in France, come back on me with appalling violence."[14] The return of the past is indicated in Wordsworth's decision to conclude the Postscript with a passage "extracted from his MSS written above thirty years ago," the first publication of what were to become lines 223–77 of Book XIII of the 1850 *Prelude*, his dedication to writing of the outwardly humble, inwardly noble men of his Lake District childhood: "Of these, said I, shall be my song" (348–9).[15] Placing this appeal to his own experience and to "individual dignity" against "clubs for the discussion of public affairs [and] political or trade-unions," and declaring that "if a single workman . . . should read these lines and be touched by them, the Author would indeed rejoice" (347), Wordsworth makes clear his reliance on the individual subject and the space of reflection that divides him from the forging of a group identity that will lead to action that Cobbett's vivid rhetoric seeks. Cobbett's nostalgia for the old days powers an active grasp of the means to shape the future of Britain; Wordsworth's meditative manner acts only indirectly.

The rapprochement of Wordsworth and Cobbett's Scots tours seems to exemplify John Stuart Mill's contemporaneous distinction between poetry and eloquence: "eloquence is *heard*, poetry is *over*heard. Eloquence supposes an audience; the peculiarity of poetry appears to us to lie in the poet's utter unconsciousness of a listener."[16] There could scarcely seem a greater contrast than that between Wordsworth, traveling invisibly through a landscape almost devoid of specific markers or consciousnesses, cherished as an escape from historical conditions, and Cobbett's crowded urban scenes, built up dialogically; but as with all polarities, the terms converge. Cobbett's rhetoric, swiveling from imagined addressee to imagined addressee, points up the artifice of Wordsworth's projected addressee, the putatively universal thoughtful man; Cobbett's political aims remind us that Wordsworth's Scots poems resonate with others in his volume, the anti-democratic "Humanity" and "The Warning," and the Postscript. As we have seen, the *ethos* of disinterestedness Wordsworth cultivates in his opening sequence serves to lend weight to his critique of "manners withering to the root" (Sonnet vi, line 8), and to ground the charges he launches in the "Sonnets, Composed or Suggested During a Tour in Scotland, in the Summer of 1833" later in the volume – and after the passage of the Reform Bill. "Despond who will," defiantly begins the twenty-first sonnet of the second sequence,

> – *I* heard a voice exclaim,
> "Though fierce the assault, and shatter'd the defence,
> It cannot be that Britain's social frame,
> The glorious work of time and providence,
> Before a flying season's rash pretence,
> Should fall: that She, whose virtue put to shame,
> When Europe prostrate lay, the Conqueror's aim,
> Should perish, self-subverted." (lines 1–8)

The confidence of the impersonal "voice" that the "sun" of English liberty will outlast the "black and dense" cloud of transient events (lines 8–10) is born of the same stepping outside time as marks the sonnet on the Earl of Breadalbane's ruined castle. Wordsworth's capacity to enter public debates without being overwhelmed by their pressures depends on the stance of being apart from them; his *dis*imagination, as Liu names it, enables an embrace of topicality lacking in the poetry of imaginative transformation of "the Great Decade."[17] When it comes, the directness of Wordsworth's involvement in current affairs measures the stylistic distance between the later poetry and the displacements of the earlier work tracked by New Historicist critics.[18]

Cobbett's exploitation of multiple forms of publication – the *Register*, the separately published *Tour*, the broadsides – also keeps us from forgetting that *Yarrow Revisited* too was a commercial enterprise, selling out what was for Wordsworth a rather large first edition of fifteen hundred copies, garnering wide reviews, and requiring a second edition in 1836.[19] Despite his insistence that he was committed merely to "a true statement of facts, derived from ocular proof," Cobbett's "eloquence," no less than Wordsworth's pretense of solitary "poetic" musing, underscores that even in travel literature *place* is unavoidably the place, and places, of rhetoric.

NOTES

1. *The Letters of William and Dorothy Wordsworth*, ed. Ernest de Selincourt, 8 vols., v, *The Later Years, Part 2: 1829–1834*, 2nd edn, rev. and ed. Alan G. Hill (Oxford: Clarendon Press, 1979), 378.
2. Quoted in Dorothy Moorman, *William Wordsworth: A Biography, The Later Years 1803–1850* (London: Oxford University Press, 1965), 465. Hereafter cited parenthetically in the text as Moorman, *Biography*.
3. The quoted phrase is from the preface to *Italy, A Poem* (London: T. Cadell, Jennings and Chaplin, and E. Moxon, 1830). Wordsworth had read the anonymous first part of the poem in 1822 "with much pleasure" (*The Letters of William and Dorothy Wordsworth*, 2nd edn, rev. and ed. Alan G. Hill, IV, *The Later Years: Part 1* [Oxford: Clarendon Press, 1978], 153), and Rogers sent him the sheets of the revised work "as the proofs came in" (P. W. Clayden, *Rogers and His Contemporaries*, 2 vols. [London: Smith, Elder, 1889], II: 9).
4. All quotations from *Yarrow Revisited, and Other Poems* (London: Longman and Edward Moxon, 1835).
5. In this the later poems differ from those of the 1803 Scots tour, about which I have written in *Reading Romantics* (New York: Oxford University Press, 1990), 241–72. For a discussion of the complex historical resonances of the 1835 sequence, see "Wordsworth at St. Bees: Scandals, Sisterhoods, and Wordsworth's Later Poetry," chapter 12 of *Reading Romantics*, and my "Cleansing the Images: Wordsworth, Rome, and the Rise of Historicism," *Texas Studies in Language and Literature*, 33 (1991): 271–326.
6. It seems appropriate to the self-extinction Wordsworth cultivates that in amplifying line 4 in a note he directs readers to Dorothy's manuscript journal of the 1803 tour alluded to rather than to any record of his own past experience (pp. 41–3), and even that the customary asterisk to alert readers to the presence of a note at the end of the sequence should have been omitted. Testimony to the past takes the form of Dorothy's words rather than his own in an extended note to the thirteenth sonnet, "Highland Hut," as well (pp. 38–40).
7. See Alan Liu, "The Idea of the Memorial Tour: 'Composed Upon Westminster Bridge,'" chapter 9 of *Wordsworth: The Sense of History* (Stanford: Stanford University Press, 1989); the quotations are from p. 491.

8. William Cobbett, *Cobbett's Weekly Political Register*, 78,8 (November 24, 1832): 468. The *Register* was printed two columns to the page, each column separately numbered. The *Tour* was published January 10, 1833, at 2*s.6d*. *Tour* and *Register* are hereafter cited parenthetically in the text.

9. On Young's *Tour in Ireland* and Johnson and Boswell's of Scotland, see Katie Trumpener, *Bardic Nationalism: The Romantic Novel and the British Empire* (Princeton: Princeton University Press, 1997).

10. See George Spater, *William Cobbett*, 2 vols. (Cambridge: Cambridge University Press, 1982), II: 504.

11. E. P. Thompson, *The Making of the English Working Class* (New York: Pantheon, 1963), 758. The most suggestive, if critical, recent study of Cobbett's rhetoric is that of Kevin Gilmartin in his *Print Politics: The Press and Radical Opposition in Early Nineteenth-Century England* (Cambridge: Cambridge University Press, 1996).

12. The first "Advice" runs from 146 to 155; the second occurs the following week in *Register* 78,4 (October 27, 1832): 199–203.

13. Compare Burke on the advisability of preserving the predominance of property in representation: "The characteristic essence of property, formed out of the combined principles of acquisition and conservation, is to be *unequal*. The great masses, therefore, which excite envy and tempt rapacity must be put out of the possibility of danger. Then they form a natural rampart about the lesser properties in all their gradations" (*Reflections on the Revolution in France*, ed. J. G. A. Pocock [Indianapolis: Hackett, 1987], 44).

14. *The Letters of William and Dorothy Wordsworth*, ed. Ernest de Selincourt, 8 vols., VI, *The Later Years, Part 3: 1835–1839*, 2nd edn, rev. and ed. Alan G. Hill (Oxford: Clarendon Press, 1982), 39.

15. He had also quoted three lines (to become V: 361–3 of the 1850 *Prelude*), similarly ascribed only to "MS.," seven pages earlier (Postscript, 341).

16. "Thoughts on Poetry and Its Varieties," *Collected Works of John Stuart Mill*, ed. John M. Robson and Jack Stillinger, 5 vols. (Toronto: University of Toronto Press, 1981), I: 348. The essay was first published in two parts in the *Monthly Repository* in January and October, 1833.

17. The sleight of time on which this position is based is neatly exposed by the "Sonnet, Composed After Reading a Newspaper of the Day" later in the volume. A note to the title claims: "This Sonnet ought to have followed No. VII in the series of 1831, but was omitted by mistake." In its acknowledgment of Wordsworth's engagement with current events, the title would have jarred with the mood of withdrawal that the 1831 sequence, and all Wordsworth's comments on the tour quoted above, seek to maintain. Whatever the "mistake," the omission made sense for a poet sensitive to the ordering of his poems, so much so that after briefly including the poem in "Yarrow Revisited" in the editions of 1836–7, Wordsworth removed the poem in 1845 to "Sonnets Dedicated to Liberty and Order."

18. A brief tour: Jerome McGann, *The Romantic Ideology* (Chicago: University of Chicago Press, 1983); Marjorie Levinson, *Wordsworth's Great Period Poems* (Cambridge: Cambridge University Press, 1986); David Simpson, *Wordsworth's Historical Imagination: The Poetry of Displacement* (New York: Methuen, 1987).

19. See W. J. B. Owen, "Costs, Sales, and Profits of Longman's Editions of Wordsworth," *The Library*, n. s. 12 (1957): 93–107.

CHAPTER 10

Burns's topographies

Penny Fielding

Where was Romantic Scotland? The act of imagining a Scotland is a subject of debate as much in the twenty-first as in the eighteenth century, and we are familiar with tensions, interplay, and acts of mutual sustaining between the romance of an imaginary Scotland and the social dynamics which both resist and produce it. To conceive of any territory must be in part a question of form and precedent, and there were plenty of generic ways of "knowing" Scotland in the late eighteenth century. Domestic tourism had given rise to a rush of printed *Tours*, "the mushroom produce of every summer."[1] The historical or anthropological tours of Johnson and Pennant produced a diachronic Scotland whose land- and townscapes inscribed a history of people moving uncertainly in their stadial progress towards advanced agricultural practices. Further underpinning the creation of a modern Scotland, the ability of Scottish landscapes to act as a source of the picturesque produced models of identification which not only enabled the tourist to know where and how to look, but also formalized a sense of the nation as being already inscribed in polite literature, obviating the need actually to go there. But the process of identifying a "Scotland," or anywhere else, must also take place at a more basic level: the nuts and bolts of location itself, the task of differentiating one place from another, or the even more difficult one of isolating place from a wider concept of space. I will return to these troublesome binaries throughout this chapter, but primarily I want to think through the more specific cultural conditions that allowed one of early Romanticism's great icons of locality, Robert Burns, to participate in topography, the writing of place.

LOCAL INSCRIPTIONS

In this chapter I explore Burns's relationship not so much with a particular locality as with the abstract processes of location and with the idea of place. "Place," however, is not an easy concept to think about. Place demands

distinctions, otherwise everywhere would be experienced as the same, yet
the borders that define it are always porous and provisional. Despite our
knowledge that maps are always arbitrary, place nevertheless seems to require physical contiguities and meetings. As Doreen Massey has pointed
out, the popular definition of place tends to shade towards "community,"
but communities, unlike places, do not need to be identified by means of
locality.[2] Similarly "region," as the name implies, evokes a specific regiment
or government to demarcate it, whereas our ability to experience "place"
does not depend on its specific political organization.[3] Burns provides us
with models for thinking about both these terms – his tax-afflicted drinking
companions in Poosie Nansie's and other hostelries, or the figure of Coila,
the muse appointed to Ayrshire – and it will be impossible to read his sense
of place without feeling their influence. But the idea of place holds out for
Burns, as it does for more modern writers and philosophers, the possibility
of the a-historical, the synchronic, and the spatial, the chance of identifying a locality which is not understood only through the contingencies of
history.

We need to be careful about thinking in terms of Burns as a "local"
poet, not least because of the extremely flexible uses to which that term
has been put in Burns's afterlife. Along with all the other paraphernalia of
Victorian and contemporary Scotland, not forgetting the practices of the
Scottish tourist board, Burns is pressed into service to stand for various
divisions: Scotland in general, the Lowlands, and the south-west of the
country.[4] Another danger presents itself if we associate Burn's locality with
his status as laboring-class poet, and both with a nostalgic sense of ideal
community. This is place imagined as the lived, the empirical, and the
communicable, the place of shared experience and story-telling, and tends
to be defined in contradistinction to an abstract "space" of alienation: "In
pre-modern societies, space and place largely coincide, since the spatial
dimensions of social life are, for most of the population, and in most
respects, dominated by 'presence' – by localised activities. The advent of
modernity increasingly tears space away from place by fostering relations
between 'absent' others, locationally distant from any given situation of
face-to-face interaction."[5] The lure of "face-to-face interaction" is – here,
explicitly – its logocentrism, the belief in the immediate, communicable
vitality of speech and the sense of loss that comes with the absence of
projected otherness. But the case of Burns underscores how impossible it
is to preserve these distinctions. In his songs, apparently imitative of the
kind of "pre-modern" modes Anthony Giddens writes of, the face-to-face is
already imbricated in the absent other. "The Northern Lass," as traditional

a love song as any by Burns, draws hypotheses of global absence: "Though cruel fate should bid us part, / Far as the Pole and Line" (123: 1–2).[6] "On a Scotch Bard Gone to the West Indies" explicitly predicates the "*merry roar*" (100: 9) of social interaction in a community defined by its localized activities on an imaginary future absence in another hemisphere: Burns's own projected but never realized emigration to Jamaica.

To consider Burns as a poet of locality thus raises two related questions: how the local can be constructed as writing, with its attendant absences, and how the structures which produce the local can be read historically. Burns still finds himself with a double reputation for being the most famous of local poets who is also expected to deliver up sentiments of universal application.[7] Such a structure of equivalence usually identifies each term with the other: Burns is universal *because* he is also local, each singular locality being alike in its very singularity, untouched by the differentiating and alienating forces of history and politics. Burns speaks, to put the matter in the most commonplace of eighteenth-century terms, with the voice of nature. Yet the local identity of the Ayrshire Ploughman rests on two prior problems: how can the singularity of any place emerge from a perceptual field, and how can this singularity be made known in textual form? To understand these questions we need to look not only at Romantic ideas about the creative imagination and its topographic function, but also at the evolution of ideas about place, writing, and difference throughout the eighteenth century.

Burns has many ways of inscribing location. "Tam O' Shanter" alone uses a strikingly wide range of referents: technical measurement (the "lang Scots miles" [321: 7] between the inn and home); local narrative (the place "Whare *Mungo*'s mither hang'd hersel" [321: 96]); European comparisons (the witches' dance is "Nae cotillion brent new frae *France*" [321:116]); and the location of natural phenomena as a global direction (the "borealis race" [321:63]). The poem reminds its readers that place is a product of discourse and that the possibility of a discrete space defined absolutely by its boundaries is purely imaginary, occurring only in the supernatural world where evil spirits cannot cross running water. Burns's own representations of a named locality are adaptable, and even Coila, his local muse and descendent of many generations of poetic *genii loci*, is not as easily "bounded to a district-space" (62: 193) as she claims to be in "The Vision." Coila does not embody locality so much as screen it: her representation of localized Scotland is projected onto her mantle in a bewildering scene which evokes not the bounded nature of the "district-space" but the openness of the sublime: "Here, rivers in the sea were lost; / There, mountains to the skies were tost" (62: 73–4). This is not the sublime as moment of inspiration, however, but rather an already inscribed language of writing; as muse, Coila does not provide a spark of inspiration but a strategic link to the written past and to places already in "*Scottish Story* read" (62: 87). Locality cannot be experienced at first hand but only as a literary structure and, in fact, Burns has already identified Coila's territorial delimitation not as a positive value, but as an empty space as yet undiscovered by Scottish writers. In the verse epistle to William Simson of Ochiltree, Burns laments that Ayrshire, again identified with Coila, has not been recognized by earlier poets:

> She lay like some unkend-of isle
> Beside *New Holland*,
> Or whare wild-meeting oceans *boil*
> Besouth *Magellan*. (59: 39–42)

The as-yet-unwritten is a space already cleared by writing; indeed Ayrshire's "unkend-of" status can only be made known *through* writing. In topographical terms, the pre-existence of Coila's territory can only be understood in the geographic discourses of eighteenth-century exploration: a globe mapped by the names of its surveyors and a New World imprinted with the names of the Old. The local is produced through global structures which are themselves the product of writing and naming.

The shifts in this poem between a narrowly identified point (Ayrshire) and a global expanse (the newly mapped continent of Australia, then known as New Holland, and the Southern Ocean) are frequent in Burns's poetry as he restlessly considers the markers by which place can be read. His references to recent exploratory activities in the South Seas draw attention to eighteenth-century concerns about geographical organization and navigation: the possibility of knowing at what "point" one might be situated on a global structure, a particularly pertinent question for late eighteenth-century Britain as it consolidated its naval powers after the fixing of the measurement of longitude.[8] The ship-board chronometer allowed the globe not only to be mapped, but also to be isotopically fixed with imaginary lines which gave the impression of objective precision and drew time into the service of place to create an apparently stable, navigable structure. This mathematization of space remained an important subject for philosophers (including Hume and Kant) and raises questions about empiricism and epistemology, allowing us to read Burns's sense of locality in relation to Enlightenment theories of spatial relations. Two further questions then present themselves: can spatial relations offer structural certainties that transcend any particular moment of experience? Or can place be understood *only* through experience? Broad though they are, these are questions not only for empirical philosophy but also for the eighteenth-century reader of fashionable verses. Throughout the century and into the nineteenth, poetry frequently returns to the problem of not only describing a place, but also inscribing it and thus recognizing writing's role in the production of place.

The fashion for the inscription of verses onto physical objects – trees, rocks, seats, windows – constitutes what Geoffrey Hartman has called "a dependent form of poetry . . . conscious of the place on which it was written."[9] To extend this line of thinking, we might also say that it is the place which is dependent on the poetry, its singularity an effect of the writing that calls it into being. This acts as an attempt to establish "place" as it is it defined by Michel de Certeau when he writes that "[a] place (*lieu*) is the order (of whatever kind) in accord with which elements are distributed in relationships of coexistence. It thus excludes the possibility of two things being in the same location (*place*)."[10] The act of inscription, then, identifies the place as singular and unique. Yet at the same time it works against any principle of rigorous exclusion; the apparent homology of place and writing in fact sets up an imaginary interiority which has already been breached by the very process which calls it into being. In order to recognize any place or point, there must already be a *structure* of identification. The role of the inscription as signpost or guide drives a wedge between subject and object, reminding the viewer of the external ways of seeing that make the scene comprehensible, and of the gaze that disrupts the calm unity of place and writing.

Hartman goes on to argue that with its development by Wordsworth, the poetry of nature-inscription undergoes an imaginative transformation which binds text and place in an ideal coexistence with the Romantic observer/author: "he gives it weight and power of its own, by incorporating in addition to a particular scene the very process of inscribing or interpreting it. The setting is understood to contain the writer in the act of writing: the poet in the grip of what he feels and sees, primitively inspired to carve it in the living rock."[11] But Burns's inscriptions cannot be seen as tending directly towards this Romantic ideal. They form an uneasy and disparate set which seems to recognize the impossible ends of the inscription form. Some follow the customary eighteenth-century pattern of summoning up a particular moment to describe a highly conventional scene. A poem with the title "Written with a Pencil over the Chimney-piece, in the Parlour of the Inn at Kenmore, Taymouth" (169) invites the reader to contemplate the unique moment of its inscription, yet this leads to a very standard prospect of Augustan nature with a homily on how the personifications of human experience can find solace in landscape. A number of other poems displace their original setting by turning it into a metaphor for the afterlife. "Verses Written on a Window of the Inn at Carron" expresses a hope that the failure of Burns's party to obtain entry to the inn may be a sign of things to come: "Sae may, shou'd we to hell's yetts come, / Your billy Satan sair us!" (165:7–8). Four "Lines Written in the Kirk of Lamington" make the same move, complaining about the coldness of both church and minister, and warning "Ye'se a' be het or I come back" (256:4). These poems argue not for the singularity of inscription but for its iterability: its capacity to be uttered with different significances in a different place.[12] If Wordsworth, as Hartman argues, uses inscription-writing to bind the poet to the place, then Burns draws in the contexts of future readings to mark the impossibility of that binding. In similar vein, and underlining this function of repetition with alterity, is "A Verse composed and repeated by *Burns*, to the Master of the house, on taking leave at a place in the Highlands, where he had been hospitably entertained" in which Burns hopes that "just [such] a Highland welcome" will be awaiting him in Heaven (173: 30). At three words longer than the verse itself, the title pulls the text away from its inscribing function (exaggerating a necessary process for the genre in general). The very supplementarity of the title invades the autonomy of the act of inscription: if the poem can invoke a complete synthesis of place and observer then there should be no need for the additional layer of description. Inscription, so far from demarcating the singular locality, shows that place can never preserve a self-sufficient and discrete interiority.

While the miniature-work of Burns's inscriptions demonstrates the impossibility of a topography of presence on a small scale, he is also interested in the wider system of reference of which each individual act of inscription is a part. Burns turns to this larger scale in his poem on Scotland and its national and global positions: "Caledonia." "Caledonia" is a rollicking celebration of Scottish history as martial force which conceals its more complex relation to the forms of otherness which constitute nationalisms. Narrating a sequence of attempted invasions driven back by the Scots, the poem structures itself round geographical patterns of interiority and exteriority. But if nationhood is to be defined by a principle of inclusion/exclusion, then the poem renders these choices difficult, in both the question of Scotland's relation to England and Britain, and that of the possibility of any fixed geographical position in the first place. Burns's personified Caledonia is a kind of supplementary Britannia whose protecting borders describe and contain Island Britain whilst undermining the completion of Anglocentric Britain. More inward-looking than her imperial sister, Caledonia is largely concerned with resisting attacks from outside her borders in the form of Roman, English, and Scandinavian onslaughts from which she emerges "bold, independent, unconquer'd and free" (253:41). Yet in preserving this discrete existence for Scottish nationhood, the poem glosses over its earlier declaration that Caledonia is already descended from a Scandinavian source in the form of her "grandsire, old Odin" (253:11). What should be excluded from Scotland is already part of its constitution. Just as any totality represented by Britannia is undermined by Caledonia's supplementary yet necessary role, so Caledonia herself fails to preserve discrete boundaries.

The poem seeks to reconcile the myths of an originatory generation which can repeat itself on the one hand, and of eternal presence on the other. Caledonia is at once within history, existing in a series of definable moments, and outside it. When Burns writes "her heavenly relations there fixed her reign" (253:7) two readings are possible: that Caledonia's governance of Scotland descends from a divine ancestry, and that her position is fixed in space and time by a set of cosmographical and mathematical relations. "Relations" are thus both historical and generational on the one hand, and structural and synchronic on the other. This secondary meaning is picked up again at the end of the poem when Caledonia is positioned in a right-angled triangle which seemingly reconciles time both with place and with eternity:

> For brave Caledonia immortal must be,
>   I'll prove it from Euclid as clear as the sun:
> Rectangle-triangle the figure we'll chuse,
>   The Upright is Chance, and old Time is the Base;
> But brave Caledonia's the Hypothenuse,
>   Then, Ergo, she'll match them, and match them always.
>
> (253: 43–8)

Burns's joky confidence in an apparently throw-away reference takes us towards some very large epistemological questions concerning time and space. In its Enlightenment context, the geometrical figure was an ideal object that could be known even though it had no material or empirical character at all. Both the sun and Euclidean geometry had appeared together in Hume's *Enquiry Concerning Human Understanding* (1748) as examples of different kinds of rational enquiry. The right-angled triangle, Hume argues, represents a mathematical axiom which remains true in the absence of any material examples in the observable world: "Propositions of this kind are discoverable by the mere operation of thought, without dependence on what is anywhere existent in the universe. Though there never were a circle or triangle in nature, the truths demonstrated by Euclid would for ever retain their certainty and evidence."[13] What is true here is not empirical fact, but structure – what Hume calls "the relationship between . . . figures" – and he draws a categorical distinction between relations of ideas and matters of fact. The latter are not relational but must seek verification outside their rational structure in the empirical world. Hume gives the example of the sun's rise: "*That the sun will not rise tomorrow* is no less intelligible a proposition, and implies no more contradiction, than the affirmation, *that it will rise.*"[14] It is only custom and experience that allow the observer to predict the sun's reappearance. From here, we are quickly in the difficult territory of cause and effect, Hume's famous discussion of billiard balls and their behavior, and the problems of philosophical skepticism. In Hume's terms, then, the sun is not clear at all but a matter of precarious inference.

At first glance, then, it seems that Caledonia is impervious to history, simply waiting around in eternity until she can be understood by rational method, her origins not dependent on any temporal configuration. Her status as the hypotenuse makes her equal to the territories governed by time and chance and tames and controls them, resolving both causal and accidental versions of history in a fixed and eternal stasis, in much the same way as the chronometer seemed to have achieved the resolution of time and space for navigation. Yet, of course, the poem is *about* history, its Humean context establishing a ground upon which abstract and transcendental structures can be seen to have a finite origin. No structure can exhaustively explain itself from within itself, in the same way that Euclidean geometry cannot be as clear as the sun; to think through the possibility of a transcendental structure requires its materialization in writing or representation. Burns announces this when he writes that the right-angled triangle is "the figure we'll chuse" to represent Caledonia-in-history: if the triangle is really a perfect, eternal structure, then it should not have to depend on any passing poet to "choose" it. In fact, the poem asserts, the "figure" of the triangle is just that: a figure, a trope, an inscription. Geometry – or any ideal structure – is always already inscribed in the empirical in that it must be produced as writing.[15]

ZONAL REPRESENTATIONS

It is his interest in the mathematicization of space and its function as representation that allows us to read Burns's response to contemporaneous notions of place. Although Burns is often read in comparison with, or sometimes as a precursor of, Wordsworth, he does not conform easily to more familiar Romantic models of place.[16] On the one hand, he is not interested in place, as Wordsworth is, as continuity and its attendant losses, memory, and internal autobiography. On the other, he does not pursue figures of deracination to the extent of later poets. Burns, it is true, does have troggers, displaced Highlanders, and betrayed women straying though his verse, but he does not develop a poetics of vagrancy, cursed exile, outcasts, Ancient Mariners, or travelers from antique lands. This is not to say that Burns was uninterested in displacement; on the contrary, he sees it as a necessary condition of the many totalizing systems of placement drawn up in the eighteenth century. The need to put things, heavenly bodies, ships, and peoples in their places drove cosmography, cartography, geography, and anthropology as sciences, but this systematizing urge was always susceptible to writers like Burns willing to point out what was left out, or left over, from such practices, and how structures which seek to explain local differences within a system may also be themselves produced by historical difference. In this section I look at Burns's relationship with one of the most popular measurements of global totalities: the theory of climatic determination.[17]

Climate theory had started as a kind of experimental positivism upon which social history could be based. Famously, Montesquieu had conducted his preliminary enquiry into the effects of heat and cold by experimenting on a sheep's tongue, but by the end of the eighteenth century the theory had taken on somatic identities as a given. Although it was still held by its supporters to give a somatic basis for empiricism, the theory being that heat relaxed the "fibres" of the body, exposing the nerves to external influence and making the subject more susceptible to external impressions, little attention was paid to these details. Opponents claimed that climate theory had no place in empiricism, or any respectable philosophy at all, and that it was consequently being passed off as a "secret" phenomenon whose effects could never be witnessed. Hume writes disparagingly of "qualities of the air and climate which are supposed to work insensibly on the body" and John Millar claims that the study of physiology has not kept pace with the extravagant claims of the climatologists: "we are too little acquainted with the structure of the human body, to discover how it is affected by such physical circumstances . . . and in the history of the world, we see no regular marks of that secret influence which has been ascribed to the air and climate."[18] By the end of the century, a well-worn global network of climatic difference had been established, no longer dependent on experimental proof. The popularity of climate theory instead depended on a fixed, zonal globe. "Climate" itself, though tending towards its modern meaning, was still primarily a spatial term, referring to the zones between the equator and the poles rather than directly to prevailing atmospherical conditions, and thus offers a more fixed and categorical structure than might ideas about the unpredictable agency of weather.[19] Climate theory was not local or contingent but dependent on a scientific and spatial overview which argued that local difference was produced by objective global structures.

Zonal theory argued that whereas geography is determining in a primary way, history itself is a product of climate: hot countries do not have history, which is a product of cold nations. Ferguson writes: "The torrid zone, every where round the globe, however known to the geographer, has furnished few materials for history."[20] Cold peoples, on the other hand, are more ready to admit the influence of political history because they are less instinctively attached to custom. Peter the Great, according to William Falconer, author of the compendious *Remarks on the Influence of Climate* (1781), "accomplished an almost entire change in the manners and customs throughout the vast empire of Russia."[21] So subordinate is history to geography that Falconer here manages to subvert with perfectly logical insouciance Hume's argument that it is political and "moral," not physical causes, that determine human behavior. The very possibility of political change, claims Falconer, is part of the differential structure of climate. Yet despite the boundless confidence of climate theorists that their structure of global totality was immune to the vagaries of history, their strategies are always undermined by historicity itself. The rigorous binary of cold/hot, which had given climate theory its original basis in empiricism, is itself produced by another, less easily defined opposition: North/South. Although it was thought that island nations were different from those with contiguous borders, the main structural force of climate theory was the bipolar axis, as it was after all the tilt of this axis that brought about climatic difference in the first place. Falconer writes that the distinction between North and South is very different from that between East and West:

Some writers have made a distinction between those people who live towards the East or West. But this is of no consequence; and the differences they remark, may be ascribed to other causes. The distinctions of this kind, found in the ancient writers, which are in some measure still kept up in modern expression, evidently refer to a difference in climate. The ancients looked upon the East, as well as the South, as the region of heat, from the countries in that quarter, with which they were acquainted, lying in a hot climate. (*Remarks on the Influence of Climate*, 169–70)

In banishing East and West to the realm of the imaginary in favor of the objective, scientific difference between North and South, Falconer is already in the territory of cultural definitions. Despite his claim that "England appears to be the country best fitted for observation, of any with which we are acquainted" (73), he never acknowledges the relativity of the compass points produced by his Anglocentric view. North and South are as much a cultural vocabulary as East and West, and in fact Falconer quite often grafts the familiar conventions of eighteenth-century orientalism onto his vindictive, violent, cunning, indolent Southerners. The cultural significances of the Eurocentric West are equally difficult for Falconer. American Indians, by this time, were already becoming identified with the tribal social organization of Goths and Celts; yet, seeming to confirm the racial othernesses of the South, they slide into both Northern and Southern characteristics, and Falconer has to hastily contain them in their separate climatic region: they live in a humid country, "over-run with woods and marshes" (165).

Burns's interactions with global taxonomy of this sort were complex. He was not averse to importing well-worn zonal difference into a poem when it suited him. After visiting the Duchess of Gordon he composed some lines to thank her for the invitation, taking the opportunity to oppose the natural freedom of Castle Gordon to the torrid zones and "the ruthless Native's way, / Bent on slaughter, blood and spoil" (175:13–14). Similarly, the familiar trope of the political liberty of Scotland and tyranny of the South makes a number of appearances: "The SLAVE's spicy forests, and gold-bubbling fountains, / The brave CALEDONIAN views wi' disdain" (496: 13–14). On the other hand, Burns has little truck with the climatologists' instance that the inhabitants of Southern regions, their passions aroused by the sun, were characterised by sexual incontinence, while the colder Northerners sublimated desire into domesticity.[22] In a song making another contrast between the rapacious but enslaved South (in this case India) and the simple freedoms of the North, "Winter's wind and rain" are no hindrance to his sexual "rapture" with the "bony Lass o' Ballochmyle" (89: 29–33). Most characteristically, Burns recognizes the provisional applications of terms like "North," which can represent either a distinct global region, home of the North wind or Northern Lights, or a relative position, as in "I Look to the North" (327), where the compass points depend on the location of the speaker and her subjective history. I want to close this discussion by looking at two poems in which Burns turns over the possibilities afforded by thinking through geography on a global scale: the troublesome relation of empirical points, the general structures which allow them to be known, and the historical forces which give those structures their determining force. Although it is impossible to think the local or particular without some form of conceptual generality, the general cannot itself act as a self-explanatory and objective totality; there is always something else at stake. What is at stake here is the whole system of Enlightenment theories of environmental determinism.

In the "Epistle to Hugh Parker" Burns returns to the question of climatic location and its influence:

> In this strange land, this uncouth clime,
> A land unknown to prose or rhyme;
> Where words ne'er crossed the muse's heckles,
> Nor limpet in poetic shackles;
> A land that prose did never view it,
> Except when drunk he stacher't thro' it[.] (222: 1–6)

The particular problems Burns is experiencing in Ayrshire – drunkenness and literary inarticulacy – were qualities commonly ascribed to Northern latitudes by the popular climate theory of the eighteenth-century. William Falconer points to the failure of Northern regions to achieve much in the way of literary distinction: "Whilst sensibility and imagination distinguished the literary productions of warm climates, judgment, industry, and perseverance were no less remarkable in those of the northern. Hence it is easy to conceive, why poetry should be little cultivated in northern countries; and indeed I know of scarce any poems that have appeared there, that deserve that name" (*Remarks on the Influence of Climate*, 64).[23] Not only this, but drinking was also a "vice increasing with the degree of latitude" (37), putting Burns squarely in the frame as a talent-free Northern alcoholic. But the poem slyly reminds its readers that the global reckoning upon which this localized difference depends is itself imaginary. In order to escape from his depressing environment Burns projects a fantastic journey around the globe, wishing he really had the power to "loup the ecliptic like a bar; / Or turn the pole like any arrow" (222: 31–2). Poles and ecliptics (the apparent annual course of the sun seen from the earth) are ideal positions that work at the level of mathematics: they are what enable global systems of location to be understood, and they produce local differences even when they themselves cannot be empirically determined. But the "ecliptic" is as imaginary as the right-angled triangle of "Caledonia"; the perfect structure never to be found in nature can only be imagined as representation or inscription. And of course the status of Burns's imaginary journey as writing descends to the empirical places of the poems' local scale. The epistle to Parker is in part Burns's own little joke about poetry and topography: just as his inscriptions show that writing cannot become place, so here he demonstrates that place cannot determine writing. Even as he is complaining that a land which has never encountered poetry is deadening his own creative imagination, he is also writing a poem.

Burns's engagement with drinking, place, and representation has its most sustained appearance in "The Author's Earnest Cry and Prayer, to the Right Honorable and Honorable, the Scotch Representatives in the House of Commons," another work whose philosophical entanglements have been overlooked because of its mock-heroic tone.[24] The poem announces that it will take displacement as its subject. Addressing himself to "Ye IRISH LORDS, ye *knights* an' *squires*, / Wha represent our BURGHS and SHIRES" (81: 1–2), Burns pitches into an extreme example of the absences upon which democracy rests. If there is always an institutional slippage between "the people" constituted as a body and their representatives, then this is doubly so in the case of Scotland. While the eldest sons of Scottish peers were still ineligible to take up seats in Parliament, their places were taken by the Anglo-Irish aristocracy. But the poem is about the representation of Scotland in more ways than one. Arguing for the fair taxation of Scotch whisky, this is another take on Burns's recurrent musings about liberty and national identity, but a vexed and ultimately uncertain one which asks not only how Scotland can be represented in Parliament, but also how any given locality can represent itself at all. The poem explores two systems of identification, political and symbolic representation, neither of which seems to be doing its job very satisfactorily.

Burns plays throughout with the fragility of "place." The term, in this poem, means parliamentary seat (the Scots representatives are warned about the vulnerability of their "place" [81: 136]) and thus can only be filled by a representative. Yet, as in the derogatory eighteenth-century term "placeman," the members' representative function is drawn not from the "place" they represent, but from the patron by whom they have been "placed" in power. "Scotland" herself keeps slipping from one representation to another: the members are invited to "paint Scotland greetan owre her thrissle" (81: 37), but this picture changes in quick succession to an impoverished woman with her pocket picked, then an Amazonian soldier running "red-wud / About her *Whisky*" (81: 95–6). Whisky is on the one hand the "Scotch Drink" of the earlier poem of that title, the "strong *heart's blood*" (77: 23) of Scotland, essential, somatic, and literally productive of a behavioral quality of Scottishness. It is beer and whisky that bring together Scottish society: drink is "the life o' public haunts" (77: 43), resolves legal arguments (77: 73–8), and generally acts as the lubricant of commercial, cultural, and convivial encounters. This, according to Falconer, is the beneficial result of the northern nations' "natural" affinity with drink.

"Drunkenness . . . is much less culpable in a cold climate, than in a hot one; as in the former the hospitable disposition of the people, and the necessity of the use of strong liquors to a certain degree, naturally lead to it" (*Remarks on the Influence of Climate*, 31). Following Falconer's line of reasoning, the "natural" propensity of cold-climate dwellers to take alcohol is the foundation of their social cohesion: "Fermented liquors have also the effect of opening the mind, and rendering social intercourse more free and chearful, and individuals more communicative . . . Perhaps the greater use of these liquors may account, in general, for the greater openness and frankness of the northern nations; and also for the great degree of hospitality practised by them" (*Remarks on the Influence of Climate*, 250). Falconer's extremely causal line of argument places liquor at the centre of the admirable democracy of the North and moves smoothly between a geographical origin and a political telos.

Yet, on the other hand, the poem is ambivalent about the association of drink and democracy, and dismisses the environmental theory that produced it:

> Sages their solemn een may steek,
> An' raise a philosophic reek,
> An' physically causes seek,
>   In *clime* an' *season*,
> But tell me *Whisky's* name in Greek,
>   I'll tell the reason. (81: 175–80)

Of course, things are not quite this simple. In his identification of Scotland with her national drink, Burns has already set foot in the "philosophical reek" of eighteenth-century climate theory when comparing the lot of "half-starv'd slaves in warmer skies" (81: 145) to that of Scotland's "freeborn, martial boys" (81: 149), picking up on the common argument that the people of hot nations were timid and easily enslaved by their rulers whereas the bolder cold nations derive strength from fighting the elements (and each other). But the poem's complex ironies cannot fix on any stable, causal linkage of national symbol with environment. The martial "freedom" afforded by whisky soon turns into somatic determinism of a different kind: the courage of Scotland's alcohol-fortified regiments to die for the British state under "royal GEORGE's will" (81: 165). Burns needs the structural location that allows him to isolate national identity: whisky is Scottish because it is not wine (81: 146), in the same way that haggis is Scottish because it is not *ragout, olio, fricassee,* or any other Southern European dish (136: 25–7). Yet whisky is also an inscription, and thus subject to politics as well as

geography: in the appeal to grant Scotland freedom to enjoy its national
drink, the very naturalness of that identification is undercut by the slippery
politics of political "place."

As ever in Burns's case, topography remains an impossible delimitation
which always subverts the convenience of characterizing him as a "local"
poet in any predetermined way. The correlation of "native soil" (72: 172)
and "the native feelings strong, the guileless ways" (72: 7) of "The Cottar's
Saturday Night" implies a kind of autochthonic spontaneous utterance
which is far from representative of his poetry in general. Burns's own
strategies both move us away from the binaries in which we have been
accustomed to think of him (rural and urban life, England and Scotland,
the local and the global) and also free him from the obligation of representing particular localities. As a poet, he is far more interested in exploring
the textual determinants of placing, than in positing a lived, pre-textual
place. Neither a "national" nor a "local" bard, Burns's complex investigation of topography allows us to consider the political and epistemological
structures of late eighteenth-century geography which produce "place" as
inscription.

NOTES

1. John Stoddart, *Remarks on Local Scenery and Manners in Scotland During the
   Years 1799 and 1800* (London: William Millar, 1801), viii. For the place of tour
   narratives in the generation of nationalist discourse see Katie Trumpener, *Bardic
   Nationalism: The Romantic Novel and the British Empire* (Princeton: Princeton
   University Press, 1997), chs. 1 and 2.

2. On the one hand, communities can exist without being in the same place – from networks
   of friends with like interests, to major religions, ethnic or political communities. On
   the other hand, the instances of places housing single 'communities' in the sense of
   coherent social groups are probably – and, I would argue, have for long been – quite
   rare. Moreover, even where they do exist this in no way implies a single sense of place.
   For people occupy different positions within any community. (Doreen Massey, *Space,
   Place and Gender* [Cambridge: Polity Press, 1994], 153)

3. For the concomitant difficulties of understanding "region" see Roberto M.
   Dainotto, *Place in Literature: Regions, Cultures, Communities* (Ithaca and
   London: Cornell University Press, 2000), 1–33.

4. By a strange twist of tartan logic, it is not unknown for Burns also to be taken
   to represent the *Highlands* of Scotland. In Len Deighton's spy thriller *Billion
   Dollar Brain*, the urbane KGB man Colonel Stok recites "To a Mouse" "with
   an excellent Highland accent." *Billion Dollar Brain* (Harmondsworth: Penguin,
   1966), 108.

5. Anthony Giddens, *The Consequences of Modernity* (Cambridge: Polity Press, 1990), 18. To give Giddens's argument its due, it might be claimed that Burns is a "modern" author representing a "pre-modern" community impossible in the 1780s. But, as post-structuralism has demonstrated, it is impossible *ever* to call up that pure presence of face-to-face communication, as all communication must evoke absence, and Burns is as good an example of this as any.
6. References are to poem and line number in Robert Burns, *Poems and Songs*, ed. James Kinsley (Oxford: Oxford University Press, 1969).
7. See, for example, Thomas Crawford's comment that "Burns's development as a poet was from the local to the national to the universal." *Burns: A Study of the Poems and Songs* (Edinburgh: Oliver and Boyd, 1960), 342.
8. See E. G. R Taylor, *The Haven-Finding Art: A History of Navigation from Odysseus to Captain Cook*, new edn. (London: Institute of Navigation, 1971). For the globalization of geographical knowledge in the eighteenth-century see Roy Porter, "The Terraqueous Globe," in G. S. Rousseau and Roy Porter (eds.), *The Ferment of Knowledge: Studies in the Historiography of Eighteenth-century Science* (Cambridge: Cambridge University Press, 1980), 285–324. For the construction of totalized systems built on this knowledge see David Harvey's account of "the time and space of the Enlightenment project", *The Condition of Postmodernity* (Oxford: Blackwell, 1989), 240–59. For the role of Scottish geographers in a "unifying discourse, designed to gather information about the globe" see Charles W. J. Withers, "Geography, Natural History and the Eighteenth-Century Enlightenment: Putting the World in Place," *History Workshop Journal* 39 (1995): 137–63 (142).
9. Geoffrey H. Hartman, "Inscriptions and Romantic Nature Poetry," *The Unremarkable Wordsworth* (London: Methuen, 1987), 31–46 (32). See also Jonathan Bate, *Romantic Ecology: Wordsworth and the Environmental Tradition* (London and New York: Routledge, 1991), 85–115.
10. Michel de Certeau, *The Practice of Everyday Life*, trans. Steven Rendall (Berkeley and Los Angeles: University of California Press, 1984), 117. See also J. Hillis Miller's account of the way Derrida deconstructs the logocentrism of topography's claim to the law of non-contradiction: "Derrida's Topographies," *Topographies* (Stanford: Stanford University Press, 1995), 291–315.
11. Hartman, "Inscriptions and Romantic Nature Poetry," 40.
12. I use the "iterability" in the sense explored by Jacques Derrida in "Signature, Event, Context," *Limited Inc*, trans. Samuel Weber and Jeffrey Mehlman (Evanston: Northwestern University Press, 1988), 1–23.
13. David Hume, *Enquiries Concerning Human Understanding and Concerning the Principles of Morals*, ed. L. A. Selby-Bigge, 3rd edn, rev. P. H. Nidditch (Oxford: Clarendon Press, 1972), 25. Hume did not offer geometrical forms as ideal objects in anything other than the philosophical sense and viewed geometry as a dangerous precedent which, because of its ability to sustain infinite divisibility, was liable to attract the attention of metaphysicians. See *Enquiries*, 156. For Euclidean geometry in the *Enquiry*, see Marina

Frasca-Spada, *Space and the Self in Hume's Treatise* (Cambridge: Cambridge University Press, 1998), 135–40.

14. Hume, *Enquiries Concerning Human Understanding*, 25–26.
15. I have confined this discussion of the poem to its eighteenth-century terms as an argument between Burns and Hume, but these questions of geometry, history, and transcendental objects have been famously revisited in the twentieth century in Jacques Derrida's first published work, his *Introduction to Husserl's "Origin of Geometry,"* trans. John P. Leavey Jr. (Lincoln: University of Nebraska Press, 1989). Derrida argues that through inscription "Historical incarnation sets free the transcendental, instead of binding it" (77). See also John Pickles, *Phenomenology, Science and Geography: Spatiality and the Human Sciences* (Cambridge: Cambridge University Press, 1985). For connections between Hume and phenomenology see R. A. Mall, *Experience and Reason: the Phenomenology of Husserl and its Relation to Hume's Philosophy* (The Hague: Martinus Nijhoff, 1973). For Hume in relation to eighteenth-century geography see Margarita Bowen, *Empiricism and Geographical Thought: From Francis Bacon to Alexander von Humboldt* (Cambridge: Cambridge University Press, 1981), 134–43.
16. For an important recent study of Burns, Wordsworth, and the representation of localities see Leith Davis, *Acts of Union: Scotland and the Literary Negotiation of the British Nation* (Stanford: Stanford University Press, 1998), 107–43. Davis argues that Burns "makes the local a place of power from which he can critique the dominant tradition" (113).
17. For an overview see Christopher Berry, "'Climate' in the Eighteenth Century: James Dunbar and the Scottish Case," *Texas Studies in Literature and Language* 16: 2 (1974): 281–92. Interest in climate theory has recently given rise to some important work on eighteenth-century gender and sexuality; see Felicity A. Nussbaum, *Torrid Zones: Maternity, Sexuality, and Empire in Eighteenth-century English Narratives* (Baltimore: Johns Hopkins University Press, 1995); and Clare Brant, "Climates of Gender," in Amanda Gilroy (ed.), *Romantic Geographies: Discourses of Travel 1775–1844* (Manchester: Manchester University Press, 2000), 129–49.
18. David Hume, "On National Characters," *Essays: Moral, Political and Literary* (Oxford: Oxford University Press, 1963), 202. John Millar, *Origin of the Distinction of Ranks*, 3rd edn (London: J. Murray, 1779), 12–13.
19. See Arden Reed, *Romantic Weather, The Climate of Coleridge and Baudelaire* (Hanover, NH and London: University Press of New England, 1983).
20. Adam Ferguson, *An Essay on the History of Civil Society*, ed. Duncan Forbes (Edinburgh: Edinburgh University Press, 1966), 110.
21. William Falconer, *Remarks on the Influence of Climate* (London: C. Dilley, 1781), 116. Further references appear in the text.
22. "As it departs from the sun . . . passion is further composed into a habit of domestic connection or frozen into a state of insensibility, under which the sexes at freedom scarcely chuse to unite their society." Ferguson, *Essay on Civil Society*, 116.

23. A belief in the literature-free environment of the North seems to have persisted into the twentieth century when Sir William Craigie was obliged to give the 1931 Alexander Lectures at the University of Toronto under the title *The Northern Element in English Literature* (Toronto: University of Toronto Press, 1933) to prove that such a tradition existed. Even so, Craigie concluded that "England has from the beginning produced a literature in which the North has a very slender share until quite recent times. Its models and its subjects have come to it mainly from the South – from actual contact with more southern countries, or from familiarity with their literatures through the centuries" (7).

24. Marilyn Butler observes that the introduction of a new Distilleries Act before the poem's publication de-fanged an already less than biting satire: "A poem already essentially light-hearted and familiar has lost any appearance of threat that it might have had." "Burns and Politics," in Robert Crawford (ed.), *Robert Burns and Cultural Authority* (Edinburgh: Edinburgh University Press, 1997), 86–112 (93). A more useful summary of the poem's tone, I think, comes from Thomas Crawford, whose description of the postscript as "remarkable . . . for the complexity of its irony" is also true of the poem as a whole. *Burns: A Study of the Poems and Songs*, 153.

CHAPTER II

At "sang about": Scottish song and the challenge to British culture

Leith Davis

In *Strange Country: Modernity and Nationhood in Irish Writing Since 1790*, Seamus Deane comments on the process of translating Irish oral sources into print:

> The sounds that issue from the mouths of the Irish – as speech, song, or wail – pose a challenge for those who wish to represent them in print . . . What is taken in by and emitted from the mouth cannot easily be represented in print. The movement from an oral to a print culture is not simply a matter of translating folk tales or customs from the mouths of the people to the page. It involves an attempt to control a strange bodily economy in which food, drink, speech and song are intimately related.[1]

For Deane, translation operates as a violent form of control, a cutting off of the organic body in an attempt to assert ideological power. In this chapter I extend and modify Deane's analysis in examining the case of Scotland in the eighteenth century and the Romantic era, as I argue that the representation of Scottish songs in printed collections served not just to promote the cultural hegemony of a London-based Britain, but in many cases to challenge the basis of its power.

Collections of notated Scottish songs – for dancing, musical instruction, and amateur playing – began circulating throughout Britain before the eighteenth century, published variously in Edinburgh, London, and even Dublin and Paris.[2] As David Johnson notes: "There was, in London in the 1680s, a flourishing genre called 'Scotch songs'; these were somewhat debased popular songs of allegedly Scottish origin, some with fake tunes, all with fake words, and Londoners liked them because they were refreshingly different from the classical productions of Purcell and Lully" (*Music and Society*, 131). While many "Scotch songs" were drawn from an "invented" traditional corpus, as Johnson suggests, others derived from (or were loosely based on) songs from actual oral sources. The translation of these songs into written music, initially in manuscript form, then in printed collections, altered them in a number of significant ways. First, notation enforced more uniformity on the songs.[3] As Michael Chanan observes, "the development of notation has the effect of shaping musical materials to satisfy its own demands, thereby marginalizing and excluding from its syntax whatever it is unable to capture."[4] In addition, the songs were presented with musical accompaniment by non-traditional instruments (German flute, hautboy, harpsichord, and, by the end of the century, pianoforte) or, in many cases, lyrics were omitted completely and only the title was retained. The process of printing also changed the relationship between music, musician, and audience implicit in the original performance of Scottish songs. The local "bodily economy" of which the original songs were part was left behind, as "Scotch songs" became commodities available in shops and performed in drawing-rooms all over Britain.

In addition to altering the nature of Scottish songs, early printed collections served to homogenize the geographical and cultural peripheries of Britain. Many of the early collections were designed to appeal to a metropolitan interest in the novelty of the provinces. Songs from both the Lowland and Highland regions of Scotland are mixed together with songs from other Celtic areas. Daniel Wright's *Aria di Camera* (London, 1725), for example, bills itself as "*a Choice Collection of Scotch, Irish, & Welsh Air's* [*sic*]," compiled by representatives of the three nations. The tunes from each nation are commingled, and there are no editorial indications of their separate national affiliations. Neither does Wright seem at all concerned with establishing an accurate transliteration of his titles. Rather, as his Italian title, *Aria di Camera*, suggests, his object is to render the tunes in a manner appropriate for chamber music. Burke Thumoth also published several other collections of songs from the Celtic periphery, including *Twelve Scotch and Twelve Irish Airs with Variations* (London, c. 1745), arranged for the German flute, violin, or harpsichord.[5] As Thumoth's case suggests, quite often publishers who had been successful with a collection of music of one nation would try their hand at another flavor of national music. John and William Neal of Dublin, for example, published *A Colection* [sic] *of the Most Celebrated Irish Tunes* (Dublin, c. 1726) as well as a similarly titled *Colection* [sic] *of the most Celebrated Scotch Tunes* (Dublin, c. 1726). Such Scottish identity as is acknowledged in these collections is designed to appeal to an audience interested in a distinctive but harmless Scottish or "Highland humour," as Playford's *A Collection of Original Scotch-tunes (full of the Highland humours) for the violin* (London, 1700) calls it. For the most part, this "humour" is characterized as natural, simple and rural, in opposition to the artificiality of metropolitan culture.

Orpheus Caledonius (London, 1725), for example, a compilation by William Thomson, a Scot living in London, begins with a poem which contrasts the "True Passion" of the lads and lasses found in songs like "Peatie's Mill" with the "Beaus and Belles so fine and fair" (1) of the capital. Early publications of Scottish music work to create a homogeneous sense of British culture with London as the cosmopolitan center to the rustic (and disembodied) Celtic peripheries.

Allan Ramsay's *Tea-Table Miscellany*, first published in 1724, represents Scottish songs in a very different context. Ramsay's collection does not cater to a London audience, as, unlike contemporary collections, the *Miscellany* does not include music to the songs.[6] Instead, it presents only lyrics and an indication of which song is to be used with each set of lyrics. At times the tune is obvious from the title of the song; at other times, Ramsay includes the instructions "To the tune of . . ." In order for his readers to fully appreciate and understand his work, they must already be familiar with the tunes of the songs. In other words, they must have some intimate knowledge of Scottish folk culture. In addition, whereas collections like the Neals' and Thompson's present music without reflection on the performance of the work, Ramsay addresses the issue of performance in his "Dedication," as he builds the participation of his readers into the meaning of his collection. Without singers "reviv[ing]" the songs with their "tunefu' notes . . . Arising saftly thro' [their] throats," he suggests, his work will fail.[7] While the songs may have been disembodied from the people who originally sang them, Ramsay imagines them being re-embodied in new contexts by the consumers of his work, "Ilka lovely British lass" who sings while she pours tea or "dances on the green" (1: v).[8]

Ramsay uses Scottish music in order to provide a positive identity for the Scots in the years shortly following the Act of Union, but he does not want the music to link Scotland simply to a nostalgic past or a rustic identity. He notes that Scots tunes are universally appreciated: "Scots tunes . . . have an agreeable gaiety and natural sweetness, that make them acceptable wherever they are known, not only among ourselves, but in other countries" (1: vii). But he presents the music as popular because it is good, not because it reflects a natural "Scotch humour." David Johnson argues that the *Tea-Table Miscellany* "was nothing less than an attempt to set up, single-handed, a complete new Scottish song repertory" (*Music and Society*, 134). It is important to keep in mind that Ramsay was establishing this new repertory in conjunction with maintaining aspects of the oral tradition. The majority of the tunes mentioned in the *Miscellany*, for example, are traditional tunes. The performance of these tunes links the singer, albeit indirectly, to the

Scottish past. Ramsay provides a number of possible lyrics for each tune, both traditional lyrics and those which he and others wrote specifically for the *Miscellany*. By including new songs, Ramsay represents Scottish song not as a fixed corpus, but as part of a dynamic and ever-changing tradition. Those songs which were written for the *Miscellany* draw more heavily on art song than folksong in a further attempt to illustrate Scotland's cultural sophistication.

Instead of reinforcing the subordination of Scotland to a hegemonic center, Ramsay works to change the model of a powerful, cosmopolitan London versus a weak, traditional Scottish periphery. He eventually expanded his project to include not just Scottish but English songs. In the new work, *The Tea-Table Miscellany: Or, A Collection of Choice Songs, Scots and English* (1737), the Scottish dominate the English songs, making the latter nation's musical contribution appear minimal. In addition, Ramsay emphasizes the international connections that Scottish music promotes. In particular, he notes the popularity of the *Miscellany* in America, as he includes the following verses by Dr. Bannerman in the Preface:

> Nor only do your lays o'er *Britain* flow.
> Round all the globe your happy sonnets go;
> Here thy soft verse made to a *Scottish* air,
> Are often sung by our *Virginian* fair.
> [Bononcini's] *Camilla's* warbling notes are heard no more,
> But yield to *Last time I came o'er the moor*;
> [Mancini's] *Hydaspes* and [Handel's] *Rinaldo* both give way
> To *Mary Scot, Tweed-side*, and *Mary Gray*. (1: viii)

Songs from the *Miscellany* serve as an indication of the power of Scottish culture to dispel the fervor for Italian opera.

Ramsay also challenges the disciplinary divisions between the arts that were being established at the time in Britain, as he implies that Scottish songs combine aspects of both poetry and music. In his Preface to the *Miscellany* he writes: "[the Scottish songs] must relish best with people who have not bestowed much of their time in acquiring a taste for that downright perfect music, which requires none, or very little of the poet's assistance" (1: viii). Ramsay intimates that music combined with poetry, which he calls "an harmonious speaking" (1: viii), is preferable to pure music. I want to explore this point a little further, situating Ramsay's commentary on Scottish song's fusion of "words and melody" within the context of what Lawrence Lipking describes as the impulse to establish the "modern rules" of the arts in the eighteenth century. According to Lipking, "Painting, music and poetry

attracted larger audiences than ever before, but their accomplishments had
not been set in order . . . For the first time many Englishmen thought it important that their arts should have a history and their tastes should have a
guide."[9] James Harris's "A Discourse on Music, Painting and Poetry" (1744)
registers this rage for order: "The Design of this Discourse is to treat of
MUSIC, PAINTING AND POETRY; to consider in what they *agree*, and in what
they *differ*."[10] Although Lipking attributes the "transformation in studies
of the arts" to a newfound interest in "both history and the arts," the urge
was also fed by nationalist interests. The founding of the Royal Academy,
the Shakespeare Jubilee of 1769, and the Handel Commemoration of 1784,
to which Lipking refers, are not just "tokens of a great surge of popular
appreciation and respect for the arts" (*The Ordering of the Arts*, 7), but
also a reflection of the desire to promote an English-dominated British
national identity by endowing it with a firm cultural foundation.[11]

The project to establish the foundations of the British arts also involved assigning relative value to the different disciplines in order to determine which of the arts "IS MORE EXCELLENT THAN THE OTHER TWO"
("A Discourse," 55), in Harris's words. And the measuring stick most often
used in this determination was the medium's imitative capacity. Harris asserts that music has the weakest power of imitation of the three fine arts.
Working from the assumption that "the *Definite* and *Certain* is ever preferable to the *Indefinite* and *Uncertain*" ("A Discourse," 80), he concludes that
music is inferior to poetry (which is itself inferior to painting in terms of
imitative ability), because "MUSICAL IMITATIONS, tho' *Natural*, aspire not to
raise the *same* Ideas, but only Ideas *similar* and analogous" ("A Discourse,"
80). John Brown echoes Harris's view, observing in his *A Dissertation on the
Rise, Union, and Power, The Progressions, Separations, and Corruptions, Of
Poetry and Music* (1763) that the "Expressions" of music are "general and
vague" in comparison with those found in poetry.[12] Music clearly ranks at
the bottom of the artistic hierarchy.[13]

By presenting Scottish song as a unique combination of words and music,
the *Miscellany* defies the conventional separation and hierarchization of
the arts in Britain and disrupts the standard assessments used to define
British culture.[14] Furthermore, by indicating that "[the Scottish songs]
must relish best with people who have not bestowed much of their time
in acquiring a taste for . . . perfect music" (1: viii), Ramsay suggests that
Scottish songs provide an alternative medium which is more accessible
to people who are not musical experts. Scottish songs are designed for a
population who take pleasure in singing, not for those who have time and
money to devote to perfecting the arts. Rather than acting as yet another

"attempt to control" Scottish oral culture, Ramsay's printed Scottish songs assert Scottish identity at the same time as they challenge the foundations of British culture.

The popularity of Ramsay's work is indicated by the fact that *The Tea-Table Miscellany* enjoyed steady republication throughout the eighteenth century.[15] A fourteenth edition was published in 1769, the same year as fellow Scot David Herd published his collection, *The Ancient and Modern Scots Songs, Heroic Ballads, &c. Now first Collected in one Body, From the various* MISCELLANIES *wherein they formerly lay dispersed.* Herd's work was in part response to Bishop Percy's *Reliques of Ancient English Poetry*, published in 1765. But it also represents an extension of Ramsay's concerns. Where Percy's *Reliques* worked to excise the "ancient poetry's" connection to music and to promote the narrative aspects of the ballad, Herd's *Songs*, like Ramsay's *Miscellany*, retains an interest in the continued existence of the song tradition in Scotland and in the connection between oral and printed (or "Ancient and Modern") sources.

Percy begins his "Essay on the Ancient Minstrels" (included as an appendix in the first volume of the *Reliques*) by acknowledging that the "ancient Bards" practiced both "the arts of poetry and music," accompanying themselves with harps.[16] He notes a division which occurred when the bards left their "German forests" for Britain, and which separated "Poets," who were "men of letters" working in monasteries, from "Minstrels," who "got their livelihood by singing verses to the harp at the houses of the great," but who also practiced the composition of verse (*Reliques*, 1: 347).[17] Percy suggests that "most of the old heroic ballads in this collection" (1: 347) were composed by minstrels who were poets and musicians, although their art began to deteriorate soon after this era. Apart from noting that the minstrels played on harps and that the name for the harp, "cithera," derives from an Anglo-Saxon not a Celtic word (1: 390), Percy is not interested in the kind of music that was played with the ballads. He is concerned with the narrative matter of the ballads, not the manner in which they were performed. In concentrating on the literary rather than the musical heritage of England, Percy concurs with the assessments of his contemporaries Harris and Brown (the latter of whom he quotes regarding the unification of "melody, poem and dance" [1: 384] in ancient minstrelsy) regarding poetry's superiority over music. In *Crimes of Writing*, Susan Stewart argues that in eighteenth-century ballad collections a single text represents "a fragment of a larger whole that is a matter not only of other versions, but of the entire aura of the oral world – such a world's imagined presence, immediacy, organicism, and authenticity."[18] Percy's project presents ballads disembodied from their particular musical sources – specific tunes – and attached instead to a general concept of orality.

The influence of the *Reliques* can be seen in the Preface of *Scots Songs* in Herd's discussion of ancient Scottish poetry's role in illustrating "the most natural pictures of ancient manners."[19] Capitalizing on the popularity of Percy's work, Herd also includes a number of "Heroic Ballads" in the second part of his book. Herd's *Scots Songs*, however, refuses a dissociation from music, as the editor "confess[es]" himself "warmly attached" to both the poetry and the music of "the original Scottish songs" (*Scots Songs*, iii). In fact, he suggests that "the merit of the one is, in many instances, equal to the other" (iii). Like Ramsay, Herd provides lyrics without any music, instead including an editorial indication of what tune is to be used in each case. The readers of the *Scots Songs*, like those of the *Tea-Table Miscellany*, must participate in recreating the songs based on their previous knowledge of Scottish song. Also like Ramsay, Herd provides traditional and newly composed lyrics to traditional tunes, fulfilling his promise of representing both the "Ancient" and the "Modern" Scots songs. He expresses his regret that "the original words to many favourite tunes, once everywhere known, are now irrecoverably lost, excepting what are to be found in the memories of country people" (*Scots Songs*, iv). But he maintains hope in the embodied knowledge of the people of the country, as he expresses his desire to gather additional material. The *Scots Songs* includes an Advertisement noting that the editor intends to publish "*other old songs as can by any means be obtained – together with several modern songs, by celebrated authors, to the old Scottish tunes, together with an ample* Glossary *for the whole, which could not be contained at the end of this volume*" (ix). In this Advertisement, Herd requests submissions from anyone "*into whose hands the following collection may come*" who is "*possessed of any Scots songs of merit, not here found*" (x).

According to Stewart, ballad collecting does not so much produce a "fixed form" but rather releases "the oral from such fixity" (*Crimes of Writing*, 104). Stewart reads the eighteenth-century "writing of folklore" as "a method for making oral genres extinct just as the zeal for trophies might ironically . . . both celebrate and eradicate a species" (104). While Herd, like Percy, does engage in a certain nostalgia for the world of oral culture, he also represents "the old Scottish tunes" as a renewable resource involving community activity and an interaction between oral and print sources. *Scots Songs* is not a finished product that preserves a dying or vanished oral culture, but an ongoing process that relies on the resources, including the singing and composing bodies, of the current Scottish community. Herd presents an alternative cultural genealogy to that suggested in the *Reliques*, one in which oral culture does not give way to a literary print culture, but in which the two coexist and replenish each other.[20]

Writing a few years after Herd, Robert Burns also draws on the radical potential of the song tradition of Scotland to trouble the homogeneity of both the British nation and its literary market. In the "Epistle to John Lapraik," for example, Burns sets up an opposition between Scottish and British literary culture, between "rhymin'" and "poetry" (lines 49–50), with the speaker of the poem coming down on the side of the "hamely" Muse that inspired his Scottish predecessors:[21]

> On Fasteneen we had a rockin,
> To ca' the crack and weave our stockin;
> And there was muckle fun and jokin,
>   Ye need na doubt;
> At length we had a hearty yokin,
>   At *sang about.*
>
> There was ae *sang*, amang the rest,
> Aboon them a' it pleas'd me best,
> That some kind husband had addrest,
>   To some sweet wife:
> It thirl'd the heart-strings thro' the breast,
>   A' to the life.
>
> I've scarce heard ought describ'd sae weel,
> What gen'rous, manly bosoms feel;
> Thought I, "Can this be *Pope*, or *Steele*,
>   Or *Beattie's* wark;"
> They tald me 'twas an odd kind chiel
>   About *Muirkirk*. (lines 7–24)[22]

The poem suggests that it is the activity of song (or "sang," as it is referred to in Scots) in particular which destabilizes British literary values. The action takes place at a "rockin" or "sang about" of a local Scottish community.[23] The narrator associates his own literary practice with oral culture, deliberately setting out his powers in opposition to the British literary tradition. He notes that "critic-folk" are outraged that he dares "To mak a sang" (line 58), and he concludes the epistle by pledging himself Lapraik's friend and servant "while I can either sing, or whissle" (line 131). Moreover, he also re-presents writers from the tradition of British *belles-lettres* within Scottish oral culture. The speaker's first reaction to the "sang" that touches him most is to conclude that it must be by Pope, or Steele, or Beattie. The ironic implication is that it would not be unusual to find works by those writers in the medium of song. In *The Making of the English Literary Canon*, Trevor Ross suggests that poets in the eighteenth century derived their authority from "the canonic masters" before them whose work they received and reproduced "for a modern audience, rendering it accessible through commentary, certifying its canonicity, consecrating it within its own hallowed temple."[24] In the "Epistle to Lapraik," Burns contests the authority of the canonic masters – and the literary economy they represent – by consecrating them within a Scottish "sang about."

Burns further destabilizes British literary culture by including songs within his published book of poetry. *Poems, Chiefly in the Scottish Dialect*, published at Kilmarnock in 1786, contains five songs. David Daiches expresses his surprise that Burns should have included "so few songs in the Kilmarnock volume," given the fact that he had "produced several charming songs by 1786."[25] Daiches suggests that:

The reason for the negligible number of songs in this volume is probably to be found in Burns's concern for the taste of the genteel audience to whom the volume was addressed . . . Burns probably felt that he would reveal a naiveté in taste if he showed a preference for songs over other kinds of poetry . . . For all his interest in song, he does not appear seriously to have associated his songs with his ambition to be a Scottish poet recognized by the genteel world. (*Robert Burns*, 209).

I contend that Burns's use of his songs – however few – is an important aspect of his poetic self-representation. Specifically, Burns used Scottish song to create an alternative cultural economy to that of the "genteel [English] world." He does not provide titles to his songs. Instead, he gives them the title "Song" or "Fragment," then, in the tradition of Ramsay and Herd, indicates the name of the tune to which the lyrics were set. This configuration sets up a different relation between reader and writer than that found in a conventional book of poetry. Instead of positioning the author as producer and the reader as consumer, Burns requires a form of production on the part of his reader who, like the readers of the *Tea-Table Miscellany* and *Scots Songs*, must draw on a knowledge of Scottish song culture. Carol McGuirk suggests that Burns's refusal to give titles to his songs demonstrates his "modesty in seeing his lyrics as mere subordinate 'vehicles to the music,'"[26] but it also illustrates his foregrounding of songs as a different genre. The "Songs" are linked within the volume as sites of alternative cultural practice. Like Herd, Burns does not represent a separation of oral and print cultures or of the musical and the poetic; rather he represents them in dynamic interaction as a challenge to conventional printed poetry.

Burns posits a similar kind of interaction between oral and print cultures and between music and poetry in "Love and Liberty" (also referred to as "The Jolly Beggars"), a work which remained unpublished during his lifetime. "Love and Liberty," like Gay's *The Beggar's Opera*, mocks operatic form with its structure of arias interspersed with "recitativos." In Burns's "ballad opera," the arias are all set to traditional folksongs, which, as in the *Poems, Chiefly in the Scottish Dialect*, are identified merely by their title. Burns selects the title of each song to reflect upon the action of the piece he has written: the "raucle carlin"'s lament for her dead husband is set to "O, An Ye Were Dead, Guidman," while the "tinkler" (tinker) sings to "Clout the Cauldron." For their part, the "recitativos" draw on both literary and oral forms. The poem begins with the "Cherry and the Slae" stanza, made famous by the Scottish Chaucerian, Alexander Montgomerie. The narrative introducing the "pigmy Scraper" is written in the "Standard Habbie" form invented by Robert Semphill in the seventeenth century, and the concluding verses concerning the "bard of no regard" use the sixteenth-century "Christ's Kirk on the Green" stanza form. Burns deliberately includes an example of every Scots poetic form that he knew. At the same time, other "recitativos" are written to fit song forms. The fight between the fiddler and the tinkler over the Highlander's widow is written in standard ballad form, while other "recitativos" are in either literary or folksong forms. The "recitativo" introducing the "martial chuck," for example, is written with alternating eight and six syllable lines using an *ababababab* rhyme. Critics of "Love and Liberty" focus on what Maurice Lindsay calls its "pure anarchism," its rejection of social, moral, and religious ideals.[27] Daiches, for example, argues that the beggars "renounc[e] organized society" (*Robert Burns*, 199), while Thomas Crawford suggests that "the world of 'The Jolly Beggars' is in opposition not simply to the aristocracy or the citizen class or the 'unco guid,' but to every kind of social stability and institutional cohesion."[28] The hybrid form of "Love and Liberty," its challenging of disciplinary and generic conventions, corresponds with and emphasizes the work's thematic focus on social disruption.

Burns's shift to the publication of songs in the latter part of his life represents his realization of the full radical potential of Scottish music within British culture. From 1787 until his death, Burns contributed songs to two publications: James Johnson's *The Scots Musical Museum*, published in six volumes from 1787 to 1803, and George Thomson's *A Choice Collection of Original Scotish [sic] Airs for the Voice*, published in eight parts from 1793 to 1818. Burns's excitement about both projects is evident in his extraordinary output and his comments in his letters. He writes, for example, regarding

Johnson's work to Reverend John Skinner, a song writer: "There is a work
going on in Edinburgh, just now, which claims your best assistance. An
Engraver in this town has set about collecting and publishing all the Scotch
Songs, with the Music, that can be found . . . I have been absolutely crazed
about it, collecting old stanzas, and every information remaining, respecting
their origin, authors, &c."[29] And his last letter to Johnson expresses his hope
for the future of the collection: "Your Work is a great one; & though, now
that it is near finished, I see if we were to begin again, two or three things
might be mended, yet I will venture to prophesy, that to future ages your
Publication will be the text book & standard of Scotish [*sic*] Song & Music"
(*Letters*, II: 381–2). Burns was eager to take part in this project for posterity
for its own sake, but he also used it as a foil to his activities in the literary
marketplace.

In *Poetry as an Occupation and an Art in Britain, 1760–1830*, Peter Murphy
argues that Burns's turn to song "relieved [him] from the oppression of authorship" and the task of having to pander to the taste of the high literary
culture of Edinburgh.[30] More than this, however, I suggest that Burns
wanted to establish the collecting of Scottish music as an alternative practice to the marketing of poetry. Burns's work for the *Scots Musical Museum*,
volumes II to v of which he edited himself, establishes a different relationship between author and reader than that involved in poetic composition.
Burns as author in fact disappears, since he does not discriminate between
songs which he writes and those which he revises or merely transmits from
available sources. In addition, the reader of the *Museum* is required to become a performer, one who will re-embody the songs by singing them.
In a spirit similar to Herd's *Scots Songs*, Burns's *Museum* invites readers to
contribute to the collective process of creating a complete repository of
Scottish song. Acknowledging that, "It has long been a just and general
Complaint, that among all the Music-Books of Scots Songs that have been
hitherto offered to the Public, not one, nor even all of them put together
can be said to have merited the name of what may be called A Complete
Collection," the first volume of the *Museum* offered the following request:
"if any Lady or Gentleman have any Song of Merit with the Music (never
hitherto Published) of the true Ancient Caledonian Strain, that they would
be pleased to transmit the same to the Publishers, that it may be submit-
ted to the proper Judges, and so be preserved in this Repository of our
National Music and Song."[31] Burns also defied the conventions of the literary marketplace by refusing to accept money for his song contributions.
In his letter of September 16, 1792, he wrote to George Thomson: "As to
any remuneration, you may think my Songs either *above* or *below* price; for

they shall absolutely be one or the other. – In the honest enthusiasm with which I embark on your undertaking, to talk of money, wages, fee, hire, &c. would be downright Sodomy of Soul!" (*Letters*, II: 149). He published his six hundred songs for the most part anonymously. Such interventions suggest Burns's contestation of the idea of the author as an individual negotiating property rights and a place for his work in the marketplace.

Burns's attempt to use Scottish music to create an alternative space to that of the literary marketplace was short-lived, however, as was his attempt to challenge the conventions of authorship. The sixth and final volume of the *Museum* (1803), published seven years after Burns's death, undoes the anonymity which Burns had desired, capitalizing on the marketability of what Michel Foucault refers to as the "author function." Johnson makes a point of indicating for the reader of volume VI which of the songs previously published were Burns's: "The Songs in the 5 preceding Volumes marked R. and B. the Editor is now at liberty to say are the production of Mr. BURNS" (Museum, VI: iv). Even though Johnson acknowledges that "Mr. BURNS requested these marks only, and not his name should be added to them" (VI: iv), he nevertheless exposes the poet's authorship. Adding insult to injury, the originals of the personal letters Burns sent to Johnson are offered for view to "subscribers."

Ironically, it is just such an emphasis on the "author function" that resulted in Burns's relegation to the margins of the canon of English literature. Wordsworth, Carlyle, and other nineteenth-century spokesmen of "high culture" used Burns as a negative example of true genius, an individual who failed to achieve greatness because of his inability to control his natural high spirits.[32] This focus on Burns the individual author has resulted in a relative neglect of the musical projects to which he contributed, because, as we have seen, Burns himself used the collection of songs to obfuscate the distinction between literary author and oral tradition. Burns has only recently become an acceptable figure in Romantic anthologies as more and more collections include his work in their contents. But in welcoming him into the center of an institution from which he has long been excluded, it is important that we avoid merely absorbing Burns into a conventional understanding of Romanticism. Rather, we need to use his example to rethink our definitions of Romanticism, indeed of literary studies in general. Reading Burns can help us challenge both the traditional period divisions between eighteenth-century and Romantic writing and the English-based model of British culture under which we tend to operate. As I have suggested in this chapter, Burns draws heavily on eighteenth-century aesthetics and popular culture – particularly Scottish song culture – in formulating his challenges to the British literary tradition. The case of Burns can also help us realize the importance of looking beyond literary works in our assessment of the cultural marketplace in the late eighteenth and early nineteenth centuries. Without an understanding of the uses made of Scottish song in the eighteenth century and the part that song played in Burns's work, we forego a real appreciation of his radical project. It is in the "sang," "catch," "crooning," and "whistle"[33] – similar to the "speech, song, or wail" of Deane's Irish population – that we hear the voice of Burns – and of Scotland – troubling the text of British culture in the Romantic era.

NOTES

1. Seamus Deane, *Strange Country: Modernity and Nationhood in Irish Writing Since 1790* (Oxford: Clarendon Press, 1997), 55.
2. Roger Fiske notes that "Scotch Songs [*sic*] of a popular type were reaching London at least by Cromwell's time, and eventually in astonishing numbers" *Scotland in Music* (Cambridge: Cambridge University Press, 1983), 1. See also David Johnson's *Music and Society in Lowland Scotland in the Eighteenth-Century* (London: Oxford University Press, 1972) and John Purser's *Scotland's Music* (Edinburgh and London: Mainstream Publishing, 1992) for more particulars on eighteenth-century Scottish music.
3. The printed texts of Scottish music would still have been open to local variation, of course. Then, as now, printing would have served to give an outline to the tune, not to constitute specific instructions. But notation of any kind, published or longhand, imposes a different system of order on music. See Michael Chanan's *Musica Practica: The Social Practice of Western Music from Gregorian Chant to Postmodernism* (London and New York: Verso, 1994), John Shepherd's *Music as Social Text* (Cambridge: Polity Press; Cambridge, MA: Basil Blackwell 1991) and Max Weber's *Rational and Social Foundations of Music*, trans. Don Martindale, Johannes Riedel, and Gertrude Neuwirth (Carbondale: Southern Illinois University Press, 1958).
4. Chanan, *Musica Practica*, 77.
5. The title-page of Thumoth's *Scotch and Irish Airs* also advertises "Two Collections of all the most favourite old and new Scotch Tunes several of them with Variations entirely in the Scotch Taste" by James Oswald.
6. Alexander Stuart published *Musick for Allan Ramsay's Collection of Scots Songs Vol: First* in Edinburgh in 1726, but it was not very popular. Johnson speculates that "fiddlers in Edinburgh had most of the Tea-table Miscellany tunes in their manuscript books, or in their heads, already" (*Music and Society*, 114).
7. Allan Ramsay, *The Tea-Table Miscellany. A Collection of Choice Songs Scots and English*, 4 vols. (London: A. Millar, 1763), 1: v. Subsequent quotations are from this edition.

8. The gendered terms and the metaphor of reproduction which Ramsay uses add to this sense of embodiment. Although the contributors of the songs are male (Ramsay himself and "some ingenious young gentlemen, who were so well pleased with my undertaking, that they generously lent me their assistance" [1: ix]), the singers he imagines are exclusively female. If the songs from the *Miscellany* succeed in stealing "into the ladies' bosoms," he suggests, the *Miscellany* will be "again reprinted" and "live . . . as long as the song of *Homer*" (1: x).

9. Lawrence Lipking, *The Ordering of the Arts in Eighteenth-Century England* (Princeton: Princeton University Press, 1970), 3.

10. James Harris, "A Discourse on Music, Painting and Poetry," *Three Treatises* (New York: Garland, 1970), 55.

11. On the construction of English national identity in the eighteenth century, see John Lucas's *England and Englishness: Ideas of Nationhood in English Poetry 1688–1900* (London: Hogarth, 1990) and Gerald Newman's *The Rise of English Nationalism: A Cultural History 1740–1830* (New York: St. Martin's Press, 1987).

12. John Brown, *A Dissertation on the Rise, Union, and Power, The Progressions, Separations, and Corruptions, Of Poetry and Music* (New York: Garland, 1971), 223.

13. Harris does offer a deviation from the aesthetic measuring stick of imitation, however, by suggesting that the real "Efficacy" of music is derived not from imitation but from its ability to raise the "Affections" ("A Discourse," 95). This, in fact, makes it the perfect accompaniment for poetry, which also aims to raise the affections; "the most sensible Impression" can be made, suggests Harris, when the "Affections . . . are already excited by the Music. *For here a double Force is made to co-operate to one End*" (97–8). Music has the power to "temper" the Mind. "From what has been said it is evident, that these two Arts can never be so powerful *singly*, as when they are *properly united*" (102). But Harris quickly compensates for his temporary diverting from the standard of value by ending with an assertion regarding the primacy of poetry: "Yet must it be remembered, in this Union, that *Poetry* ever have the *Precedence*; its *Utility*, as well as *Dignity*, being by far the more considerable" (102).

14. The *Miscellany's* conflation of music and poetry finds an echo in James Beattie's *Essays: On Poetry and Music* (1776), as Beattie argues that a combination of music and poetry is even more powerful than just poetry: "I am satisfied, that though musical genius may subsist without poetical taste, and poetical genius without musical taste; yet these two talents united might accomplish nobler effects, than either could do singly" (*Essays: On Poetry and Music* [London: Routledge/Thoemmes, 1996], 120).

15. The *Miscellany* went through nineteen editions by 1793. It was republished both as "a collection of Scots songs" and "a collection of choice songs, Scots and English" and packaged variously in four volumes, two volumes, and a single volume.

16. Bishop Percy, *Reliques of Ancient English Poetry*, ed. Henry B. Wheatley, 3 vols. (London: George Allen and Unwin, 1927), 1: 345–6. Subsequent references are to this edition.

17. Percy notes that "minstrel" in English properly designated "one who sung to the harp, or some other instrument of music, verses composed by himself, or others," but he suggests that "the term was also applied by our old writers to such as professed either music or singing separately . . . Music, however, being the leading idea, was at length peculiarly called minstrelsy, and the name of the minstrel at last confined to the musician only" (1: 385).

18. Susan Stewart, *Crimes of Writing: Problems in the Containment of Representation* (Durham, NC and London: Duke University Press, 1994), 104.

19. David Herd, *Ancient and Modern Scots Songs* (Edinburgh: Martin and Wotherspoon, 1769), ii. Subsequent references are to this edition.

20. Many other Scots followed Percy's lead in concerning themselves primarily with the narrative ballad in an attempt to provide Scotland with a distinctly literary heritage. Most notable among these were Walter Scott in his *Minstrelsy of the Scottish Border Consisting of Historical and Romantic Ballads*, ed. T. F. Henderson, 4 vols. (Edinburgh and London: Blackwood and Sons; New York: Charles Scribner, 1902) and William Motherwell, *Minstrelsy Ancient and Modern* (Glasgow: John Wylie, 1827). While the title of Robert Jamieson's two-volume *Popular Ballads and Songs* (Edinburgh: Cadell and Davies; London: John Murray, 1806) suggests the editor's interest in both genres, the work itself neglects any reference to music. Instead, the editorial comments shape both ballads and songs so as to make them representative of the "RELIQUES OF ANCIENT SCOTISH [sic] POETRY" (Dedication, n.p.).

21. In *Devolving English Literature*, Robert Crawford argues that such juxtapositions work to "upset established categories, raising questions about the way in which we casually assign cultural value" (Oxford: Clarendon Press, 1992), 89.

22. *The Poems and Songs of Robert Burns*, ed. James Kinsley, 3 vols. (Oxford: Clarendon Press, 1968), II: 85. Subsequent references to Burns's poetry are to this edition.

23. Burns picks up on the tradition of verse epistles begun by Allan Ramsay and William Hamilton of Gilbertfield (*Robert Burns: Selected Poems*, ed. Carol McGuirk [London: Penguin, 1993], 204).

24. Trevor Ross, *The Making of the English Literary Canon: From the Middle Ages to the Late Eighteenth Century* (Montreal and Kingston: McGill-Queen's University Press, 1998), 4.

25. David Daiches, *Robert Burns* (New York: Macmillan, 1966), 209.

26. *Robert Burns: Selected Poems*, ed. McGuirk, xvi.

27. Maurice Lindsay, *Robert Burns: The Man, His Work, The Legend* (New York: St. Martins Press, 1979), 91.

28. Thomas Crawford, *Burns: A Study of the Poems and Songs* (London: Oliver and Boyd, 1960; Edinburgh: Canongate, 1994), 132.

29. *Letters of Robert Burns*, ed. G. Ross Roy and J. De Lancey Ferguson, 2 vols. (Oxford: Clarendon Press, 1985), 1: 168.

30. Peter Murphy, *Poetry as an Occupation and as an Art in Britain, 1760–1830* (Cambridge: Cambridge University Press, 1993), 80.
31. *The Scots Musical Museum*, 6 vols. (Edinburgh, 1787–1803), 1: iii.
32. For expansion of these ideas, see my *Acts of Union: Scotland and the Literary Negotiation of the British Nation, 1707–1830* (Stanford: Stanford University Press, 1998), chapters 4 and 6.
33. All mentioned in "Epistle to Lapraik."

CHAPTER 12

Romantic spinstrelsy: Anne Bannerman and the sexual politics of the ballad

Adriana Craciun

The late eighteenth-century ballad revival, inspired by Thomas Percy's *Reliques of Ancient English Poetry* (1765) and taken to a new level of scholarly ambition in Walter Scott and John Leyden's *Minstrelsy of the Scottish Border* (1802–3), helped shape canonical Romanticism's developing theories of genius, primitivism, and authenticity. The ballad revival was particularly significant in Scotland because "the influence of the ballad was – and is – the strongest continuing influence in Scottish poetry."[1] Not only is the ballad central to the tradition of Scottish literature, but Scottish literature as a whole is central to the historical development and theorization of Romanticism, as this volume bears witness. Scottish poetry profoundly impacted what has until recently been considered "English Romanticism" not only through the vibrant oral Scots tradition popularized by Burns, but also in the heroic bardic tradition of Ossian. Macpherson's role in constructing a national epic is analogous to the Scottish ballad collectors' role in reconstructing a body of national literature in the wake of the failed 1745 rebellion. Macpherson fabricated a national tradition, while antiquaries like Scott, Ramsay, Leyden, and Jamieson attempted to reconstruct one in their ballad anthologies, complete with an elaborate scholarly apparatus designed to authenticate (and safely historicize) the ballads' primitive passions and heroism.[2]

Percy's *Reliques* also inspired a revival of interest in distinctly English poetry, a nationalist celebration of stylistic "simplicity" (as opposed to German sensationalism) culminating in Wordsworth's claims for a new poetry based on simplicity, authenticity, and passion in the *Lyrical Ballads*. Wordsworth acknowledged his debt to Percy's *Reliques*, "so unassuming, so modest in their pretensions," and argued that modern English "Poetry has been absolutely redeemed by it."[3] The influence of Bürger's supernatural ballads, on the other hand, while significant for the *Lyrical Ballads*, was downplayed by Wordsworth in a characteristic effort to elide the German Gothic's influence on what he considered to be English simplicity and sincerity.[4]

Thus one little-studied yet significant aspect of the ballad revival (of which Wordsworth and Scott were fully aware) is its role in developing the Gothic as a poetic genre. Today the Gothic is predominantly studied as a narrative genre, i.e., as the novel, but I want to reintroduce the Gothic into current debate on the ballad revival (and vice versa), in order to illuminate the larger cultural significance of the Romantic-period Scottish ballad, and to better understand the relationship between Gothic and Romanticism.[5] Thus, both the ostensibly "authentic" ballads in the antiquarian collections of Percy, Scott, Ritson, and others, and the overtly "imitation" Gothic ballads of Lewis, Southey, and Coleridge, share an important role in the development of Romanticism and of Scottish literature.

Scott and Leyden's work in the *Minstrelsy of the Scottish Border* rehearses this fundamental tension between what in retrospect are distinguished as "Romanticism" and "Gothic," and does so in a distinctly Scottish context. Thus, in order to appreciate the full significance of Scottish poetry at the turn of the nineteenth century, we need to consider (in addition to the ballad's centrality to Scottish literature and Scottish literature's centrality to Romanticism) the role of the Gothic. And, second, we need to consider the role of gender and the significance of women writers, because both the Gothic and the ballad are culturally feminized forms. "Once we look beyond the invention of the minstrel tradition," writes Susan Stewart, "we find a genre predominantly continued by women in both its 'authentic' and its imitated forms."[6]

I want to explore this complex nexus of poetic production in Romantic-period Scotland – the interplay of the ballad revival, Gothic, and gender – by considering the ballads of the Edinburgh poet Anne Bannerman (1765–1829). In the first decade of the nineteenth century, Bannerman published ballads, odes, and sonnets in such volumes as *Poems* (1800), *Tales of Superstition and Chivalry* (1802), and *Poems, A New Edition* (1807).[7] Bannerman's volume of supernatural ballads, *Tales of Superstition*, was greeted by critical hostility and sold poorly, despite the approbation of influential admirers like Scott, Percy, and Robert Anderson. Following this commercial failure, Bannerman's literary career foundered, and she struggled to make her living as a governess. Bannerman had deliberately situated her writing in the tradition not of Scott's *Minstrelsy* but of Matthew Lewis, author of the scandalous *The Monk* (1796) and editor of the critically maligned ballad volume *Tales of Wonder* (1801). The hostile reception of Bannerman's ballads helps illuminate the sexual politics of the Scottish ballad revival (in addition to its nationalist politics, more often studied), and its uneasy relationship to the rise and fall of the Gothic.

SPINSTRELSY OF THE SCOTTISH BORDER

Minstrelsy of the Scottish Border is a landmark text in Scottish and Romantic literature, a product of the literary collaboration of a Scottish literary circle that included Anne Bannerman. Bannerman's marginal position in this circle, and the limited opportunities through patronage that were available to her as a woman, illustrate the impact of Gothic and gender on shaping our canon of Scottish literature. *Minstrelsy* was a cooperative venture published in Scott's name; in fact, as John Sutherland acknowledges, John Leyden was "the project's workhorse and its architect," "whose name should have been on the title page as joint-editor," although his influence was afterwards downplayed by Scott and his biographers.[8] Leyden[9] (1775–1811) was a close friend – and perhaps a romantic interest – of Bannerman's, and an important early Orientalist whose antiquarian interest in Scottish ballads led readily to his studies of Asian languages and literature.[10]

The source of several of the romantic ballads in the *Minstrelsy* was Anna Gordon Brown (1747–1810) of Falkland, "the most important single contributor to the canon of English and Scottish ballads."[11] Brown's ballads contain a concentration of supernatural and witchcraft themes "unprecedented in earlier balladry," some of which were also published in Lewis's *Tales of Wonder*.[12] Along with Lady Wardlaw, who contributed some of the most influential ballads in Percy's *Reliques*, Brown emerges as a central figure in the Scottish ballad revival.[13] In fact, the "ballad was almost exclusively preserved and transmitted by women," writes Catherine Kerrigan: "The same pattern can be seen in the major male collectors of the ballad – Burns, Scott, Hogg, Greig-Duncan – all of whom refer to women as a prime source of their material" (*An Anthology*, 2). Scott did name Brown as a source of the *Minstrelsy*, yet his overall vision of the collection championed the masculine and heroic nature of the "historical" martial ballads, which Scott believed were originally composed by a male minstrel in courtly society.

At Leyden's suggestion, however, Scott included romantic ballads (immensely popular in rural oral culture) and modern imitation Gothic ballads (popular with contemporary readers) in what turned out to be a multi-volume collection. Leyden, himself raised in rural poverty, acknowledged the collective, folk, and feminine origins of the ballad, while Scott favored the aristocratic bardic model of the minstrel put forward by Percy (and famously denounced by the more scrupulous Joseph Ritson).[14] Writing in 1801 to the bibliophile and scholar Richard Heber, Leyden reports on the progress of the "Border Ballads, which Scott (in my opinion with some degree of affectation) persists in stiling [*sic*] the *Minstrelsy* of the Border. I have urged the claim of a term of similar composition *Spinstrelsy*!! without effect, tho' I think the one not much inferior to the other either in propriety or in affectation."[15] Leyden's perceptive critique of his collaborator attests at once to the class and, more unusually, the gender pretensions of Scott's model of minstrelsy. The more democratic title of "Border Ballads" would accommodate the ballads' collective and largely feminine mode of transmission and creation, though Scott's antiquarianism (like his novels) intended to avoid precisely such a democratizing effect. Spinsters, "old wives," nurses, milkmaids, and grandmothers remained the sources of Scottish ballads, romantic as well as heroic, a fact well known to those who, like Leyden, were themselves from poor rural backgrounds, and gathered ballads from oral sources.

Like those other renowned ballad singers Carolina, Baroness Nairne (author of "The Laird o' Cockpen") and Lady Anne Lindsay (author of "Auld Robin Gray"), Anna Brown and Lady Wardlaw did not seek public recognition in print but instead often circulated their ballad books among select circles, and likewise performed their ballads before a limited audience. How then would a woman poet enter into the literary marketplace during this Scottish ballad revival, when the source material produced by women poets and singers often appeared only in the published works of male scholars? Given the widespread authority of Scott and Percy's minstrel model, how would a woman publish as a poet in this emerging Scottish tradition? The question was all the more acute for an unusually educated, urban woman poet who was not an aristocrat and lacked the financial support or social respectability provided by a husband or father.

Bannerman never married, and struggled unsuccessfully to maintain a professional literary career, despite her (marginal) membership in the most influential literary circle in Edinburgh. I say that Bannerman was a marginal member of this masculine literary circle because it is literally only in the margins of the correspondence of Scott, Percy, Heber, Cooper Walker, Erskine, Park, Leyden, and others that one finds traces of Bannerman's life and work. Beyond her published volumes, virtually no traces of her exist in her name. As her friend Leyden would have understood, she is thus also a member of another important literary circle, that of Romantic "spinstrelsy," in which gender severely limits the access to patronage that made possible the professional careers of male counterparts like Leyden, Campbell, and Scott. Unsurprisingly, we do catch glimpses of Bannerman throughout the correspondence of the above-named men, glimpses that reveal the contours of spinstrelsy in Romantic-period Scotland, a gendered literary landscape essential for understanding both Scottish minstrelsy and Romantic poetry in general.

LIFE AND WORK OF ANNE BANNERMAN

What little we know about Bannerman's life we know largely through Robert Anderson's letters about her, detailing his efforts to help her publish, and her destitution and depression after the death of her brother and mother in 1803. Her father had been a "running stationer," a street merchant authorized to sell and sing broadside ballads in Edinburgh. Bannerman's familiarity with the ballad tradition, both literary and oral, is evident in her strongest work, *Tales of Superstition and Chivalry*. Anderson, the editor of the influential thirteen-volume *Complete British Poets* (1792–5), sent his literary friends copies of Bannerman's first volume, *Poems*, along with Campbell's first volume (*The Pleasures of Hope*), warmly praising both poets' first efforts. Anderson noted her poetry's "splendor & energy," and marveled that "[s]o opulent a mind at such an age is a phenomenon."[16] He also organized her 1807 volume, *Poems. A New Edition*, by subscription as a means of relieving her impoverishment; although this effort largely failed, Thomas Park did secure £20 for her from the Royal Literary Fund.

In his letters, Anderson increasingly recommended that she renounce the hope of becoming a self-supporting writer, and urged her to become a governess, which she eventually did in 1807, ending her publishing career. In September 1829 Bannerman died, an invalid and in debt, in Portobello. The following year Scott praised her in his "Essay on Imitations of the Ancient Ballad," noting in particular the evocative quality of her ballads that reviewers had long remarked upon:

Miss Anne Bannerman likewise should not be forgotten, whose *Tales of Superstition and Chivalry* appeared about 1802. They were perhaps too mystical and too abrupt; yet if it be the purpose of this kind of ballad poetry powerfully to excite the imagination, without pretending to satisfy it, few persons have succeeded better than this gifted lady, whose volume is peculiarly fit to be read in a lonely house by a decaying lamp.[17]

Bannerman's ballads are indeed "too mystical and too abrupt," and as Scott recognized, their genius lies in their consistent thwarting of their reader's will to truth. Bannerman mastered the ballad form that Bürger, Lewis, and Coleridge are renowned for, and endowed it with a higher degree of generic self-awareness by foregrounding the enigmatic significance of femininity for the Gothic and the ballad.

Reviewers of *Tales of Superstition and Chivalry* consistently complained of the ballads' narrative ambiguity, which "excites expectations of something very great" but leaves the resolution of these expectations in obscurity.[18] In five of her ten *Tales of Superstition and Chivalry*, these unresolved narrative expectations are embodied in female figures that are never satisfactorily unveiled: "The Dark Ladie," "The Prophetess of the Oracle of Seäm," "The Penitent's Confession," "The Prophecy of Merlin," and "The Festival of St. Magnus."[19] By exciting but refusing to satisfy our desire to unveil the feminized ideal, Bannerman foregrounds the ideal's power and centrality in ballads, and simultaneously foregrounds the power of the poet in so expertly seducing her readers. I want first to look briefly at two ballads, "The Dark Ladie" and "The Prophetess of the Oracle of Seäm," in terms of the Gothic anti-narrative poetics embodied in their veiled female figures, before considering Bannerman's ballads in their larger Scottish and Gothic context.

"THE DARK LADIE"

Bannerman's "The Dark Ladie" is a good place to begin to consider her work within existing critical accounts of the ballad revival, because of her poem's relationship to Coleridge's "Introduction to the Tale of the Dark Ladie" (first published in the *Morning Post* [1799] and the *Edinburgh Magazine* [1800], and revised in the *Lyrical Ballads* [1800 onwards] as "Love"). In Coleridge's narrative, a poet relates the story of "the cruel scorn, / that craz'd [a] bold and lovely Knight" to his virginal beloved in order to seduce her.[20] Coleridge uses the Belle Dame figure as a pawn in a masculine sexual economy: the example in the tale of the "beautiful and bright" female Fiend becomes a weapon of seduction. After the poet's lover swoons into his arms, the poem concludes with a promise that will remain unkept for over thirty years: "I promis'd thee a sister tale / Of man's perfidious cruelty: Come, then, and hear what cruel wrong / Befel the Dark Ladie" (II: 1059). Although apparently written in 1798, Coleridge's "The Ballad of the Dark Ladie" would not be published until 1834. It is a traditional ballad of a woman who pines for the treacherous knight to whom she has given what she "can ne'er recall" (I: 294).

Bannerman included her own "sister tale," "The Dark Ladie," in *Tales of Superstition and Chivalry*; it first appeared in the March 1800 *Edinburgh Magazine*, with a footnote directing readers to Coleridge's "Introduction to the Tale of the Dark Ladie," published in the same journal one month earlier. Bannerman's "Dark Ladie" differs in several respects from Coleridge's. Instead of providing yet another tale of women's victimization, Bannerman focuses on the Ladie's terrifying revenge on the Christian crusaders who took her from the Holy Land. Her supernatural ballad also resists the covert misogyny of the Romantic idealization of women reproduced in Coleridge's "Introduction to the Tale of the Dark Ladie." While Coleridge's balladeer tells his tale of women's cruelty in order to seduce both the listener (his idealized beloved) and the reader, in fact producing another potential Dark Ladie in his beloved, Bannerman's multiple male narrators compulsively tell the tale of the Dark Ladie's seduction because, like the Ancient Mariner, they are cursed to do so. Her poem thus replies to Coleridge's call for a sister tale by avenging the seduction that takes place in his own poem.

Bannerman's Dark Ladie imprisons her captor and a succession of other knights, compelling them to repeat the tale of her seduction – the traditional tale of women's sexual victimization introduced by Coleridge. But Bannerman's Dark Ladie, unlike Coleridge's, forces the knights to repeat this predictable narrative in order to destroy them, not simply to elicit their pity. Bannerman's poem begins with the knights' celebration upon their return from the crusades. The Dark Ladie's spectacular entrance into this excessively masculine scene emphasizes the power of her gaze and the impotence of her male audience:

> For thro' the foldings of her veil,
> Her long black veil that swept the ground,
> A light was seen to dart from eyes
> That mortal never own'd.
>
> And when the knights on Guyon turn'd
> Their fixed gaze, and shudder'd now;
> For smother'd fury seem'd to bring
> The dew-drops on his brow.
>
> But, from the Ladie in the veil,
> Their eyes they could not long withdraw,
> And when they tried to speak, that glare
> Still kept them mute with awe! (*Tales of Superstition*, 5–7)

After this terrifying visit, the knights are haunted by the Dark Ladie in their sleep, and the reader eventually hears her story through a succession of fragmented accounts, as each knight tells the others of his haunting. The reader is left wondering if these knights will waste away in the castle, held in thrall by the Ladie's lamentable tale like Keats's "pale kings and princes."

Bannerman's poem ends with a narrative deferral characteristic of her ballads, in which one knight repeats an account of the Dark Ladie's origins that he has heard second-hand from a mysterious, "hoary-headed" Ancient

Mariner figure. Through this series of unreliable (perhaps mad) narrators, we learn that she had been taken from her husband, child, and home in the Holy Land after the Christian knights had murdered the "infidels" "beneath the blessed Cross" (9). The knight's account of the Ladie's tale, like the second-hand tale on which it is based, is enigmatic and unreliable, and leaves unresolved for the reader (as for the knights) the truth of the Ladie's death, and the truth of who or what she actually is, since she cannot be unveiled. The poem concludes with a series of unanswered questions, the last of which inquires: "why it cannot be remov'd / That folded veil that sweeps the ground?" (16).

The Dark Ladie's double veils (both white and black), in addition to signaling her racial and religious otherness, suggest an endless veiling, an absence of depth and its latent meanings. The absence she embodies is the absence of Woman herself, and by extension, the absence of the Romantic ideal. If Coleridge's "Introduction to the Tale of the Dark Ladie" relies on two traditional stereotypes of Woman (the Beloved and the Dark Ladie, or the bride and the fiend), then Bannerman's Dark Ladie embodies both these extremes, literalized in her veils of pure light and pure darkness. She proceeds to use this double construction against the very men – the balladeers – who proliferate such images of fallen women through their seductive narrations. Bannerman also draws upon the revenant ballads popular throughout the eighteenth century, and perhaps also upon "The Gypsy Laddie," a traditional Scottish abduction ballad collected in Allan Ramsay's *Tea-Table Miscellany*. Bannerman's ability to move with ease between literary ballads like Coleridge's, and popular versions like "The Gypsy Laddie," originates in the combined influence of her father's profession as street ballad singer and her own unusual literary education.

According to Bannerman's response to Coleridge, then, the tales men tell of the Dark Ladie originate not in the fantasies of male speakers/poets, nor in the "true" voices of oppressed women, but in a model of narrative as a powerful curse to which narrators and poets are alike subject, and in which all language is repetition. The haunted knights alternate between uncontrollable repetition and speechlessness in the Ladie's presence, especially when struck by her unearthly voice, which "came forth, dull, deep, and wild, / and O! how deadly slow!" (13). This displacement of discursive authority mirrors the creative role of balladeers within a larger cultural matrix, figured as an evolving popular tradition in which (Romantic) authenticity is not a privileged value.

The sexual politics of feminine idealization and demonization prevalent in supernatural ballads thus emerges as a central preoccupation in

Bannerman's work, as it did in Coleridge's. As I have argued in *Fatal Women of Romanticism*, Bannerman's work shares significant affinities with Coleridge's early poetry in this respect, particularly in both poets' fascination with the ambiguities of the femme fatale tradition. Both poets' careers likewise suffered because of their antipathy to narrativity and the hostile reception this received (particularly in the case of "Christabel"). We should also keep in mind that the same reviews that complained of Bannerman's obscurity and narrative confusion also dismissed Coleridge's "Ancient Mariner" as "a rhapsody of unintelligible wildness and incoherence,"[21] leading Wordsworth to remove it from its position as the first poem in *Lyrical Ballads*.

"THE PROPHETESS OF THE ORACLE OF SEÄM"

Bannerman's "The Prophetess of the Oracle of Seäm," like "The Dark Ladie," is an anti-narrative that centers on a female figure that cannot be unveiled. From an undersea cave, the Prophetess of Seäm destroys passing ships with her voice and invites specific men – priests – behind the veil of her shrine to meet a fate that is literally unspeakable. Bannerman's use of the veiled feminine ideal is proto-feminist, for her priestess of the oracle is active, not an ideal and absent object of male pursuit. As in "The Dark Ladie" we see that the victims of this female presence, as her volume's title suggests, are the patriarchal institutions of religion and marriage (alternatively, superstition and chivalry). And, significantly, Bannerman never reveals the priestess, so that we do not know what it was, if anything, that the priest saw behind the veil of the shrine, only that its presence – or absence – shattered his faith and reduced him to a living phantom.

"The Prophetess of the Oracle of Seäm" uses a complex and deliberately disorienting series of narrative frames, or more precisely cycles, to undermine the possibility of narrativity itself. The ballad "begins" on a doomed ship with a priest, Father Paul, repeating the legend of the Prophetess who destroys passing ships like a siren, as he has heard it from the sole survivor (another priest) of such a shipwreck:

> "And he told them of the Prophetess
> And the Oracle below!
>
> "He told the tale of Seäm's isle,
> He told the terrors of its caves,
> That none had passed them with life
> When that sleep was on the waves!

"He told them, when the winds that roar'd
Around that isle had ceas'd to breathe,
Was the fated night of sacrifice
In the gloomy vaults beneath.
. . .
"But when he came to tell, at last,
What fearful sacrifice had bled,
His agony began anew,
And he could not raise his head!

"And he never spoke again at all,
For he died that night in sore dismay:
So sore, that all were tranc'd for hours
That saw his agony!" (*Tales of Superstition*, 22–5)

As in Father Paul's tale, the ship is destroyed and he alone is taken beneath the sea to the oracle. The narrative spirals through a series of second and third-hand accounts of previous priests' encounters with the enigmatic Prophetess, whose identity (or actual existence) is never confirmed, as in "The Dark Ladie."

Bannerman's Christian priests enter the shrine, though she never resolves for us what precisely their sin is, or if they even commit one, or what divine or infernal deity, if any, awaits them. She leaves all possibilities open, so that we readers are in the same position as those who listen, spellbound, to the legendary tale of the oracle's powers. All priests (and faithful readers) collapse into one another, and the mystical revelation at the heart of each of their narratives emerges as an effect of the endless creation, pursuit, and deferral of presence in readings of poetry that search for authentic truths. Bannerman's complex narrative cycles represent an innovative outgrowth of the incremental repetition characteristic of eighteenth-century ballads in their oral form. Her mastery of the ballad form, oral and literary, allows her to take the Gothic ballad to new levels of narrative complexity, amplifying the ambiguity of the enigma of femininity.

It is significant that Bannerman's ballads, while preoccupied with the force of the inescapable past (as Gothic texts always are), are not primarily set in Scotland's historical past.[22] The "end" of "The Prophetess" moves forward suddenly by forty years, so that we realize that the series of accounts we had heard had happened long ago. This shift to the present allows for an intriguing comparison with similar techniques used in later poems. As Robert Crawford points out, Scott's abrupt shift to the present in *The Lay of the Last Minstrel* (1805) anticipates Keats's use of this technique in "The Eve of St. Agnes": "Scott forcefully details past actions, and then abruptly jolts us back across the centuries into the present, making the past appear both vivid and remote."[23] Scott does this as part of his larger "anthropological" and aesthetic project of presenting Scotland's past. Leith Davis argues that "Scott's attitude in the *Minstrelsy* anticipates the ambiguity found in much of his later work, as he both regrets the passing of the old ways of life and normalizes their passing."[24] Bannerman's presentation of the past does not share the anthropological mode of the *Minstrelsy*. Like the *Minstrelsy*, *Tales of Superstition* is accompanied by scholarly notes, yet instead of tracing the historical authenticity or specificity of the ballads, her notes emphasize their literariness, and the wide-ranging education of the poet. Because they are for the most part set in feudal Catholic Europe (much like the English Gothic romances of Radcliffe and Lewis), Bannerman's ballads do not share the "thematic core of the Scottish Gothic" that Ian Duncan argues "consists of an association between the *national* and the *uncanny or supernatural*."[25]

Although she does explore national conflict in "The Dark Ladie" and "The Murcian Cavalier," the "uncanny recursion of an ancestral identity alienated from modern life"[26] in Bannerman's Gothic is not national but sexual. Typically, a demonized ancestral past returns to avenge a sexual crime, not a national one, and does so in the form of a female revenant. In "The Perjured Nun," "The Festival of St. Magnus," and "The Penitent's Confession" the revenants are seduced or murdered women, while in "The Murcian Cavalier" the revenant knight is a demon lover who seduces the woman who loves him. In "The Murcian Cavalier," Bannerman, like Charlotte Dacre, dwells on the sexual ambiguities of revenant ballads, featuring a Queen of Castile who becomes a fugitive "wanderer at will" in order to follow her revenant cavalier.[27] Female victims of revenants are traditionally horror-struck when the lover reveals himself to be undead, but in "The Murcian Cavalier," this unveiling reveals "unearthly beauty":

> O'er ev'ry feature clear she saw
> Unearthly beauty wave!
> The purest white, the softest red,
> The eye alone was glaz'd and dead,
> As the sleeper's in the grave! (*Tales of Superstition*, 103)

Transforming the grisly appearance of Coleridge's Life-in-Death, Bannerman takes the errant nature of desire to its "logical" conclusion, with the Queen of Castile becoming a phantom Ladie of the Wood: "Her face is pale, her air is wild, / And her looks are toward heaven!" (108). The liberties Bannerman took with Coleridge's ballads (like those he took with other works) attest to the rich intertextuality of the ballad revival. As Bannerman wrote in defense of her revisions of popular legend in "The Prophecy of Merlin," "it is all fairy-ground, and a poetical community of right to its appropriation has never been disputed" (*Tales of Superstition*, 144).

THE SCHOOL OF LEWIS

By embracing and indeed amplifying the poetics of the Gothic in her ballads, Bannerman linked her work to the fate of *Tales of Wonder*, *Tales of Terror*, "*Tales of Plunder*," *Tales of the Devil*, and so on – (self-)parodic excesses from which early practitioners like Scott and Leyden eventually distanced themselves as they assumed respectable positions as editors, orientalists, and antiquarians.[28] Yet *Minstrelsy of the Scottish Border* and *Tales of Wonder*, the two most significant ballad collections to appear on the scene at this critical juncture, shared key similarities. The easy interplay between these kinds of ballads, ancient and imitation Gothic, would have been readily apparent to contemporary readers, though today these two phenomena are typically studied in different contexts: Scottish literature and the Gothic. The two collections shared contributors (also with the overtly parodic *Tales of the Devil* [1801] and *Tales of Terror* [1801]), and together map the true range of the ballad revival, from "historical" ballads like (Lady Wardlaw's eighteenth-century) "Sir Patrick Spens" (in *Minstrelsy*), to overt imitations of the Gaelic like Leyden's "The Mermaid" (in *Minstrelsy*) and Scott's pseudo-Scandinavian "The Fire King" (in *Tales of Wonder*). *Tales of Wonder* also contains parodies of its own ballads, such as the anonymous "The Cinder-King" and Lewis's self-parody "Giles Jollup the Grave and the Brown Sally Green," which he liked so much he also included it in later editions of *The Monk*. *The Monthly Mirror* was appalled at this desecration of the "justly popular" "Alonzo the Brave," warning that Lewis's self-parody would "pervert the effect of the original."[29] But Lewis's self-parody in *The Monk* and *Tales of Wonder*, and his perversion of the very terms of originality, illustrates why he is a master of Gothic poetics.

Scott reflected that Lewis "remained insensible of the passion for ballads and ballad-mongers having been for some time on the wane, and that with such alteration in the public taste, the chance of success . . . was diminished. What had been at first received as simple and natural, was now sneered at as puerile and extravagant."[30] Yet Scott's argument that Gothic ballads were originally valued for being "simple and natural" is unconvincing, since these ballads were self-conscious imitations, deliberately "extravagant," as in the case of Dacre, Coleridge, and especially Lewis. We need to remember that Scott was anxious in retrospect to excuse his own enthusiasm for extravagant Gothic ballads, and more specifically his participation in *Tales of Wonder*. After all, as Albert Friedman reminds us, "Scott, who was a master of ballad lore from boyhood, did not take to writing ballads as a result of collecting and studying the Border ballads, but rather as a consequence of his enormous admiration for the German artistic imitations of the ancient style with their love of supernatural terrors."[31]

The neglect of the Gothic in Scott scholarship and Romanticism in general (with the recent exceptions of Ian Duncan's and Fiona Robertson's studies) has reproduced a critical oversight of the Gothic's central function not only in Scott's writing, but of the Romantic period as a whole. In one of the rare studies to consider the impact of Gothic poetry, André Parreaux makes a crucial connection between Scott and Lewis: "Today the pioneer's part played by Lewis tends to be forgotten, although the revolution in taste effected by Scott's poetry, important as it was, owed its birth largely to the example and the influence of Lewis."[32] Parreaux wrote this in 1960; in 1830, Scott acknowledged much the same in his "Essay on Imitations": "finding Lewis in possession of so much reputation, and conceiving that if I fell behind him in poetical powers, I considerably exceeded him in general information, I suddenly took it into my head to attempt the style of poetry by which he had raised himself to fame."[33] If we reconsider this lost critical thread linking what we today distinguish as the Gothic and Romanticism, Anne Bannerman's "opulent" ballads will appear less like an anomaly and more like the end result in a dangerous experiment; dangerous because, of all the literary traditions with which women writers could be associated, the "school of Lewis" was the most controversial due to its explicit eroticism. Charlotte Dacre is a rare example of a woman writer who successfully positioned herself in this tradition through her scandalous Gothic romances, most notably in *Zofloya* (1806), her revision of *The Monk*.[34]

Leyden also clearly appreciated the eroticism of Lewis's work, as well as its parodic perversions. His papers contain a manuscript copy of George Watson-Tyler's satirical Lewis parody "The Old Hag in the Red Cloak," circulating unpublished in their Edinburgh circle, in which Lewis's terrors are revealed to originate in the juvenile imagination of Mother Goose.[35] Yet Leyden's love letters to Jesse Brown repeatedly quote Lewis's incantation from the Bleeding Nun episode: "thou art mine, and I am thine, Body and Soul for ever."[36] Writing after his departure for India, Leyden again indulges in Gothic excess: "I think of nothing but clasping you in my arms, all the tedious night . . . I will not lose you tamely. You are mine soul & body, & theere [*sic*] exists not a being living that can tear you from me."[37] Leyden's private letters, like Dacre's published writings, explored the eroticism of Lewis's Gothic while remaining open to its parodic possibilities.

The association of Bannerman's poetry with Lewis's *Tales of Wonder* and the *Tales of Terror* seems to have been particularly damaging. *Tales of Superstition*'s anonymous publication in 1802 no doubt fueled speculation as to the volume's relationship to these volumes of the previous year. The *British Critic's* review noted that "This beautiful little book belongs, as its title implies, to the family of Tales of Wonder," and complained that its fancy "is fancy perverted to the purpose of raising only horror."[38] Park tried to head off precisely this association by recommending in 1802 that Bannerman change the title to the more respectable *Metrical Legends; or Tales of Other Times*, though the *Tales of Superstition* appeared as planned.[39] Bannerman avoided the explicitness of Lewis's (and Dacre's) eroticism, yet she remained tainted by her association with the ballads in *The Monk* and *Tales of Wonder*.

Bannerman's ballads were written in the overtly anti-narrative, deliberately inauthentic tradition of the early Coleridge, Lewis, and Scott, so much so that Anna Seward denounced Bannerman's poems as parodies of Coleridge:

the Tales of Superstition are meant to *burlesque* that species of writing, of late so fashionable. In that point of view, the chaos of horrid images, without story, without connection, "without form & void," presented in Miss B's volume, are good satire. It seems particularly aimed at Coleridge's *Ancyent Marinere*, as the language, & phrase, & manner of writing, so often parody that composition; which is a fine original wild thing on the whole.[40]

What Seward deliberately overlooks is that Coleridge's ballads are themselves consciously inauthentic. Like Bannerman's ballads, they are imitations of imitations, whose aesthetic value lies to a large extent in the self-critical gesture of inauthenticity. The ideology of authenticity, which would eventually gain critical ascendancy (as "Romanticism"), cannot accommodate the poetic accomplishments of Bannerman, Dacre, and Lewis (and to a significant degree, of the 1798 Coleridge). Instead, canonical Romanticism was established in part through the "authenticity" of the *Minstrelsy* and the *Reliques*, the "simplicity" of the *Lyrical Ballads*, and the historicist "maturity" of the Waverley novels. Hence Seward's further complaint that Bannerman's ballads also "adopt lines & half lines also, from Mr. Scott's noble epic ballads, – but it is impossible their author cou'd mean to ridicule what are in themselves of faultless excellence."[41] The effort with which Seward distinguishes between the epic nobility of the *Minstrelsy* and the extravagance of *Tales of Superstition* belies the proximity of these two formidable modes within the ballad revival.

The dangers of Lewis's extravagant Gothic proved to be visual as well as verbal. The brief scandal caused by the fourth engraving ("The Prophecy of Merlin") in *Tales of Superstition* offers a final insight into the sexual politics of publishing with which Bannerman and other women poets had to contend. Called "offensive to decency" by one reader,[42] the engraving features a naked Queen of Beauty, Venus, offering her charmed cup to King Arthur. It is a striking and unusual image to find in a volume of poetry published by a woman in 1802. Bannerman's patron Thomas Park acted swiftly to prevent further embarrassment: as her self-appointed "knight-errant," he took "up the gauntlet of opprobrium" by removing the engraving from review copies.[43] Park's ironical indulgence in a heroic posture reveals that patronage remained central to literary publication in 1802, although poets and patrons clearly had an uneasy relationship to this system and the lack of independence (and "manliness") associated with it.[44] For women poets, patronage was even more vexed, carrying with it suggestions of sexual exchange.

Park and Anderson were relieved when Bannerman relinquished her attempts to find publishers through their aid, since, as they repeatedly confided to each other, she "was not likely to have such personal connexions [*sic*] among the rich and powerful" in London as one would need.[45] Yet Scottish intellectuals cultivated the idea of untutored Scottish genius rising from poverty, such as Burns, Leyden, Hogg, and Campbell. Campbell and Leyden are particularly apt examples of the sexual inequality women poets faced even in this land of "untutored genius," since both men were part of Bannerman's Edinburgh literary circle, and succeeded in the same system of literary patronage in which she continued to struggle. Anderson lauded Campbell's 1799 *Pleasures of Hope* in the same letters as he did Bannerman's first volume, *Poems* (1800), and Campbell went on to secure a comfortable literary career as editor of the *New Monthly Magazine*, thanks in part to the help of his influential male patrons. His letters reveal a consistent anxiety over his dependence on patrons such as Anderson and the powerful Lord Minto, whose secretary he was and in whose houses he lived.

Park's usual high praise of Bannerman occasionally slipped into faint praise indeed, especially when he compared Campbell's work to her own "Gothic" ballads: "Is Miss Bannerman printing her ingenious imitations of the gothic ditty, & is T. Campbell proceeding in his career to high poetic fame?"[46] Park characterizes Bannerman's work in terms of a material reproduction of popular verse, ephemeral printed imitation, and Campbell's in terms of "high poetic fame" and a professional "career." Park's distinction between these two poets, their literary modes, and their careers amounted to a self-fulfilling prophecy. Writing in his journal in 1826, Scott reflected on Campbell's "youthful promise": "I wonder often how Tom Campbell, with so much real genius, has not maintained a greater figure in the public eye." Later that same day, Scott "[g]ave a poor poetess £1."[47] Whether in Park's forward-looking speculation or Scott's retrospect, these influential men of letters reinforced their own professional self-fashioning through such distinct expectations for "real genius" and "poor poetess."

CONCLUSION

Patronage and membership in a literary circle were central to literary publication in Romantic-period Edinburgh. Robert Anderson's home at Heriot's Green was the leading Edinburgh literary salon of the day, to which Anne Bannerman had access, as had other peripheral poets (and daughters) like Jessie Stewart and Margaret Anderson. Yet in the memoirs of Edinburgh writers we see the prominence of the private club in literary culture, whether Masonic (particularly significant for Scott, Erskine, and Leyden, who was writing a history of Freemasonry), university-related (such as the German seminar that launched the ballad revival by introducing Scott, Erskine, and others to the works of Schiller and Bürger), or the more traditional private club like the Knights Companions of the Cape (for the ballad collector David Herd) and the Poker Club (for Robert Burns). "Thoroughly democratic institutions"[48] like the Knights Companions excluded women, whose literary successes were necessarily "marginal," once we realize that the "remarkable feature of literary society in Scotland was the familiar fraternity in which these men lived."[49]

If we shift our focus to this female periphery, however, we see how Bannerman both attempts to position her work through actual and desired connections to central figures (male and female), and how she influences other peripheral poets. For example, Thomas Park noted with approval that Jessie Stewart had "watched the bold flights of Miss Bannerman with the eye of a parnassian eaglet."[50] Joanna Baillie, a Scottish woman writer who succeeded in London, is particularly significant for Bannerman. Bannerman sent Baillie a presentation copy of her *Poems* in 1800, and in "Verses to Miss Baillie, on the Publication of her First Volume of Plays on the Passions"

(1807), after comparing Joanna Baillie to Shakespeare, Bannerman elevated herself to this visionary company:

> Yes! tho' these lines the feeble effort own,
> The soul that stamps them bears another tone!
> Thro' realms of beauty, and thro' darkest night,
> That soul hath trac'd thee in thy towering flight. (*Poems* [1807], 110)

Early reviews of Bannerman's *Poems* had admired precisely "the sublimer and more energetic" qualities of her writing, typically "the productions of a *masculine spirit*": "Anne Bannerman's Odes may be quoted as an irrefragable proof that the ardour, whatever be its gender, which gives birth to lofty thought and bold expression may glow within a female breast."[51] Through this exploration of sublimity, Bannerman aspired to the heights of Baillie's talent (as Stewart did to Bannerman's), and through it we also see a Scottish women's tradition emerging. Stuart Curran has perceived Bannerman's influence in the Shetland poet Dorothea Primrose Campbell, even more (geographically) isolated than Bannerman. And of course the lines of (mutual) influence also undoubtedly run through Leyden and Scott, whose works have rarely been considered in terms of female poetic influence.

While Park and Anderson understood the complex factors involved in publishing success and failure, the most important criterion in both of their assessments of Bannerman's stalled publishing career remained her gender, and its incompatibility with that of a poet. The problem finally lay in "her having received an education above her condition" and her stubborn resistance to returning to this condition.[52] The issue here is not class but gender, for when disenfranchised Scottish poets such as Leyden (the son of a shepherd) and Campbell (the son of a merchant) received educations above their station, this reinforced the myth of the meritocratic effects of the "exceptional" Scottish educational system, which supposedly resulted in nearly universal literacy in the late eighteenth century. Yet historians have begun to question this myth of widespread Scottish literacy, in part due to the large gender gap on which the myth depends.[53] This double standard is visible in Anna Seward's distinction between the commendable Robert Bloomfield, son of a shoe-maker and author of *The Farmer's Boy*, and Bannerman, for "the sensible, interesting, and unaffected worth" of this "self-educated bard" cannot be compared "with the stilted abortions of Miss Bannerman's volume."[54] Both her gender and her class (as the daughter of a street ballad singer) severely limited Anne Bannerman's professional opportunities, but only the former was incompatible with a serious poetic vocation in the eyes of her patrons.

In publishing her ballads in her own volumes, Anne Bannerman challenged the prevailing sexual politics of the Scottish ballad revival, in which women were expected to provide the popular, oral sources for male scholars' published volumes. Moreover, the boldness of her supernatural female figures, and the controversies surrounding her association with the "School of Lewis," attest to the significance of her work for our understanding of the complex interdependence of "Gothic," "Romanticism," and the Scottish ballad. Bannerman's commercial struggle in Edinburgh remains an instructive example of the fate many other women writers faced in the Romantic period, casualties of what Clifford Siskin has termed "the Great Forgetting" of women writers, which made possible the Great Tradition: women were "excluded not by the increasingly porous distinction of gentility, but by the newly valorized professional criterion of earned expertise – a criterion that, for the work of writing, was increasingly regulated . . . by the burgeoning institutions of criticism."[55] Scott, Park, and Anderson envisioned Campbell and Leyden as fellow professional writers, editors, and critics, and Bannerman, ultimately, as a governess with an opulent imagination, printing her "ingenious imitations" of Gothic verse. These persistent characterizations of women poets, and of Gothic poetry's relationship to the now-canonical high Romanticism, were essential features of the Scottish literary landscape at the turn of the nineteenth century. Spinstrelsy, as John Leyden acknowledged in 1801, lay at the heart of minstrelsy.

NOTES

1. Catherine Kerrigan (ed.), Introduction, *An Anthology of Scottish Women Poets* (Edinburgh: Edinburgh University Press, 1991), 5.
2. Robert Crawford, *Devolving English Literature* (Oxford: Clarendon Press, 1992); Katie Trumpener, *Bardic Nationalism: The Romantic Novel and the British Empire* (Princeton: Princeton University Press, 1997); Leith Davis, *Acts of Union: Scotland and the Literary Negotiations of the British Nation, 1707–1830* (Stanford: Stanford University Press, 1998).
3. Wordsworth, "Essay, Supplementary to the Preface" (1815), *Literary Criticism of William Wordsworth*, ed. Paul Zall (Lincoln: University of Nebraska Press, 1966), 180.
4. Bürger was himself inspired by Percy to create German ballads; see Stephen Maxfield Parrish, "Dramatic Technique in the *Lyrical Ballads*," *PMLA* 74 (1959): 85–97.
5. See also Anne Williams's *Art of Darkness; A Poetics of Gothic* (Chicago: Chicago University Press, 1995), Robert O'Connor's dissertation, *Gothic Ballads in Romantic Literature* (Bowling Green University, 1979), and Michael Gamer's *Romanticism and the Gothic* (Cambridge: Cambridge University Press, 2000).

6. Susan Stewart, "Scandals of the Ballad," *Crimes of Writing: Problems in the Containment of Representation* (Oxford: Oxford University Press, 1991), 102–31 (119).
7. Anne Bannerman, *Poems* (Edinburgh: Mundell & Son; London: Longman & Rees, 1800); *Poems. A New Edition* (Edinburgh: Mundell, Doig and Stevenson, 1807); *Tales of Superstition and Chivalry* (London: Vernor and Hood, 1802). Bannerman may have written the *Epistle from the Marquis de La Fayette, to General Washington* (Edinburgh: Mundell & Son; London: Longman & Rees, 1800), and also published poems in periodicals and edited volumes. For a full discussion see chapter 5 in my *Fatal Women of Romanticism* (Cambridge: Cambridge University Press, 2003). An electronic edition of *Tales* is available through the British Women Romantic Poets Project at the University of Califonia at Davis (http://www.lib.ucdavis.edu/English/BWRP/) and through the *Scottish Women Poets* electronic archive edited by Stephen Behrendt and Nancy Kushigian (Alexander Street Press, 2002).
8. John Sutherland, *The Life of Walter Scott* (Oxford: Blackwell, 1995), 79.
9. Leyden's learning was legendary, as a linguist, antiquary, Orientalist, and medical doctor (see John Reith, *Life of Dr. John Leyden, Poet and Linguist* (Galashiels: A. Walker [n.d.])). An important overview of his career remains Scott's "Biographical Memoir" (1811) and the editor's "Supplement to Sir Walter Scott's Biographical Memoir," in *Poems and Ballads by Dr. John Leyden*, ed. Robert White (Kelso: Rutherford, 1858). Scott's influential account of Leyden as a poor, high-strung, struggling scholar who benefitted from his patronage and mentorship is self-serving. As the "Supplement" pointed out, "As a literary character, Leyden was in point of fact, on their first acquaintance, more distinguished in Edinburgh than Scott. He was the right arm of [the publisher] Constable, and the subsequent manager of the chief periodical then published in Scotland."
10. Nigel Leask, "Towards an Anglo-Indian Poetry? The Colonial Muse in the Writings of John Leyden, Thomas Medwin and Charles D'Oyly," in Bart Moore-Gilbert (ed.), *Writing India 1757–1990* (Manchester: Manchester University Press, 1996), 52–85; John Leyden, *An Anglo-Indian Poet, John Leyden*, ed. P. Seshardi (Madras: Higginbottom, 1912).
11. David Fowler, *A Literary History of the Popular Ballad* (Durham, NC: Duke University Press, 1968), 294.
12. *Ibid.*, 298.
13. On the controversy surrounding Lady Wardlaw, see Mary Ellen Brown, "Old Singing Women and the Canons of Scottish Balladry and Song," in Douglas Gifford and Dorothy McMillan (eds.), *A History of Scottish Women's Writing* (Edinburgh: Edinburgh University Press, 1997). In the same volume, see also Kirsteen McCue, "Women and Song 1750–1850."
14. See Stewart, "Scandals of the Ballad," 102–31.
15. Leyden to Heber, National Library of Scotland (NLS), MS 3380.
16. Anderson to James Currie, June 28, 1800 (Mitchell Library, Glasgow). Anderson's correspondence remains the most easily accessible source for

information on Bannerman. See Bishop Thomas Percy, *The Correspondence of Thomas Percy and Robert Anderson*, ed. W. E. K. Anderson, vol. IX of *The Percy Papers*, general eds. Cleanth Brooks and A. F. Falconer, 9 vols. (New Haven: Yale University Press, 1988); John Nichols, ed., *Illustrations of the Literary History of the Eighteenth Century*, 8 vols. (London: JB Nichols, 1848), vol. VII. See also Daniel Elfenbein, "Lesbianism and Romantic Genius: The Poetry of Anne Bannerman," *ELH* 63 (1996): 929–57.

17. Scott, "Essay on Imitations of the Ancient Ballad," *Minstrelsy of the Scottish Border*, ed. T. F. Henderson, 4 vols. (Edinburgh: William Blackwood, 1902), IV: 16–17.

18. *Critical Review* 2, 38 (1803): 110–11.

19. "The Festival of St. Magnus" and "The Black Knight of the Water" were omitted from the 1807 volume.

20. *The Complete Poetical Works of Samuel Taylor Coleridge*, ed. E. H. Coleridge, 2 vols. (Oxford: Clarendon Press, 1912), II: 1056.

21. *Monthly Review*, 2nd series, 29 (June 1799): 204; *British Critic* 14 (October 1799): 365.

22. "The Black Knight of the Water" is set in Scoone and features King Robert. "The Prophecy of Merlin" is based on Arthurian legend.

23. Crawford, *Devolving English Literature*, 117.

24. Davis, *Acts of Union*, 156.

25. Duncan, "Walter Scott, James Hogg, and Scottish Gothic," in David Punter (ed.), *A Companion to the Gothic* (Oxford: Blackwell, 2000), 70.

26. *Ibid.*

27. On revenant ballads, see Adriana Craciun, "'I Hasten to be Disembodied': Charlotte Dacre, the Demon Lover and Representations of the Body," *European Romantic Review* 6 (1995): 75–97.

28. On Lewis's ballads, see Joseph James Irwin, *M. G. "Monk" Lewis* (Boston: Twayne, 1976), 97–128; Syndy Conger, *Matthew Lewis, Charles Maturin, and the Germans* (Salzburg: Universität Salzburg, 1977); André Parreaux, *The Publication of The Monk: A Literary Event* (Paris: M. Didier, 1960).

29. Review of Lewis, *The Monk*, 4th edn, *The Monthly Mirror* 5 (March 1798): 157–8; quoted in Parreaux, *The Publication of The Monk*, 59.

30. Scott, "Essay on Imitations," 49–50.

31. Friedman, *The Ballad Revival: Studies in the Influence of Popular on Sophisticated Poetry* (Chicago: University of Chicago Press, 1961), 287.

32. Parreaux, *The Publication of The Monk*, 55.

33. Scott, "Essay on Imitations," 49–50.

34. See my Introduction in *Zofloya*, ed. Adriana Craciun (Peterborough, Ont.: Broadview, 1997).

35. NLS MS 3220. Watson-Tyler published the poem in *The School of Satire* (1802).

36. Leyden to Jesse Brown, February 6, 1802, NLS MS 3383.

37. Leyden to Jesse Brown, April 2, 1803, NLS MS 3383.

38. *British Critic* 21 (1803): 78. See also *Critical Review* 2, 38 (May 1803): 110.

39. Park to Anderson, January 1802, NLS MS 22.4.10.

40. Seward to Bannerman (1802?), in Park's letter to Anderson, October 10, 1812 (NLS, MS 22.4.10). Park did not send this letter to Bannerman. See also *The Letters of Anna Seward*, 6 vols. (Edinburgh: Constable, 1811) v: 324–25.
41. Seward to Bannerman (1802?), in Park's letter to Anderson, October 10, 1812 (NLS, MS 22.4.10). See also Steven Jones, *Satire and Romanticism* (Basingstoke: Macmillan, 2000).
42. Park to Anderson, November 29, 1802, NLS MS 22.4.10.
43. Park to Anderson, *ibid.* I discuss this scandal in detail in *Fatal Women of Romanticism*.
44. See for example: "Strictures on Literary Patronage," *Scots Magazine* 64 (1802): 807–10, and Dustin Griffin, *Literary Patronage in England, 1650–1800* (Cambridge: Cambridge University Press, 1996).
45. Park to Anderson, May 23, 1803, NLS MS 22.4.10.
46. Park to Anderson, January 30, 1801, NLS MS 22.4.10.
47. Scott, *Journal of Sir Walter Scott*, ed. W. E. K. Anderson (Oxford: Clarendon, 1972), 217, 218.
48. Hans Hecht, *Songs from David Herd's Manuscripts* (Edinburgh: William Hay, 1904), 37–8.
49. H. G. Graham, quoted in *ibid.*, 34.
50. Park to Anderson, December 9, 1801, NLS MS 22.4.10.
51. Original emphasis; review of *Poems*, in *Critical Review*, 2, 31 (1801): 438–8.
52. Anderson to Joseph Cooper Walker, December 4, 1805, Edinburgh University MS La II 598.
53. R. D. Anderson, *Education and the Scottish People 1750–1918* (Oxford: Clarendon Press, 1995).
54. *The Letters of Anna Seward*, v: 338.
55. Clifford Siskin, *The Work of Writing: Literature and Social Change in Britain 1700–1830* (Baltimore: Johns Hopkins University Press, 1998), 218, 222.

CHAPTER 13

"The fause nourice sang": childhood, child murder, and the formalism of the Scottish ballad revival

Ann Wierda Rowland

In a 1787 letter, Walter Scott attributes his poetical pursuits to his lifelong love of "ballads and other romantic poems," poems which he has "read or heard" from the "earliest period of [his] existence" as a "favourite, and sometimes as an exclusive gratification."[1] It would seem, however, that not all of Scott's beloved ballads provided gratification exclusively, for he continues:

> I remember in my childhood when staying at Bath for my health with a kind aunt of mine, there was an Irish servant in the house where we lodged, and she once sung me two ballads which made a great impression on me at the time. One filled me with horror. It was about a mason who because he had not been paid for work he had done for a certain nobleman, when that lord was absent, conveyed himself into the castle with the assistance of a treacherous nurse and murdered the lady and her children with circumstances of great barbarity.[2]

The ballad Scott describes here is "Lamkin," one of the many Scottish ballads that contain an account of infanticide. In most versions of this ballad, a "false nurse" helps Lamkin achieve his revenge. Together, the nurse and the mason fatally wound the infant son so that its cries will bring the mother down the stairs to meet her own death. When the nobleman returns at the end of the ballad, he rights these wrongs by hanging, burning, or boiling Lamkin and the nurse to death.

The ballad takes its name from Lamkin's revenge, but the figure of the nurse is the most horrifying, precisely because she uses the forms and practices of her traditional role to kill her charge rather than care for him. In most versions of the ballad, it is she who tells Lamkin to "Stab the babe to the heart wi a silver bokin" and encourages him to kill her mistress. In at least one version, the mother calls down to the nurse to comfort the crying child, saying "There is a silver bolt lies on the chest-head; / Give it to the baby, give it sweet milk and bread." The next stanza describes what the nurse does instead: "She rammed the silver bolt up the baby's nose / Till the blood it came trinkling down the baby's fine clothes."

But the perversion of the nurse's care is most clearly seen in the ballad's central image of Lamkin and the nurse around the cradle: "Then Lamkin he rocked, and the fause nourice sang, / Til frae ilkae bore o the cradle the red blood out sprang."[3] As the nurse sings to the dying child, she mocks her usual practice of singing to amuse and comfort, and the ballad itself becomes implicated in her crimes. Women who worked as nurses and mothers were the most common ballad singers in eighteenth-century Scotland and the most significant source of traditional ballads for antiquarian collectors. In these lines the ballad effectively recreates the scene of its own production, suggesting troubling connections between the "fause nourice" and the nurse commonly singing the ballad, between the child in the cradle and the child listening to the ballad's tale. This self-reflective moment, in which the gruesome contents of the ballad spill over into the context of its singing, suggests something potentially horrifying about the traditional forms of ballad singing more generally, about who sings to whom and to what end.

Scott does not include "Lamkin" in his *Minstrelsy of the Scottish Border*, but not out of any residual squeamishness about the barbarity of the tale. He includes two other infanticide ballads, one of which also features a "fause nourice" and which reminds Scott of a third that he "often heard sung in my childhood."[4] Furthermore, he discusses "Lady Anne," the fragment of "The Cruel Mother," and "The Queen's Marie" with no apologies for their sordid content, no acknowledgment or expression of horror whatsoever. In publishing these ballads of child murder, Scott reproduces what was standard fare in ballad revival collections: tales of familial violence in all its possible manifestations, as well as stories of illicit, incestuous affairs and illegitimate children. Ballads of infanticide and child murder, in which mothers and nurses murder their children, often without hesitation or remorse, form a significant share of these tales, and they place representations of motherhood and nursing in front of Romantic readers that directly challenge the period's investment in the acculturative role of domestic women.

This chapter is an attempt to read both the horror and the absence of horror that the infanticide ballad produces within the Scottish ballad revival. It thus hopes to answer the larger question of how the Scottish ballad collections of the Romantic period accommodated the scandalous content of their ballads within the nationalist frame of their project. The "ancient ballads," "reliques," and "primitive poetry" contained in these collections constitute an "inheritance of Ancient National Minstrelsy"; their rescue and preservation is a "bounden duty on all true and patriotic Scotsmen."[5] Yet the stories they tell are often far from being the "celebration of the acts of Kings, and the warlike deeds of Heroes" that antiquarians such as

Peter Buchan claimed them to be.[6] There is a sharp contradiction between the tales of the ballads, particularly those considered "romantic ballads," and the national value they are made to bear; tales of family violence challenge visions of national continuity, strength, or historical perseverance. Ballad collectors dealt with these challenges in different ways. Infrequently, they offered brief apologies for the subject matter, as Scott does in his introduction to "The Bonny Hynd," a ballad about sibling incest. Slightly more often, the antiquarian firmly assigned the violence and perversion of the ballad's story to the primitive period of its production, as if such things as incest or infanticide no longer occurred or appealed to readers in a "more refined age."[7] But most frequently, the scandalous contents go unnoticed altogether. Scott and his fellow antiquarians simply fail to comment on such material beyond noting different versions, historical accuracies or anachronisms.

The lack of comment on the ballads' sensational stories is less a sign of antiquarian tolerance than it is a strategy for coping with the contradictions and embarrassments created when "popular" literature is redefined as a "national treasure." The ballad collections manage their difficult content, I will argue, by producing a reading practice that disregards content and privileges form as a vehicle of national cultural transmission. The impressive scholarly apparatus that the ballad revival bequeaths to British literature is, in fact, a way of *not* reading or responding to the contents of popular literature; it thus models how a "refined" editor and reader might appreciate popular poetry while still maintaining a proper, critical distance. It also models how the nation can maintain a proper historical distance from the violence of the primitive past while still claiming cultural continuity with that past.

One of the ways the antiquarian resists responding to the contents of the ballads is to locate any responsive, unmediated relationship in his own early childhood. Childhood, both personally recalled and metaphorically conceived, is a critical imaginary field for the ballad revival, one, as we will see, that is intimately involved in the revival's formal practice. In the introductory essays that are customary for the collections, the editor often recalls his original childhood attachment to popular poetry before detailing his adult scholarly practice, claiming for that practice a refinement and credibility based largely on the absence of those first emotional charges. Both the child's original ardor and the adult's subsequent stolidity together provide authenticity and authority for the antiquarian project. What is surprising, however, is that this idea of the child's affective response to the ballads goes along with that of the child as the ideal formalist. In the antiquarian imagination, the child's original, powerful attachment to the ballads is less an unmediated response to their contents than it is a pure channeling of their form.

It is ultimately this image of the child formalist – and, consequently, the viability of antiquarian formalism – that is threatened by the infanticide ballad. The ballad of child murder significantly troubles the revival's practice of disregarding content and emphasizing form. Within a literature that defines its project as preserving national culture, infanticide ballads tell stories of failed transmission and reproductive crisis, of mothers and nurses central to the course of acculturation violating their sacred trust, of children who are the privileged vehicles of cultural transmission wounded by the culture they are made to carry. How does Scott understand this violation and violence when he no longer expresses horror? What is at stake when a nurse is false, when a child is killed, in a ballad of the Scottish revival?

THE NATIONAL MUSE IN THE NURSERY

Well aware that "these relics of the old *natural literature* of my native coun-try" pose problems for readers about *how* they should be read, Robert Chambers admits in the preface to the third edition of his *Popular Rhymes of Scotland* that he "cannot help feeling anxious that the articles collected may be viewed in a proper light." He proceeds to offer the reader the following advice:

The reader is therefore not to expect here anything profound, or sublime, or elegant, or affecting. But if he can so far upon occasion undo his mature man, as to enter again into the almost meaningless frolics of children – if to him the absence of high-wrought literary grace is compensated by a simplicity coming direct from nature – if to him there be a poetry in the very consideration that such a thing, though a trifle, was perhaps the same trifle to many human beings like himself hundreds of years ago, and has, times without number, been trolled or chanted by hearts light as his own, long since resolved into dust – then it is possible that he may find something in this volume which he will consider worthy of his attention.[8]

Chambers's collection of rhymes, tales, and riddles are all "nursery" pro-ductions, simple and "befitting the minds which they were to regale."[9] To read them properly, he suggests, one must "undo his mature man" and "enter again into the almost meaningless frolics of children." Chambers views children as particularly adept at playing with and appreciating the "almost meaningless." To do so is to "undo" adult reading practice, and it is precisely this child-like response that Chambers wants from his readers.

Chambers shares with Scott and other Scottish antiquarians an acute interest in the state of childhood. Old ballads, songs, and rhymes were customarily sung to children. The antiquarian's manuscripts and precise transcriptions are thus always supplemented by the aura of memory; his historical commentary always punctuated by recollections from childhood. Just as Scott dates his love of ballads to the "earliest period of [his] existence," William Aytoun dedicates his collection to his "dearest mother" and describes Scottish ballads as "the firstlings of my memory"; Robert Jamieson recalls being a "lover of poetry from his childhood," naturally "fond of popular ballads and songs."[10] Chambers displays characteristic nostalgia when he confesses that:

I must own that I cannot help looking back with the greatest satisfaction to the numberless merry lays and *capriccios* of all kinds, which the simple honest women of our native country used to sing and enact with such untiring patience, and so much success, beside the evening fire in old times . . . There was no philosophy about these gentle dames . . . It never occurred to them that children were anything but children – "bairns are just bairns," my old nurse would say.[11]

Here reminiscence blurs cultural and individual childhoods, reaching backward toward a state of simple equivalencies where "bairns are just bairns." Chambers wants a simple equivalency between personal and collective memory, as a later rhetorical question betrays: "What man of middle age, or above it, does not remember the tales of drollery and wonder which used to be told by the fireside, in cottage and in nursery, by the old women, time out of mind the vehicles for such traditions?"[12]

The fact that oral literature is traditionally sung to children and remembered from childhood makes the "old women" who care for children – the nurses, mothers, grandmothers, aunts, and domestic servants – the central "vehicles for such traditions." Indeed, the notes in Scott's *Minstrelsy* list their sources as "taken from the recitation of an old woman, residing near Kirkhill"; "communicated to the Editor by Mr. Hamilton, Music-seller, Edinburgh, with whose mother it had been a favourite"; "from the recitation of an old woman, long in the service of the Arbuthnot family"; often "from the recitation of a lady, nearly related to the editor"; or simply "from the memory of an old woman."[13] Katie Trumpener has argued that Scottish and Irish literature represents these women as the successful inheritors of the bardic tradition; according to Trumpener, the nurse in particular retains "bardic authority," embodying oral culture and enacting cultural transmission through her songs and stories.[14] The ballad collections are, in fact, quite ambivalent about the authority the nurse has in the work of child-rearing

and acculturation, as one can see in a ballad such as "Lamkin." Furthermore, the conventional homage to "Ancient National Minstrelsy" usually
included in the introductions to these collections tends to describe an exclusively male oral tradition and to posit the antiquarian, rather than the
nurse, as the final inheritor and arbiter of bardic value.[15]

Nevertheless, the image of an old woman singing to children remains
an important validating scene for the ballad collections. The significance
of the scene, however, is as much a function of the child's early, authentic
listening as it is of the nurse's authoritative singing. The importance of
childhood aurality and memory to the Scottish ballad revival is most vividly
evident in the descriptions of Anna Gordon's (Mrs. Brown of Falkland)
ballad singing career. Scott credits Alexander Tytler's transcription of Anna
Gordon's ballads as a significant source for his volume and quotes Tytler's
account of how she learned her ballads in full:

"An aunt of my children, Mrs. Farquhar, now dead . . . a good old woman, who
spent the best part of her life among flocks and herds, resided in her latter days in
the town of Aberdeen. She was possest of a most tenacious memory, which retained
all the songs she had heard from nurses and countrywomen in that sequestered
part of the country. Being maternally fond of my children, when young, she had
them much about her, and delighted them with her songs, and tales of chivalry.
My youngest daughter, Mrs. Brown, at Falkland, is blest with a memory as good
as her aunt, and has almost the whole of her songs by heart."[16]

Here the transmission of ballads from "nurses and countrywomen" to child,
and then, when that child is herself an old woman and aunt, to a new
generation of children, establishes oral tradition as an ongoing series of
exchanges between old women and children. But it is the fact that both the
old aunt and Mrs. Brown learned their ballads as children and remembered
them from childhood that establishes both the age and authenticity of these
ballads.[17] Jamieson, who also used Mrs. Brown's ballads in his collection,
defends their authenticity simply by noting that she "learnt most of them
before she was twelve years old, from old women and maid-servants; what
she once learnt, she never forgot."[18]

It is in Brown's own comment that she "never saw any of [the ballads]
either in print or Manuscript but have kept them entirely from hearing them
sung when a child" that we begin to see the full importance of childhood
to the ballad revival.[19] Brown's "by-corners" of memory become preserves
of childhood and orality marooned in an adult mind and a textual world.
The antiquarians describe Brown as an exceptional "depository" of Scottish
oral poetry, her memory a "hoard" of old ballads, her mind neatly divided

between the oral culture of her childhood and the print culture of her educated adult life.[20] As Robert Anderson reports to Thomas Percy:

It is remarkable that Mrs. Brown . . . never saw any of the ballads she has transmitted here, either in print or MS., but learned them all, when a child, by hearing them sung by her mother and an old maid-servant who had been long in the family, and does not recollect to have heard any of them either sung or said by any one but herself since she was about ten years.[21]

Brown's ballads exist apart from any others she might read or even hear; the purity of their form a function of how separate they are from any current time and context. It is not simply that childhood is associated with orality in the discussion, which becomes, at times, a debate, about Brown's exceptionally "tenacious" memory.[22] Childhood represents a privileged oral/aural state, one in which what one hears passes unmediated into memory and what one remembers persists intact, protected, unchanged. The persistence of childhood memory, its pure preservation within the adult mind, holds the promise of renewed access to oral culture. The scene of an old woman singing to a child thus lends authenticity to the ballad collections from both the child's presumably incorruptible hearing and the nurse's access to the childhood "by-corners" of her mind.

If ballads are dated and authorized from the childhood of the singers, antiquarians, and collectors, they are also dated from the "childhood" of national culture; they are child-like because they represent the poetry of a primitive nation. The importance of childhood to traditional, oral literature is also seen in the idea of a national infancy. Scott makes this point repeatedly: the "early poetry of every nation" represents "a chapter in the history of the childhood of society"; his collection offers a "glimpse of the National Muse in her cradle," allowing one to "hear her babbling the earliest attempts at the formation of the tuneful sounds"; the ballads are repeatedly described as the "infancy of the art of poetry."[23] According to Scott, the figure of the "national muse" is neither bard nor nurse, but child.

Chambers also describes the songs and ballads of the nursery as those which "breathed of a time when society was in its simplest elements."[24] For Chambers, this description of simple society is also a description of childhood; thus the childhood of the individual and of the nation come together in the nursery through the singing of ballads and telling of traditional stories. The Scottish child of the "old nursery system":

might be said to go through in a single life all the stages of a national progress. We began under a superintendence which might be said intellectually to represent the Gothic age; and gradually, as we waxed in years, and went to school and college, we advanced through the fourteenth and sixteenth centuries; finally coming down to the present age, when we adventured into public life. By the extinction of the old nursery system, some part of this knowledge is lost.[25]

Writing in 1826 when the nursery has been "revolutionized," Chambers regrets the lost knowledge of the nation's primitive past, knowledge that every child used to learn through the ballads and tales of his nursemaid. Indeed, it is the loss of this nursery culture that makes Chambers "anxious" about how his collection will be read. The idea that one goes through "in a single life all the stages of a national progress" is a fantasy of recapitulation that makes national history available to the experience of every individual, or, since few will have the "tenacious memory" of Mrs. Brown, at least *lost* to each individual only as the earliest memories of childhood are lost. Changes in nursery culture aggravate the ironic fact that the nation's "old natural literature" may present itself as alien and unintelligible to the nation's modern, adult subjects.[26] The figure of the child thus represents not only the authenticity of national, oral literature, but also the way in which such primitive poetry might remain part of the lived, albeit dimly remembered, experience of the modern, refined nation.

Given the importance of childhood to antiquarian representations of oral tradition, it is not surprising that, when advising his readers on how to appreciate properly the stories and rhymes of his collection, Chambers asks them, in effect, to become children again. To read like a child becomes a way to "enter again" into the course of cultural transmission that oral tradition represents (translated now into a purified, more reliable written form), as well as a way to relocate or recreate the original scene of national literature in the present time. But for Chambers, the child-like reader is mostly important for his or her ability to appreciate the "almost meaningless." Indeed the "trifles" of his collection, he advises, are meaning*ful* only because they constitute a continuous form of meaninglessness through hundreds of years of national history; it is the "same trifle" sung "to many human beings like himself hundreds of years ago." Here, the sameness of the trifle produces the "likeness" of the human beings across so many years; what the trifle is means nothing, that it has stayed relatively the same and produced the same cultural effect gives it significance. Chambers's invitation to read like a child is thus also an evaluation of traditional popular literature that empties it of what we typically call "content" and emphasizes the continuity of what we might call its cultural "form," its shape as a vehicle of cultural transmission. By disregarding the content of these rhymes and tales, Chambers, in fact, encourages a formalist attention to popular literature.

NOTES AND OCCASIONAL DISSERTATIONS

Disregarding content is a characteristic gesture of antiquarianism, although the typically excessive number of headnotes, footnotes, and introductory essays all commenting on the language and stories of the ballads seems to suggest otherwise. Scott's *Minstrelsy* exemplifies the scholarly excess of the ballad revival: its three introductory essays and lengthy "Notes and occasional Dissertations" introducing the individual ballads – including, for example, the eighty-two page introduction to the "Tale of Tamlane," itself only fourteen pages in length – demonstrate Scott's self-proclaimed interest in contributing "to the history of my native country; the peculiar features of whose manners and character are daily melting and dissolving into those of her sister and ally."[27] Scott's attention to the details of the ballads would seem to signal a keen interest in their contents as well as the kind of attention he expects from his readers. But his interest in the "history of my native country" is not that of an historian; it is that of a nationalist antiquarian whose sense of the past is both of that which is in danger of being lost and that which is capable of being rescued and recovered. The antiquarian, in other words, is less interested in history than in history's artefacts and "remains," less interested in the past than in the "relique," the object collected and preserved from the past. Ultimately the ballads are important to Scott less as historical records than as antiques – objects or cultural forms that have survived the flux of history.[28]

Scott, in other words, is interested in the content of the ballads in order to prove their form as a vehicle of national cultural transmission. This explains both the excess and arbitrariness of his scholarly commentary: these notes are produced for reasons beyond what the content of the ballads demands. The effect throughout the *Minstrelsy* is that of a rather arbitrary accumulation of stories, facts, and definitions, one that does not explain or illuminate the ballads so much as call attention to its own supplementary information.

This scholarly apparatus becomes necessary because of Scott's insistence that the ballads have little literary or poetic merit. In his "Introductory Remarks on Popular Poetry," Scott ventures that "even a reader of refined taste will have his patience rewarded, by passages in which the rude minstrel rises into sublimity or melts into pathos."[29] But such passages "occur seldom," and Scott enumerates exactly how and why popular ballads display "tenuity of thought and poverty of expression," "loose and trivial composition," "sameness and crudity."[30] If there are "grand and serious beauties" in the ballads, they "occurred but rarely to the old minstrels; and, in order to find them, it became necessary to struggle through long passages of monotony, languor, and inanity."[31] In a strong and notable revision of his earlier tribute to the ballad as the source of both gratification and horror, Scott's ballads begin to sound like Chambers's rhymes: inane and "almost meaningless."

What most compromises the poetic merit of these ballads is the "joint-stock" of rhymes and phrases that the "ballad-maker" uses, "thereby greatly facilitating his own task, and at the same time degrading his art by his slovenly use of over-scutched phrases." Even worse, "ballad-mongers" use these stock lines to spare themselves the "labour of actual composition."[32] Clearly Scott is running up against the ways in which popular literature – first oral tradition, then a commercial, print-culture of "ballad-mongering" – refuses to conform to a high poetic ideal of individual inspiration and composition.

But Scott's discussion of the ballad's poetic shortcomings is most striking for the extent to which he defines the problems of "over-scutched phrases" and "dull and tedious iteration" as products of the ballad's formal charge. The repetition of words and phrases simply aids transmission, as Scott writes: "If a message is to be delivered, the poet seizes the opportunity of saving himself a little trouble, by using exactly the same words in which it was originally couched, to secure its being transmitted to the person for whose ear it was intended."[33] Indeed, when the exact words are *not* used, the integrity of the ballad tradition is threatened. Scott describes the course of "innumerable instances of transmission" *not* as vital oral tradition, but as corrupting the "authenticity" of the ballad. He asks us to consider that over the "long course of centuries," the ballads "have been transmitted through the medium of one ignorant reciter to another, each discarding whatever original words or expressions time or fashion had, in his opinion, rendered obsolete, and substituting anachronisms by expressions taken from the customs of his own time." The trouble with these ignorant reciters, however, is that they were not ignorant enough:

And here it may be remarked, that the desire of the reciter to be intelligible, however natural and laudable, has been one of the greatest causes of the deterioration of ancient poetry. The minstrel who endeavoured to recite with fidelity the words of the author, might indeed fall into errors of sound and sense, and substitute corruptions for words he did not understand. But the exercise of a slight degree of ingenuity on the part of a skilful critic could often, in that case, revive and restore the original meaning; while the corrupted words became, in such cases, a warrant for the authenticity of the whole poem.[34]

The desire "to be intelligible," to have the ballad mean something to its audience, results in "deterioration." An interest in content threatens the ballad's integrity as a vehicle or form of transmission. Far better for the minstrel to recite something he cannot understand, learning the sounds of words rather than the meaning of words. The "errors of sound and sense" that may result are then not only easily repaired, they are also "warrant" for the ballad's age and authenticity.

In Scott's description of oral tradition, the content and form of the ballad are opposed to and work against one another. The preservation of the ballad's form requires either repetitive, degraded content or total lack of attention to content. In the *Minstrelsy*, this representation of oral transmission leads to an aesthetic evaluation of popular literature that encourages a particular reading practice. Scott insists that the ballads have little poetic merit or significant meaning and suggests that their value instead lies in their ability to serve as a vehicle back to the "childhood of society." The "moral philosopher," the "historian of an individual nation," and the "admirers of poetry as an art" should be interested in these ballads not because of their content, but because of their capacity for what we now call cultural transmission, their formal ability to shape and carry a continuous, national culture.[35] Since this quality only becomes evident through the scholarly apparatus that frames each ballad, Scott's notes and introductions produce a reading practice that makes their own erudite commentary central to the proper appreciation of popular literature.

In this way, Scott's "Introductory Remarks on Popular Poetry" exemplifies Pierre Bourdieu's account of how an aesthete approaches popular art. "Whenever he appropriates one of the objects of popular taste," Bourdieu writes, the aesthete "introduces a distance, a gap – the measure of his distant distinction . . . by displacing the interest from the 'content', characters, plot etc., to the form, to the specifically artistic effects which are only appreciated relationally, through a comparison with other works which is incompatible with immersion in the singularity of the work immediately given."[36] Here Bourdieu uses "form" in the sense of "artistic effects" and not in the cultural and antiquarian sense of "artefact" or "vehicle." But his description of the way in which the aesthete resists "immersion in the singularity of the work immediately given" perfectly describes Scott's editorial practice in the *Minstrelsy*, allowing us to see his excessive production of notes and commentary as, in fact, resistance to immersion in an individual ballad.

Like Scott, Bourdieu's aesthete aims to appreciate a work "'independently of its content,'" and does so by a tendency to "bracket off the nature

and function of the object represented and to exclude any 'naïve' reaction –
horror at the horrible, desire for the desirable, pious reverence for the
sacred . . . in order to concentrate solely upon the mode of representation,
the style, perceived and appreciated by comparison to other styles."[37] The
aesthete's formal knowledge and reading practice establish his class status and its cultural capital. Bourdieu's analysis of the aesthetic disposition
is useful for our discussion of Scott's antiquarianism because it suggests
that Scott's denigration or disregard of the ballads' contents is precisely
what establishes his proper, scholarly, and refined response to this popular
literature.

Romantic antiquarianism is well aware that the appeal of "popular"
ballads to the "people" is their sensational contents. In the introduction to
his collection, *Minstrelsy Ancient and Modern*, William Motherwell points
out that many ballads present "domestick Tragedies" and attributes this to
the "appetite in the vulgar mind for true incident."[38] Motherwell follows
Scott's example of paying little notice to the contents of the ballads, but he
does discuss the problems created by editors who do not follow this practice
of disregard. The "Ancient Minstrel," according to Motherwell, does not
hesitate to "call a spade a spade," and "the Modern affects to shudder at the
grossness and vulgarity of antiquity," stigmatizing the "Muse of Antiquity as
being rather 'high kilted.'"[39] This obviously clichéd way of distinguishing
oneself from the vulgar content of popular literature is both misguided and
hypocritical, according to Motherwell:

In truth, it is by such impertinent and pernicious labors [of re-appareling the
"high-kilted" Muse in a "trailing gown"] that the obscenities of early writers become disgustingly obtruded on the publick eye. Had they been allowed to pass
uncommented on, they would never have called a blush to the innocent cheek, or
in the unaffectedly pure mind have wakened one unhallowed thought . . . In their
bitter wrath and in their lachrymose exclamations against the licentiousness of ancient song . . . these well-meaning individuals not unfrequently manifest a lurking
affection for their task, and a perfect acquaintance with its subject, seldom to be
found in conjunction with that unspotted purity and extraordinary refinement
and maiden-like delicacy which they profess.[40]

Editorial attention of any kind to the sensational content of the ballads
becomes, in this passage, evidence of a "lurking affection" for that content,
a desire no different than the vulgar mind's unending appetite for shocking
incident. Motherwell would rather demonstrate how *not* to respond to the
content of popular ballads, how to let their scandals "pass uncommented
on." His aim is instead to produce a reading practice that can appreciate
popular literature without participating in popular response.

The result is, once again, exemplary formal attention: discussion of style at the level of variations, corrections, "authenticity," and an interest in the details of the tale only as they can be traced back to a geographical or historical origin. Motherwell's formal reading practice has its best example in the notes to his version of "Lamkin," entitled "Lambert Linkin." His introduction to the ballad lists and assesses its other published versions, suggests that his version establishes the correct name of the builder, and complains that discovering the location of the ballad's castle has proven as difficult as fixing the "topography of Troy." The stabbing of the infant and beheading of the mother, the nurse's suggestion to Lamkin that "ye'll be laird o' the Castle, / And I'll be ladye," Lamkin's eventual hanging and the nurse's burning, are never mentioned. Indeed, Motherwell's one footnote to the ballad exemplifies his determination not to acknowledge the content of the tale. To the lines describing the central scene of the ballad – "Belinkin he rocked, / And the fause nurse she sang, / Till a' the tores o' the cradle / We' the red blude down ran" – Motherwell attaches this note: "*Tores*. The projection or knobs at the corners of old fashioned cradles, and the ornamental balls commonly found surmounting the backs of old chairs. Dr. Jamieson does not seem to have had a precise notion of this word. *Vide* iv. Vol. of his Dictionary, *voce Tore*."[41] Calling attention to the structure, style, or *form* of the cradle, Motherwell ignores its contents, even as those contents overflow that form. The difficulty of these lines for Motherwell, the anxiety provoking the pedantry of this footnote, is that they dismantle the original, authenticating scene of the ballad, that of the woman singing to the child, and undermine his formal practice to the extent that it relies on the smooth and repeated transmission of ballads from woman to child, from woman to child again.

MEN AT WORK, CHILDREN AT PLAY

The formalism of these ballad collections works not simply to model the appropriate, detached relationship to the sensationalism of popular literature, nor simply to establish and reinforce the differences between popular and refined literatures. It is also motivated by the desire to claim a continuous national culture which is as free as possible from the familial and other "border" conflicts that these ballads otherwise insist upon. Reviving the literature of the past and describing it as "national" always risks reviving the conflicts and violence of that past. Scott and his fellow antiquarians manage this risk largely through their formal appreciation of the ballads and the scholarly apparatus it generates. Their editorial practice, by what it revives and what it resists, enacts what we might call a formal nationalism, one that defines the nation around the continuity of cultural forms, rather than in the stories, characteristics, and creeds that these forms express.[42]

The formal nationalism of the antiquarians and its favorite form, the ballad, thus conceive of nation and literature quite differently than the literary form more usually associated with the nation, the epic. The move from epic to ballad as the privileged form of national literature involves a number of adjustments in how the nation is imagined: scenes of domestic women and children on knees replace those of courtly bards and royal audience; the work of transcription replaces that of translation; primitive origins replace heroic foundations. While the antiquarians often claim the legacy of Homeric bards and heroic minstrelsy in the prose introductions to their collections, the ballads necessitate a radically different relationship to the national past. Rather than relating the modern nation through elegiac reverence towards an idealized version of itself projected back into an absolute and inaccessible past, the ballad equates personal with national nostalgia and makes longing and loss its central affective orientations towards an equally inaccessible past.[43] For the ballad, the nation is located not in a particular past or official story, but in an authentic scene of oral transmission. To put it crudely: the epic imagines a nation of strong content and kings; the ballad imagines a nation of unchanging form and children.

The formal practice of the ballad revival embraces the child as its ultimate formalist. Able, according to Chambers, to enjoy "meaningless frolics," children are also able to approach the all too meaningful as meaningless, hearing, even learning by rote, ballads they do not fully comprehend. The child, equipped with the incorruptible hearing and memory we saw attributed to Mrs. Brown, thus becomes Scott's desired "ignorant" reciter, the ignorance cleansed of vulgarity and translated into the idealized form of childhood innocence. Not fully understanding the ballad's story, the child learns its words more by sound than by sense; and what the child learns, she never forgets. This ideal child is thus able to "recite with fidelity the words of the author," producing something more like a "fixed text" of the written word than a re-creative ballad of the oral. Penny Fielding has described the paradox troubling Scott's *Minstrelsy* as his investment in both orality's purity of origins and its impurity of transmission.[44] The figure of the child acquires its significance for Scott and his fellow antiquarians by resolving this paradox, by inhabiting a pure oral, pre-literate state and, at the same time, enacting a pure transmission. The ideal child represents what Scott wants the form of the ballad to be, but what he must always lament it is not: a fixed text in oral form, an embodied text.

The child's formalism not only promises a pure, formal transmission; it also represents the fantasy of cultural innocence persisting within the forms and practices of cultural knowledge. Understanding childhood as an oral, original state places the child on the cusp of the cultural world; the definitive object of acculturation, she is not yet fully a cultural subject, not yet fully subjected. The child who knows not what she sings represents an illusory, because imaginary, relationship to culture in which one can play with and participate in cultural forms without being subjected to their power. Bourdieu's aesthete becomes again relevant to our discussion:

To be able to play the games of culture with the playful seriousness which Plato demanded, a seriousness without the "spirit of seriousness," one has to belong to the ranks of those who have been able, not necessarily to make their whole existence a sort of children's game, as artists do, but at least to maintain for a long time, sometimes a whole lifetime a child's relation to the world. (All children start life as baby bourgeois, in a relation of magical power over others and, through them, over the world, but they grow out of it sooner or later.)[45]

The aesthete's detachment from economic urgency here becomes a child's relation of "magical power" over others and the world. The child has "magical power" over the world to the extent that all its stories, songs, pictures, images are equally available and suitable for games and play, all are equally meaningful and meaningless. The adult aesthete retains this magical power in his belief that "beautiful" art can be made "from objects socially designated as meaningless . . . or as ugly and repulsive . . . or as misplaced."[46] But this belief that all objects are equally meaningful and meaningless, all equally suitable for artistic production, relies on a firm sense that these objects are fundamentally not related to or determinative of one's self. The "baby bourgeois" who never grows up maintains a confidence in his detachment from cultural objects, in his power to play with, interpret, and evaluate cultural forms without in any way being a part or product of those forms.

Bourdieu's "baby bourgeois" helps us understand one more connection between the antiquarian and the child: the child represents a relation to culture that the antiquarian would have for himself, particularly as he revives the scandalous stories of popular ballads. In dwelling on the childhood of Mrs. Brown, in recalling his own early love of ballads, the antiquarian is less interested in differentiating between his adult, scholarly practice and the child's naïve enthusiasm, than he is in connecting his own formal practice to a playful, original formalism. Chambers's invitation to approach traditional, oral literature as a child, to "undo [one's] mature man, as to enter again into the almost meaningless frolics of children," implies that antiquarian pursuits and childish games share a delicate, even paradoxical, cultural negotiation: their meaningless frolics make them national, bring them into culture, at the same time that they manifest an original innocence or enduring autonomy within the national, cultural field.

To these ideals of childhood the ballad of child murder poses a particular threat. Such child-like or formal reading practices may work well when the "trifle" of oral literature is a nursery rhyme, but can a ballad such as "Lamkin" or "The Cruel Mother" also be read as "almost meaningless"? To suggest that one appreciate a ballad of child murder as a child would is obviously problematic: do the stories become trifles or does the child-like reader become all the more vulnerable to their contents? The answer, from what we have seen, is both. The antiquarians publish the various infanticide ballads without commenting on their contents or by dismissing them as examples of primitive practice and superstition. Scott's introduction to "Lady Anne" is typical in noting that "stories of this nature are very common in the annals of popular superstition," and he also supports the authenticity of the ballad by commenting that it "corresponds with that of a fragment . . . which I have often heard sung in my childhood."[47] Here Scott's childhood recollection both establishes the "ancient turn" of the ballad and lays claim to that version of childhood hearing and memory that transforms even the most horrifying ballad into a trifle "often heard sung."

But the strain exhibited, for example, in Motherwell's footnote to "Lamkin"'s most gruesome image – "Till a' the tores o' the cradle / We' the red blude down ran"; *"Tores.* The projection or knobs at the corners of old fashioned cradles" – suggests that the formal or child-like practice of antiquarianism does become vulnerable to the contents of the infanticide ballad. The contents of "Lamkin," "The Cruel Mother," "Lady Anne," or "The Minister's Daughter of New York" – each of which contains the scene of a mother or nurse deliberately killing an infant or infants – ultimately threaten the formal production of the ballad itself, its status as a vehicle of national, cultural continuity.[48] These ballads transform the authenticating scene of woman singing to child from one of cultural transmission to one of cultural crisis; antiquarian sensibility is given the most crude and violent reminder that form is never a pure, decontextualized vehicle, but is always contingent upon the scene of its production. The culturally innocent and incorruptible child loses his "magical powers" and instead becomes acutely vulnerable to cultural forms. Indeed, the practices and traditions of accul-turation, of making a child into a national, cultural subject, reveal their violence; the child risks being wounded in being reared. To the idealized child of the ballad revival, the fantasy of a pure, innocent relation to and transmission of national culture, we must now add the image of the child murdered, the image of cultural situation and subjection.

Scott, whose recollection of childhood horror upon hearing "Lamkin" suggests that he was quite different from Chambers's and Bourdieu's unflappable kids, is, of all the antiquarians, the most sensitive to the tension between the revival's idealization of childhood and ballad scenarios of violence against children. If Scott associates ballads with the "earliest period of [his] existence," he also associates "false nurses" and the threat of infanticide with early childhood; the gratifications of ballads and the horrors of child murder are intimately linked. Scott remembers one nurse who almost "murdered" him as a child by concealing her own illness. Most striking is his account of the nurse at Sandy-Knowe, his grandparents' farm, who "contracted a sort of hatred at poor me" as the reason she was unable to join her lover in Edinburgh. Her hatred growing to a "sort of delirious affection," the nurse eventually confessed to a housekeeper that "she had carried me up to the Craigs, meaning, under a strong temptation of the Devil, to cut my throat with her scissors, and bury me in the moss.[49] She "was dismissed, of course, and . . . became afterwards a lunatic," Scott concludes, reporting the nurse's fate in the same blithe tone with which he recalls the threat to "poor me."

Yet the story establishes an ominous connection between ballads, childhood, and child murder. Sandy-Knowe is where Scott first learned from his grandmother the "songs and tales of the Jacobites," as well as "many a tale of Watt of Harden, Wight Willie of Aikwood, Jamie Telfer of the fair Dodhead, and other heroes."[50] His account of the Sandy-Knowe nursemaid betrays these ballad and romance associations, for her absent lover, her scissors and plan to bury the child in the moss, her disgrace and eventual madness, place her squarely in the ballad revival tradition of infanticidal women.

In this anecdote from his "private history," Scott "balladizes" his early childhood.[51] More interested at this moment in representing a private, autobiographical child than a national, collective childhood, Scott nevertheless moves between personal and cultural fields, borrowing between them to enhance his position in both as a genial survivor. But his resort to traditional ballad stories in this autobiographical narrative forces him to acknowledge the class rancor that often characterizes them and to record the fate of those false nurses who are "dismissed" to illness and insanity. Only the "healthy peasant" who succeeded them is "still alive to boast of her *laddie* being what

she calls *a grand gentleman.*"⁵² While the formalism of the ballad revival
avoids the recognition that the antiquarian nation is not of, by, and for the
same people, the content is clear: only the properly deferential nurses and
the magically preserved children survive to sing the song.

NOTES

1. Walter Scott, *The Letters of Sir Walter Scott, 1787–1807*, ed. H. J. C. Grierson
   (London: Constable & Co., 1932), 4.
2. *Ibid.*
3. Francis James Child, ed., *The English and Scottish Popular Ballads*, 5 vols. (New
   York: Dover Publications, 1965), II: 323, 326.
4. Walter Scott, *Minstrelsy of the Scottish Border*, 3 vols. (Edinburgh: Cadell &
   Co. 1830), II: 234.
5. William Motherwell, *Minstrelsy Ancient and Modern* (Glasgow: John Wylie,
   1827), iv, and Peter Buchan, *Ancient Ballads and Songs of the North of Scotland*
   (Edinburgh: W. & D. Laing, 1828), iii.
6. Buchan, *Ancient Ballads*, iii. Susan Stewart identifies the contrast between the
   revival's emphasis on the ballads' martial qualities and the thematics of the
   ballads themselves. *Crimes of Writing: Problems in the Containment of Representation* (Durham, NC and London: Duke University Press, 1994), 114–15.
7. See Scott, *Minstrelsy*, III: 100–1; and, in reference to infanticide, George
   Kinloch, *Ancient Scottish Ballads* (London: Longman, 1827), 44.
8. Robert Chambers, *Popular Rhymes of Scotland* (London: W. & R. Chambers,
   1870), vi.
9. *Ibid.*, 48.
10. William Aytoun, *The Ballads of Scotland* (Edinburgh: William Blackwood and
    Sons, 1858), xvii, and Robert Jamieson, *Popular Ballads and Songs* (Edinburgh:
    Constable and Co., 1806), i–ii.
11. Chambers, *Popular Rhymes*, 12.
12. *Ibid.*, 48.
13. Scott, *Minstrelsy*, II: 250, 276; III: 36, 59, 79. Charles Kirkpatrick Sharpe is also
    typical in proclaiming that his ballads have been "mostly gathered from the
    mouths of nurses, wet and dry, singing to their babes and sucklings." *A Ballad
    Book* (Edinburgh: William Blackwood and Sons, 1823, rpt. 1880), vi.
14. Katie Trumpener, *Bardic Nationalism: The Romantic Novel and the British
    Empire* (Princeton: Princeton University Press, 1997), 211–12.
15. Penny Fielding has discussed the ways in which Scott develops his sense of the
    "highly gifted individual," the Minstrel or Bard, as the "author" of the bal-
    lads. *Writing and Orality: Nationality, Culture, and Nineteenth-Century Scottish
    Fiction* (Oxford: Clarendon Press, 1996), 57.
16. Scott, *Minstrelsy*, I: cxxxii–cxxxiii.
17. The fact that one can recall a ballad from one's own childhood, or can refer
    to an individual who recollects a ballad from infancy becomes an important

credential that the antiquarian frequently mentions to establish the age and authenticity of the ballad. See Scott's introduction to "Fause Foodrage" as just one example; *Minstrelsy*, III: 3.

18. Jamieson, *Popular Ballads*, ix.
19. Letter from Mrs. Brown to Fraser Tytler quoted in David Buchan, *The Ballad and the Folk* (East Lothian: Tuckwell Press, 1997, first published 1972), 66. Brown begins by remarking that "I have lately by rumaging in a by-corner of my memory found some Aberdeenshire ballads which totally escaped me before."
20. These terms are taken from a letter of 1800 from Robert Anderson to Thomas Percy. Quoted in John Bowyer Nichols, *Illustrations of the Literary History of the Eighteenth Century* (London: J. B. Nichols and Son, 1848), 89 and 90.
21. *Ibid.*, 89.
22. Robert Anderson expresses doubts about the authenticity of Brown's ballads. *Ibid.*, 90.
23. Scott, *Minstrelsy*, I: ix, x, xi.
24. Chambers, *Popular Rhymes*, 48.
25. *Ibid.*, 12. Hugh Blair has a similar understanding of how the childhood of man and the childhood of society represent the same state. See his *Critical Dissertation on the Poems of Ossian*, in James Macpherson, *The Poems of Ossian and Related Works*, ed. Howard Gaskill (Edinburgh: Edinburgh University Press, 1996), 346.
26. Ian Duncan discusses this sense of discontinuity haunting the Scottish romance revival through the important figure of the uncanny. See his *Modern Romance and Transformations of the Novel* (Cambridge: Cambridge University Press, 1992), 9 and "The Upright Corpse: Hogg, National Literature and the Uncanny," *Studies in Hogg and his World* 5 (1994): 34–6.
27. Scott, *Minstrelsy*, I: cxxxvii.
28. Fielding notes that the ballads are not "themselves historical" in Scott's understanding, although he does understand the language of the ballads as more "representational than creative." See Fielding, *Writing and Orality*, 55–6.
29. Scott, *Minstrelsy*, I: xi.
30. *Ibid.*, I: xii.
31. *Ibid.*, III: xii.
32. *Ibid.*, I: xiii.
33. *Ibid.*, I: xiii, xiv.
34. *Ibid.*, I: xvi–xvii.
35. *Ibid.*, I: ix, x.
36. Pierre Bourdieu, *Distinction: A Social Critique of the Judgement of Taste*, trans. Richard Nice (Cambridge, MA: Harvard University Press, 1984), 34.
37. *Ibid.*, 53–4.
38. Motherwell, *Minstrelsy Ancient and Modern*, xxvi.
39. *Ibid.*, viii.
40. *Ibid.*
41. *Ibid.*, 296, 297.

42. Jack Kerkering has recently discussed an instance of what I consider formal nationalism in "'We are Five-and-Forty': Meter and National Identity in Walter Scott," *Studies in Romanticism* 40 (Spring 2001): 85–98.

43. For a discussion of epic as national form, see Stewart, *Crimes of Writing*, 74–8; M. M. Bakhtin, *The Dialogic Imagination*, ed. Michael Holquist (Austin: University of Texas Press, 1981), 13–40; and David Quint, *Epic and Empire* (Princeton: Princeton University Press, 1993).

44. Scott, *Minstrelsy*, I: xvii; Fielding, *Writing and Orality*, 53.

45. Bourdieu, *Distinction*, 54.

46. *Ibid.*, 35.

47. Scott, *Minstrelsy*, II: 234–5.

48. "Mary Hamilton" or "The Queen's Marie" is the other important infanticide ballad that I leave out here because it does not emphasize the scene or moment of child murder as prominently as the others.

49. J. R. Lockhart, *Life of Sir Walter Scott* (Edinburgh: Adam and Charles Black, 1853), 14.

50. *Ibid.*, 15 and 17.

51. *Ibid.*, 1.

52. *Ibid.*, 13.

Index

Jeffrey, Francis 5, 33, 64, 69–70, 98–9, 147
Jewett, William 147
Johnson, David 188, 190
Johnson, James 197–9
Johnson, Samuel 4, 7, 49, 59, 64, 123, 125, 170; *Journey to the Western Islands of Scotland* 38–9, 51–4, 158
Johnstone, Christian Isobel 7
Jones, Sir William 95
Joyce, James 128

Kaiser, David Aram 31
Kames, Henry Home, Lord 3, 59, 62, 98
Kant, Immanuel 1, 10, 20, 23, 25, 26, 30, 31–2, 173
Keats, John i.8, 115, 210; "Eve of St. Agnes" 117, 213
Kerrigan, Catherine 206
Kidd, Colin 8
Kracauer, Siegfried 84

"Lamkin" (ballad) 225–6, 230, 237, 240–1
Leavis, F. R. 4, 6
Lefebvre, Henri 40
Leibnitz, Gottfried Wilhelm 25
Lewis, Matthew 117, 205, 206, 208, 214, 215–17, 218
Leyden, John 97, 98, 104, 204, 205, 206–8, 216–17, 218, 219, 220, 221, 222
Lipking, Lawrence 191–2
Lindsay, Lady Anne 207
Lindsay, Maurice 197
Liu, Alan 156
Livy (Titus Livius) 60
Locke, John 25, 30, 42
Lockhart, J. G. 7, 13
Lukács, Gyorgy (Georg) 4, 114–16, 129
Lynch, Deidre 53
Lyotard, Jean-François 89

Macaulay, T. B. 98
MacDiarmid, Hugh 6
MacIntyre, Alasdair 20
Mackenzie, Henry 67
Mackintosh, Sir James 25, 98
MacLeod, Fiona 1
Macpherson, James 4, 8, 9, 11, 20; *Poems of Ossian* 1, 3, 4, 7, 9, 11–12, 21, 34, 38, 39, 40, 46–52, 67, 68, 204; *Fingal* 3, 47–9; *History of Great Britain* 69
Makdisi, Saree 14, 149
Malcolm, Sir John 96–7
Malthus, Thomas 157, 161
Manning, Peter 14
Manning, Susan 8, 12, 40
Marshall, David 45

Massey, Doreen 171
McGann, Jerome 13, 20
McGuirk, Carol 196
McIlvanney, Liam 8
McLaren, Martha 97
McLuhan, Marshall 40
Mellor, Anne K. 148
Michelet, Jules 77–8
Mill, James 95, 98, 104
Mill, John Stuart 29–30, 165–6
Millar, John 2, 11, 64–5, 95, 178
Mills, Charles 106
Milton, John 6, 46
Montesquieu, Charles-Louis 178
Moore, Thomas 101, 104, 105
Morier, James 104
Morning Chronicle 163
Motherwell, William 236–7, 240
Muir, Edwin 6, 7
Munro, Thomas 96–7
Murphy, Peter 198

Nairn, Tom 7–8, 21
Nairne, Baroness Carolina 207
Neal, John and William 189
New Dictionary ... of the Canting Crew 58
Nietzsche, Friedrich 89

O'Brien, Flann 119
Osborne, Peter 40, 51, 80

Pannwitz, Rudolf 49
Park, Thomas 207, 208, 218–19, 220, 221
Parreaux, André 216
Pater, Walter 35
Peabody, Norbert 97
Pennant, Thomas 170
Percy, Thomas: *Reliques of Ancient English Poetry* 193–4, 204, 205, 206, 207, 217, 231
Phillips, Mark 63, 66, 84
Pinch, Adela 148
Pinkerton, John 98
Pitt, William 11
Pittock, Murray 8
Poe, Edgar Allan 6
Pope, Alexander 195
Potkay, Adam 46
Powys, John Cowper 128
Pushkin, A. S. 21
Pynchon, Thomas 119

Radcliffe, Ann 214
Ramazani, Jahan 48
Ramsay, Allan: *Tea-Table Miscellany* 190–3, 194, 196, 204, 211
Ramsay, John, of Ochertyre 82, 83